SEX SCANDAL

SEX SCANDAL

THE DRIVE TO ABOLISH
MALE AND FEMALE

ASHLEY McGUIRE

REGNERY
PUBLISHING
A Division of Salem Media Group

Regnery® is a registered trademark of Salem Communications Holding Corporation

Cataloging-in-Publication data on file with the Library of Congress

ISBN 978-1-62157-581-8

Published in the United States by
Regnery Publishing
A Division of Salem Media Group
300 New Jersey Ave NW
Washington, DC 20001
www.Regnery.com

Manufactured in the United States of America

10 9 8 7 6 5 4 3 2 1

Books are available in quantity for promotional or premium use. For information on discounts and terms, please visit our website: www.Regnery.com.

Distributed to the trade by
Perseus Distribution
www.perseusdistribution.com

For Brian

CONTENTS

INTRODUCTION

S ex has become scandalous.

    I don't mean the "sex" you're thinking of—the thing that men needle each other about in the locker room, that women talk about in hushed tones over glasses of wine, that men and women have been fighting over and laughing about since the dawn of humanity. That kind of sex has always been a little bit scandalous, and it still is, even in today's anything-goes world.

I'm talking about sex as it demarcates male and female, the basic biological and physiological differences that tell us with scientific certainty whether a human being is a man or woman, and all that that entails.

That right there has become a matter of national scandal.

Somehow, it has become a violation of the accepted code of conduct to suggest that men and women are different, and to act accordingly.

The very word "sex" in the sense of basic biological difference is no longer used in everyday life; it's been replaced by "gender," which itself has been rendered practically meaningless. The scientific and medical communities still have clear definitions of sex and gender. Society denies them almost entirely.

LIVING IN DENIAL

Indeed, we live in a world of sexual denial. We are increasingly trying to treat men and women as if they were exactly the same. And then we're surprised by the growing sexual confusion.

Take romance, for example. Women lament its demise, and men hardly know how to be affectionate toward a woman, or even treat her with respect, without finding themselves in danger of sexism or chauvinism. Men can't win. If they don't hold a door, pull out a chair, or pay for dinner, they're jerks; if they do, they're patronizing. Women are just as confused. They say they want real romance, but they're content to move in with a guy, do his laundry, and cook his meals for little more in return than the chance of Valentine's Day tickets to see *Fifty Shades of Grey*.

You may have noticed the whitewashing of sexual difference in one small way or another. But if you look closely, you will see strands of sex-denial everywhere.

Maybe a toy or activity disappeared from your child's school for "gender equity" reasons. Maybe your high school son was elected to Homecoming Court, only to be crowned as a unisex "Royal," because calling him Homecoming King would be offensive. Maybe a battle is brewing in your school district about whether high school boys should be allowed access to the girls' locker room.

Maybe you're a college student who is majoring in gender studies—and just got invited by the cute guy who lives on your floor and showers in your bathroom to a "Secretaries and Bosses" party at the frat down the street. Or maybe you've graduated and are on the dating scene—or rather, wishing you knew where exactly that scene is, and why casual sex seems to be the price of admission to any meaningful contact with the opposite sex. Or maybe you're with your girlfriends at a nail salon, reading magazines and wondering how it came to be that a man who won a gold medal at the Olympics as a decathlete is complaining that "choosing clothes is the hardest part about being a woman" or why everyone suddenly seems to agree that women should be drafted into the military and sent into combat.

Maybe you are a professional who was recently required to undergo workplace training where you were taught that gender is fluid and a meaningless label. You had to spend five hours discussing male and female characteristics that make up the supposedly "socially constructed" "gender binary"—which you can't help thinking has a lot to do with biology. Or maybe you are an employer terrified by the prospect of being slapped with a $200,000 fine if you refer to an employee by the wrong pronoun. In some cases, it seems, sexual difference still does matter.

Feeling confused? I don't blame you.

It seems like you woke up one day and suddenly it was normal for kindergartens to ban Legos® as sexist, for high school boys to shower in the girls' locker room, and for America to send the mothers of toddlers to defend us from our enemies. But the reality is that the denial of sexual differences has been unfolding before us for decades.

"THE BATTLE OF THE SEXES"

On September 20, 1973, tens of thousands of people crammed into the Houston Astrodome in the scorching afternoon heat. About 90 million more sat in front of their televisions in eager anticipation. Everyone was dying to watch what had been dubbed "the Battle of the Sexes."

Bobby Riggs, one of the greatest tennis stars in history, had challenged female tennis star Billie Jean King to a match for show. Riggs, who made no effort to hide his sexist disdain for women in sports, had been taunting King, who had collected ten singles titles before turning thirty, for some time. Riggs was constantly provoking King and other rising female tennis stars with misogynistic jeers like "the best way to handle women is to keep them pregnant and barefoot," or "women belong in the bedroom and kitchen, in that order," and "Women play about 25 percent as good as men, so they should get about 25 percent of the money men get."[1]

One woman had already taken Riggs's bait. Margaret Cook, then the highest-ranked woman in tennis, agreed to play him for a cash prize of $10,000. In what became known as the "Mother's Day Massacre," Riggs walloped her 6-2, 6-1. Making things worse, Cook told reporters afterward that she was outmatched. "We girls don't play like that," she said.

But Riggs wasn't satisfied; he wanted to beat Billie Jean King, whom he called a "women's libber leader." He challenged her repeatedly, saying, "I'll play her on clay, grass, wood, cement, marble or roller skates. We got to keep this sex thing going. I'm a woman specialist now."

To everyone's shock, King finally agreed to an exhibition match with a $100,000 purse. Before a combined live and TV audience of nearly 100 million, at the time the biggest audience for any tennis match in history, King entered the arena dressed like Cleopatra and carried by men in togas, while Riggs was wheeled in by half-naked women labeled "Bobby's bosom buddies." King gifted Riggs with a baby pig, and Riggs gave King a giant "Sugar Daddy" lollipop,[2] which he described as "the largest sucker I could find for the biggest sucker I know."[3]

But "the Battle of the Sexes" was not a circus spectacle. Despite the gimmicks, it was truly emblematic of women's struggle to lay claim to a broader role in society and to establish whether new opportunities for them on paper meant anything in reality.

In what many have called a turning point for women, Billie Jean King beat Bobby Riggs fair and square in all three sets. The History Channel later reported that "the Battle of the Sexes turned King into arguably the first superstar female athlete in the United States." King went on to form a public truce with Riggs, and the two became lifelong friends. King had an illustrious career, at the end of which she founded the Women's Sports Foundation, which still advocates for girls and women in sports today.

King later said of the Battle of the Sexes, "I thought it would set us back 50 years if I didn't win that match. It would ruin the women's tour and affect all women's self-esteem."[4]

Yet fifty years later, it appears as though things are backsliding. Billie Jean King and other female champions staked out a space for women's sports, which earned the respect of the American people and the legal backing of Congress. They fought for that space on the grounds of their sex. But what happens to women's sports in a world where the very reality of sexual difference is in dispute?

MAKING SPORT OF SEX

In 2013, mixed martial artist Fallon Fox, who had "been a woman to her training partners and opponents for the last five years" and had been "tearing through her [female] opponents,"[5] came out as having been "born in a male body." After much deliberation, the UFC allowed the biological male to continue fighting against women. The following year, Fox sent a female opponent, Tamikka Brents, to the hospital after just two minutes of fighting. Brents suffered a broken skull and a concussion, and needed seven surgical staples.[6] She said of the match, "I've never felt so overpowered ever in my life. I've fought a lot of women, and never felt the strength I felt in a fight as I did that night."

Even after being hospitalized, Brents knew she had to toe the P.C. line: "I can't answer whether it's because she was born a man or not, because I'm not a doctor. I can only say, I've never felt so overpowered ever in my life, and I am an abnormally strong female in my own right."[7]

That a female athlete landed in the hospital because of her opponent's patently obvious biological advantage did not matter. Hinting at that reality was the scandal. "MMA Fighter Fallon Fox Is a Woman, Get Over It," barked the title of a Paris Lees article on *Vice*: "People get hurt. All the time. It's their job. I appreciate your gut reaction may be one of sympathy toward Fallon's vanquished opponent, Tamikka Brents, but a china doll she isn't. She's a successful MMA fighter who could have opted out of the fight beforehand if she truly believed Fallon had an unfair advantage over her." There's no cause for concern, "Because biological sex isn't black and white."

Except that it is. As this book will detail, science offers a pretty plain definition of what sex is. But increasingly, top decision makers, from the bureaucrats at the Department of Education to the members of the International Olympic Committee (IOC), have decided that science no longer applies. The 2016 Olympic games in Rio de Janeiro marked the first time that athletes could compete against members of the sex with which they self-identify, not the sex with which they are categorized by science. And yes, that means men can compete in women's events.[8]

Dare to raise a hand in protest, even on the grounds of basic fairness, and *you* are the scandal.

YOU'RE IN THE ARMY NOW

Somewhere along the line, the battle of the sexes turned into the scandal of the sexes. Speaking of battle, it has even become a sign that you're insufficiently committed to equality if you argue against literally sending women into battle, even if it's against their will. Young women now face the very real prospect of being forced to register for Selective Service. Advocates for drafting women will brush off the significance of that fact: "We aren't going to have another draft!"

Then why is it so important that women be forced to sign up?

The end goal of an elite segment of our society is the eradication of any distinction between the sexes. Equal treatment sounds nice, but as is often pointed out in the context of economics, equal treatment does not necessarily yield equal outcomes. You give a young man and a young woman a rifle and a hundred-pound pack and the exact same training and send them into war, and they will most certainly face unequal odds of surviving unscathed. You fill a frat house with men and women and booze and turn off the lights, and there will be unequal outcomes. A man and a woman have sexual intercourse, and nine months later they can end up in very unequal situations.

The willful blindness to basic biological difference under the mantra of equality ultimately disempowers women. It forces them to compete on male terms and punishes them when they fail. It creates a societal preference for the masculine, the physically stronger, and the more aggressive, putting women at a disadvantage. It gives us a world where movies about torture sex are considered romantic, but Shakespeare is banned from college classrooms because his maleness is a threat.[9] A world where ROTC cadets are forced to wear high heels to show solidarity with rape victims,[10] but female midshipmen at the Naval Academy aren't allowed to wear skirts to graduation.[11] A world where a woman with a "Sugar Daddy" isn't just a prop in a Bobby Riggs tennis spectacle, but a woman just using her sex appeal as a perfectly valid means to pay for her Ivy League education. A world where the Midwife Alliance of North America feels pressured to call pregnant women "birthing individuals" lest someone be offended by the notion that it is women, and only women, who bear children.[12]

Sex needn't be a scandal. It should be a source of potential and the starting point for true equality. The things that make us different can't be changed, but understanding them can help us to build a better and more just society that gives both men and women the chance to live freely and authentically.

I mean it entirely differently when I echo Bobby Riggs in saying, "We got to keep this sex thing going." But first, we have to remind ourselves what "sex" actually means.

CHAPTER 1

THE KIDS ARE NOT ALRIGHT

*Nature wants children to be children
before being men.*

—Jean-Jacques Rousseau, *Emile*

"Don't Let the Doctor Do This to Your Newborn," reads a scary headline that pops into my Facebook newsfeed. With a baby due in mere weeks, I take the bait and click.

Imagine you are in recovery from labor, lying in bed, holding your infant. In your arms you cradle a stunningly beautiful, perfect little being. Completely innocent and totally vulnerable, your baby is entirely dependent on you to make all the choices that will define their life for many years to come. They are wholly unaware (at least, for now) that you would do anything and everything in your power to protect them from harm and keep them safe. You are calm, at peace.

Sounds nice.

The article goes on to describe a scene in which an ominous obstetrician walks in with a suspicious grin and "gloved hands reaching for your baby insistently."

"It's time for your child's treatment," he says menacingly. The article goes on:

> Obstetricians, doctors, and midwives commit this procedure on infants every single day, in every single country. In reality, this treatment is performed almost universally *without even asking for the parents' consent*, making this practice all the more insidious.

"Well, what the heck is it?" I wonder frantically. Finally, I reach the answer:

> It's called infant gender assignment: When the doctor holds your child up to the harsh light of the delivery room, looks between its legs, and declares his opinion: It's a boy or a girl, based on nothing more than a cursory assessment of your offspring's genitals.

Embarrassed, I realize that I've been punk'd. What I expected to be a serious, scientific article about a medical procedure performed on newborn babies in hospitals against the wishes of mothers like myself was actually just another gender theory diatribe in *Slate*.[1]

I never knew a newborn's genitals could be so scandalous. And yet they are. There are people in America who consider it criminal and abusive to identify children by their biological sex. And they are coming for yours.

PRINCESSES NEED NOT APPLY

Just about every mom will readily admit that Target is one of the best places to shop for kid stuff. The clothes are cheap and adorable—

whether it's a pair of pink jellies for a little girl or baseball jammies for a baby boy—and so is just about everything they sell. The store is well organized, making it very easy for frazzled parents to head directly for the sections they need. Clothes and shoes are well arranged and clearly labeled by age and sex, as are bedding, backpacks, undies, you name it.

Or they were until the gender radicals got to them.

In August of 2015, Target announced a new corporate policy: they would be moving away from "gender-based" signage.

Apparently, it was hurting some people's feelings. As a post on Target's corporate website explained, the signs had led to certain customers feeling "frustrated or limited by the way things are presented. Over the past year guests have raised important questions about a handful of signs in our stores that offer product suggestions based on gender."

One can hardly be blamed for wondering who these guests are. Certainly not frazzled parents just trying to do some shopping without getting swept up in a battle about gender dysphoria.

Nope, not those guests. Because these mystery customers had enough spare time to pressure Target into making children the target of the latest trend in sex denial in America. Target agreed to eliminate all "gender-based signage" in its toy, home, and entertainment sections, and clarified that in the toy section, they would even cease using "pink, blue, yellow or green paper on the back walls of our shelves."[2]

Finally, no more offensive yellow walls! (Said no parent, ever.)

Target left clothing alone, for now. But kids' clothes are certainly up next.

When I clicked on a recent Huffington Post article that came floating through my newsfeed—"13 Empowering Photos Show There's No 'Right' Way to Be a Boy"—part of the #ABoyCanToo hashtag campaign, the first image that appeared was one of a young boy in a wide-brimmed hat and ruffled dress. He was dressed as Scarlett O'Hara.[3]

As Ruth Margolis wrote for the *Week*, "Liberal parents did some celebratory fist pumping when Target announced last week that it would bend to customer criticism and stop separating toys into boys' and girls' sections. It's heartening that Target is bringing its floor plans into the

21st century, where—I hope—it's a given that some little girls play with cars and some boys like dressing up Elsa dolls. But if the retailer really wanted to advance equality of the sexes for kids, they'd tear down the gender divide in their children's clothing section." Margolis boycotts Target because they don't sell "gender-fluid garb" for tots.

Plenty of moms share Margolis's frustration with the princess-heavy nature of the girls' clothing section. And yet my daughter's clothes come almost exclusively from Target, and I've never bought a thing with a princess on it. There are plenty of non-Disney options in the girls' clothing section at Target. But that doesn't stop Margolis from wondering "if they assume that once the infant phase is over, we're all gagging to put our squishy, sexless toddler girls in insipid florals?"[4]

Actually, yes. And hipster jeggings, boho eyelet tops, and rompers with Native American stitch work. My daughter is dressed that way, and many of her Target-purchased clothes are in styles I would buy for myself. None of her clothes scream, "My life goal is to marry Prince Charming," but they're recognizably feminine.

It's one thing to fret about the princess culture and the messages it sends to girls. It's entirely another to think clothing that reflects a girl or boy's sex is scandalous.

And just what is "gender-neutral" or "gender-fluid" clothing? For girls, it's certainly less girly.

Does a toddler boy seem less like a boy in single color, frill-free t-shirts, which Margolis suggests as more ideal and practical for today's parents? No.

Does a toddler girl seem less like a girl in that same outfit? You bet.

In fact, what people call "gender-neutral" clothing is just clothing washed of feminine characteristics. Girlish traits are dropped in favor of a more boyish look.

There have been some exceptions. One successful attempt at breaking free of "gender stereotypes" in kids clothing without washing out femininity is Princess Awesome, a self-funded company started by two moms looking for girls' clothes that are more than just "pink dresses adorned with princesses or flowers or ruffles."[5] Their clothing line, which advertises itself as "a different kind of girly," offers things like the "She-Rex" Dinosaurs Twirly Play Dress" or the "Super Secret Hidden Ninja Play Dress."[6]

But while Princess Awesome still allows girls to wear dresses, plenty of "gender-neutral" clothing companies for tots, such as those that are a part of the "Clothes Without Limits" campaign, drip with virtue signaling, using advertising lines like, "We create baby clothes that break down stereotypes," or our clothes "flip the script on gender clichés" or "We believe that ALL kids should be #freetowearpink regardless of their gender."[7] For parents perfectly comfortable dressing their boys and girls as girls and boys, it's all a bit exhausting.

Anyway, Target sidestepped clothing for now to focus on more low-hanging fruit: toys.

No doubt the suits in corporate felt pressure when one woman's tweet about her shopping experience at Target went viral. The tweet included a picture of a Target sign advertising "Building Sets" and underneath, "Girls' Building Sets."[8]

The sign is admittedly cringe-worthy. But the woman was not a random Target shopper. Turns out the mom behind the viral photo is Abi Bechtel, an outspoken activist and writer who has been published in

Courtesy of Abi Bechtel

places like *xoJane* and *Time* and who describes herself on her Twitter page as, among other things, a "sexual libertine" and "conversational terrorist."[9]

After her Target tweet "went viral," she went on a media tour harping on Target for sorting things for kids by sex—exactly the kind of nightmare scenario that makes head honchos freak out, even if ninety-nine percent of their customers would still like to be able to find girls' bedding without having to dig through a pile of Thomas the Tank Engine comforters for "gender equity" reasons. One loud customer who takes to the media can drown out one million others who are too busy to politicize their everyday shopping.

To be fair, there are concerns about "gendered toys" that are not radical or insane. For example, while mothers of all political stripes worry about what has become known as "the princess culture," that concern doesn't mean hating everything related to princesses; it's a dislike for the gaudy and sparkly Disney retail world that presents the ideal woman as a damsel in distress with a two-inch waist.

It's hard to tell how much of the princess culture is explained by girls' seemingly innate inclination toward all things princess, and how much of it can be chalked up to Disney's marketing savvy. As Peggy Orenstein reported for the *New York Times*, "'Princess,' as some Disney execs call it, is not only the fastest-growing brand the company has ever created; they say it is on its way to becoming the largest girls' franchise on the planet."[10]

Indeed, the Disney princess world is a $5 billion industry, with what can seem like a monopoly on girl products. These days, "Keeping a 3-year-old girl away from Disney's princesses is a lot like trying to get through January without hearing about the Super Bowl," to use one journalist's comparison.[11] Many parents worry that the princess culture heightens the pressures on today's girls to look and act a certain way, and cultivates a sense of entitlement that won't work out so well in adulthood.[12]

Newer Disney offerings like *Frozen* and *Sofia the First* seem designed to quell the growing anti-princess fervor among today's more feminist mothers. They're refashioning the princess as smart, practical, and independent. And a recently launched Disney campaign dubbed "Dream Big, Princess" seeks to "[bring] girl power to the masses." A blog post announcing the campaign said, "There's nothing in the world quite like a Disney Princess. Whether it be Rapunzel's go-getter spirit, Mulan's diehard ambition, or Ariel's thirst for a better life in a better world, women and children alike have been inspired and moved by countless tales of these classic female protagonists."[13]

Sure, it's a marketing pitch, but they have a point. A thoughtful review of pre-*Frozen* Disney heroines reveals they aren't merely damsels in distress. Belle walks around town with her nose in a book and sought something more than "this provincial life." Ariel takes a major risk to explore a totally different world. Cinderella wins the heart of the prince because she isn't the fawning fool that he's used to. Captain Smith winds up relying on Pocahontas to save his life.

To Disney's credit, while many of their princesses have unrealistic figures and expose too much skin, they're actually pretty courageous women who win their men primarily because of their virtues. They are kind when others are cruel. They are fearless when others are afraid. They are intelligent when others are not. Ultimately, they win happiness for themselves, often with a prince and kingdom thrown in.

Perhaps the princess culture, flawed as it may be, is one way girls celebrate what makes them stand apart, an instinctive expression of their different-ness from boys that begins when they start understanding sexual difference. And perhaps the princess culture's not-so-great aspects are a reflection of rampant commercialization and materialism more than anything else, a materialism that influences the clothing and toys geared toward boys as well.

But some feminists were so upset about the princess culture that they decided to launch an ad called "Potty-Mouthed Princesses." In the ad, girls dressed in princess outfits make fun of princess-speak and yell a litany of profanities and tired feminist talking points at the camera: "I'm not some pretty [expletive] helpless princess in distress. I'm pretty [expletive] powerful and ready for success. So what is more offensive, a little girl saying [expletive], or the [expletive] unequal way society treats women? So listen up grown-ups, here some words more [expletive] up than the word [expletive]: pay inequality!"[14]

I'll stop there, and spare you the remaining two minutes of six-year-olds dropping f-bombs and yelling about rape. It's as appalling as it sounds, bordering on child abuse. At the end of the ad, just after a few boys dressed in princess outfits come out and yell, too, women who are presumably the mothers of these underage political props appear and hawk t-shirts saying "This is what a feminist looks like," sold by the ironically named company FCKH8.

The ad's "Potty-Mouthed Princesses" made the rounds on the web, racking up lots of acclaim from radical feminists. Lane Moore, the sex and relationships editor for *Cosmopolitan* magazine, wrote that seeing girls "dressed as princesses" and "cursing like sailors to spread the message of feminism" is "like a gift I didn't know to ask for."[15] *Jezebel* called the girls "awesome."[16]

The problem is that the little girls in the ad come off looking like caricatures of the lewdest teenage boy imaginable. They look angry and aggressive, more like drunk men than little girls.

Is this really a pro-woman message? Why should the price of equality be that girls abandon their girliness?

SEX DENIAL IN THE CLASSROOM

Princesses aren't the only toys standing in the way of "gender equity." In the mind of one kindergarten teacher, Legos propagate gender differences, too—so she banned boys from playing with them.

The idea, according to Seattle elementary school teacher Karen Keller, was that if boys couldn't play with Legos, girls would be more inclined to use them, instead of gravitating toward toys like dolls, as they typically did. "I always tell the boys, 'You're going to have a turn'—and I'm like, 'Yeah, when hell freezes over' in my head," she told a local news outlet. "I just feel like we are still so far behind in promoting gender equity," she continued.[17]

Her decision drew national attention in the fall of 2015, at which point the school received a deluge of enraged phone calls from parents, the teacher's name disappeared from its website, and the school issued a statement saying that the Lego ban for boys was an "isolated, short-term practice" that "ended in October. All students in all classrooms have and will continue to have access to all instructional and noninstructional materials."[18]

As the Lego kerfuffle suggests, American schools are the latest battleground over whether students and parents are allowed to acknowledge even the most basic differences between the sexes. Children are now actively encouraged to "explore" their gender—by schools that are actively encouraged to sow sexual confusion among children.

A recent CNN story, for example, urges schools to foster a "welcoming" environment for "gender nonconforming students" and find ways to "accommodate children who are opening up about gender identity as early as kindergarten." Suggestions include making sure boys and girls are never separated by sex and using gender-neutral greetings like "good morning, class" instead of "good morning, boys and girls." The article quotes one teacher as saying, "We need to be sure we don't create structures and artifices to reinforce binaries that limit and constrain the ways in which we behave and express ourselves."[19]

One Milwaukee elementary school recently held what it called "Gender Bender" day, in which boys were encouraged to dress like girls and vice versa. After parents balked, the day was renamed "Switch It Up Day," but the event went on.[20] At some high schools, it's no longer permitted to refer to a homecoming "king" or "queen." One must use the genderless "royal" instead. As a Wisconsin principal told the *Today Show*, about his school's move to ban "king" and "queen," the elected "royal couple" could even be "off the binary spectrum."[21] An elementary school in South Carolina was forced to cancel its annual father-daughter dance, also a successful fundraiser for the school's parent-teaching organization, over complaints that the dance was not "inclusive" of all genders. This despite the fact that, as the school district's spokeswoman stated, "it was never an event that was exclusive to only fathers and daughters. Mothers and anyone else who wanted to show up at the dance were certainly welcome to attend."[22]

But increasingly, the sexual confusion begins right in the classroom, with the rise of curricula that teach gender is a "fluid social construct" and sex is a meaningless label assigned at birth. In Virginia's Fairfax County, for instance, the school board issued a report in 2015 recommending that a new sex-ed curriculum teach middle and high school–aged children "that there is a broader, boundless, and fluid spectrum of sexuality that is developed throughout a lifetime."[23]

Despite being a liberal county, a bastion of Washington, D.C.'s wealthy elite, parents freaked. According to a *Washington Post* story about the school board meeting at which the proposal was discussed and voted upon, "The 10-to-2 vote Thursday night came amid shouts of anger and howls of frustration from a raucous crowd that largely stood in opposition to the curriculum changes." In an indicator of what's yet to come, the board had initially proposed moving parts of the curriculum out of sex-ed and into the health class. Parents can opt their children out of sex-ed. Health class is mandatory. In a last-minute concession, the board relented on the class switch, and parents were assured that, for now, they can pull their kids out of classes that are teaching that gender is a meaningless and malleable construct.[24] Fairfax County joins other schools around the country in enshrining sexual confusion into curricula designed for children. In Washington State, the confusion begins long before middle school: the state educational governing body lists "Understand there are many ways to express gender" as a "core idea" in the realm of "sexual health" *for kindergartners.*[25]

But schools' shift away from using sex as the basis of children's identity has implications beyond playtime and sex-ed.

THE END OF WOMEN'S SPORTS?

Bernice Sandler, dubbed the "Godmother of Title IX,"[26] called the legislation that she helped to draft "the most important step for gender equality since the 19th Amendment gave [women] the right to vote." Title IX is just thirty-seven words buried in a major education bill passed in 1972—"37 words that changed everything" when it came to women's sports, according to espnW, ESPN's online vertical for women. Those words run, "No person in the United States shall, on the basis of sex, be excluded from participation in, be denied the benefits of, or be subjected to discrimination under any educational program or activity receiving Federal financial assistance."

In an interview with espnW, Sandler admitted that girls' sports were not at the top of the priority list when the legislation was in the works. "The only thought I gave to sports when the bill was passed was, Oh, maybe now when a school holds its field day, there will be more activities for the girls." But Title IX turned out to be a major boost for girls' sports; ESPN notes that female participation in high school sports soared 1079 percent over the following four decades, and rose at a similar rate among college students. Male participation at the high school level grew by 22 percent in the same time.[27]

Though plenty of change that arose during the sweeping social upheaval of the seventies was deeply divisive and remains so today, increasing opportunities for women to play sports offered some common ground. A new generation of girls grew up enjoying sports as a healthy outlet and a place to cultivate friendships and leadership skills. For some, talent and hard work led to great professional and financial opportunities. That generation, which I am part of, grew up knowing that women could succeed in sports without sacrificing what it meant to be a woman. Sports was not a man's domain, and being a female athlete didn't mean you were just like "one of the guys."

We grew up watching the likes of Florence Griffith Joyner, known affectionately to Americans as "Flo Jo," an Olympic track and field athlete who is still considered the fastest woman of all time. She was known not just for the world records she still holds, but also for her feminine beauty and her dazzling nails. As the *Los Angeles Times* once described her, in a story about the way she inspired an entire generation of high school girls to pursue their athletic passions, Flo Jo was, "The great track athlete. The lovely lady with the long fingernails and great clothes."

Her husband, Al Joyner, also an Olympic gold medalist, said that "what Florence always wanted" was "[t]o see track prosper and to see more girls want to run."[28] Title IX was an essential part of making that happen for hundreds of thousands of girls who have run track in high school and beyond.

But for the first time in forty years, the opportunities that Title IX created for female athletes are under threat. Women's sports face a major test in the fallout from sex-denial: biological males on girls' sports teams. For decades, Title IX kicked in when a girl wanted to play a sport but no girls' team was offered at her school. A school had to make an effort to offer equal athletic opportunities for boys and girls, and when it could not, it had to allow girls to play on the boys' team. But now, under the "gender theory" regime, Title IX is being co-opted to permit boys to play on girls' teams, too.

The phenomenon went mostly unnoticed until 2011, when male high school senior Will Higgins competed in a girls' state swim meet in Massachusetts. He won the fifty-yard freestyle race and broke the meet record[29]—with a time that would not have even qualified him to compete in the same race in the boys' division.[30]

The lead paragraph of a *Boston Globe* article covering the controversy that ensued was Orwellian: "The governing body that regulates high school athletics in Massachusetts is taking a closer look at the controversy surrounding mixed-gender swim teams, and will soon address the issue of boys breaking girls' swimming records."[31] That same fall, boys competed on eight different high school girls' swim teams in Massachusetts, and several of the boys qualified to compete at the state level.

The *Globe* summed up the situation: "Athletic officials are limited in what they can do. In the eyes of the MIAA [Massachusetts Interscholastic Athletic Association], there's no stopping boys from competing on girls' swim teams because state law mandates equal access to sports for both genders. If a boy wants to swim and there is no boys' swimming program offered at his school, he is allowed to swim with the girls."

The same issue came up for debate in Pennsylvania in 2013, prompted by a surge in boys playing on girls' sports teams. One survey conducted by the Pennsylvania Interscholastic Athletic Association (PIAA) found that approximately thirty percent of schools reported having boys on a girls' sports team. When worried parents of girls began to protest, the state dug in its heels, taking the position that gender equity in sports means blindness to sexual difference. Pennsylvania's then attorney general said, "Athletic equity is required by the Pennsylvania [Equal Rights Amendment] and the ERA will not allow a rule barring boys from participating or playing on girls teams, just as the ERA will not allow a rule barring girls from participating or playing on boys teams."

Unsurprisingly, the pushback came from women. The Women's Sports Foundation, founded by none other than female tennis legend Billie Jean King of "Battle of the Sexes" fame, argued that a proper reading of Title IX protects the rights of women to have their own space for athletics, and that separating the sexes athletically gives girls and women a truly equal opportunity to succeed. Like the concerned parents of girls, the Women's Sports Foundation argued that allowing boys onto girls' sports teams could reverse the advances that female athletics has made and threatens girls' opportunities for scholarships. The foundation pointed out, "While courts have found girls to have the right to compete on boys teams under Title IX, the courts have not granted boys the same access to girls' teams."[32] This is to ensure that women are not deprived of athletic opportunities or scholarships. Despite great gains for women since the 1970s, the foundation's website notes, female high school athletes still have 1.3 million fewer athletic opportunities than men. Female college athletes have 63,000 fewer opportunities at NCAA schools and receive $183 million less in athletic scholarships at NCAA schools.[33]

Title IX remains very popular with the American public, boasting the support of eight in ten voters spanning political and familial demographics. "The American public," the foundation states, "believes that sports participation is as important for our daughters as it is for our sons."[34]

Eventually the PIAA took the issue to court, asking the Pennsylvania Supreme Court to reopen its 1973 decision ruling on Title IX as it applied to high school athletics. The PIAA made the same case as the Women's Sports Foundation, that the purpose of Title IX was not to mandate complete sex-blindness when it came to sports, but rather to ensure that women have the same chance to compete athletically as men. Allowing boys onto girls' teams threatened that equality.

The PIAA cited a mountain of data, such as the differences in height and weight between the average high school male and female that have resulted in different standards in various sports: a "lower net in [girls'] volleyball," a "smaller basketball" for girls' teams, "a shorter difference from tee to green in [girls'] golf," and so on. "[T]o even qualify to compete against boys in the PIAA track and field championship, a high school female would need to break a female state record.... in cross-country running, in 2012, 75 percent of all male athletes finished ahead of the fastest female athlete."

Allowing boys to compete with and against girls, the PIAA argued, "defeats the purpose of separate classifications, reducing participation opportunities for girls, providing teams using boys with unfair competitive advantages, and enhancing risks of injuries for girls."

The general counsel for the PIAA summed the issue up with a series of questions: "When equal treatment creates fundamentally unequal and unfair competition, should gender-blind equality trump fairness? Also, if boys and girls can each—and without limitation—play sports designated for the other gender, does there remain any legitimacy in having teams classified by gender? If not, should the classifications be merged and all teams be considered co-ed since gender is not a limitation on which team a student plays?"

"Such an approach would likely devastate female athletics at the high school level and is not a realistic, or at least a practical, option," he wrote.

The Pennsylvania Supreme Court ruled that it could not stop the PIAA from enacting a policy that barred boys from playing on girls' teams. But the opinion issued a warning: "If the past, as William Shakespeare noted in *The Tempest*, is truly a prologue, then any such policy may be challenged in a court of law on equal protection grounds."[35]

Just a few years later, Flo Jo's sport got national attention when Nattaphon Wangyot, a high school senior and biological male who self-identifies as female, was given permission to compete on the girls' track team. He went all the way to Alaska's state competition, placing third and fifth in two events and earning All State Honors, the kind of accolades that appeal to college scholarship officials.[36]

Families and students were timidly uncomfortable, with one student telling local news, "I'm glad that this person is comfortable with who they are and they're able to be happy in who they are, but I don't think it's competitively completely 100-percent fair."

A male athlete competing on the boys' team stated the obvious: "I don't know what's politically correct to say, but in my opinion, your gender is what you're born with. It's the DNA. Genetically a guy has more muscle mass than a girl, and if he's racing against a girl, he may have an advantage."

One mom said allowing a biological boy to compete against girls is "not fair and it is not right for our female athletes. We have a responsibility to protect our girls that have worked really hard, that are working towards college scholarships."[37]

The Alaska School Activities Association passed the buck: its board voted unanimously to accept any local school district's decision as to whether to allow members of one sex to compete on the opposite sex's team, and it won't hear any appeals from school districts competing against one another with conflicting policies. In the event that a school or district does not have a policy, the default policy is that a student must compete on teams with his or her own sex.[38]

When I spoke with Neena Chaudhry, a Title IX expert at the National Women's Law Center, she affirmed that Title IX was designed to protect women, not men. She told me that despite great gains for girls and women in sports, many "are still not getting opportunities to play; in college and high school, only 40 percent of opportunities to play sports are provided to women." Chaudhry said she is currently working on twelve different Office for Civil Rights complaints from twelve different school districts related to unequal opportunities for girls and boys. She said she's seen girls have to raise money for an ice hockey team when a boys' team already exists with school funding, and has heard about unequal facilities, like a spiffy new baseball field for the boys, but a rundown softball field for the girls.

So I was stunned when I asked her about biological boys who self-identify as females playing on girls' sports teams, and she brushed it off as nothing to be concerned about. "The differences within the genders can be greater than the differences between the genders," she said, and argued that "respect" for gender identity is paramount. "If we start drawing lines" based on gender stereotypes, she said, and saying "this is okay and this is not," that can lead to harmful discrimination.

Just moments before, Chaudhry had affirmed Title IX as a protection for girls, saying that "boys are already getting their fair share" of athletic opportunities, and allowing a boy onto a girls' team is simply "taking a spot from a girl."[39] I was left wondering about the same question the attorney for the PIAA asked: "Should the classifications be merged and all teams be considered co-ed since gender is not a limitation on which team a student plays?"

It's no longer a rhetorical question: If sex doesn't matter—if we are going to pretend there are no important biological differences between boys and girls—then why have girls' sports at all?

Nancy Hogshead-Makar, a three-time Olympic gold medalist in swimming, a sports law professor and Title IX expert, and then senior director of advocacy for the Women's Sports Foundation, has argued that keeping girls and boys sports separate is the only way to ensure that girls have the same access to sports participation. In an interview with the *Pittsburgh Post Gazette*, she said, "Sports are unique. Other than bathrooms, they are the only sex-segregated area because of the physical differences between boys and girls."[40]

Might we see the downfall of both?

LEGOS FOR GIRLS

In 2013, the Danish company Lego announced that it had seen a twenty-five percent boost in its revenue the year before, with sales nearly triple those of just five years before.[41]

The reason?

Legos for girls. Working in consultation with actual girls, Lego had developed a new product line aimed exclusively at girls called Lego Friends.

As one executive put it, "The girls we talked to let us understand that they really wanted a Lego offering that mirrors what the boys experience, but in a way that fulfills their unique desire for redesign and details and combined with realistic themes in community and friendship."[42]

The new line of products features scenes of girls doing things like hanging out at "City Park Cafe," getting artistic at "Emma's Creative Workshop," or visiting "Heartlake Hair Salon." Not every product choice is manifestly girly; the line offers more "gender-neutral" choices like "Heartlake Airport," "Olivia's Exploration Car," and "Adventure Camp Archery." But the collection comes in every offensive shade of purple and pink, and heavily features scenes that seem plucked right out of the lives of normal girls today, with an emphasis on creativity and community.[43] It quickly became Lego's fourth-bestselling product line; Lego said in a press release that it had been unable to keep up with demand after it was launched.

Lego even came out with a giant Disney Castle set, which writer Jonathan Last called a Lego "Death Star for Girls," "a big, 4,080-piece step toward gender equality," and "the kind of set that would make a girl scream uncontrollably on Christmas morning."

"What Lego finally seems to understand," Last wrote, "is that however much some people might wish it otherwise, more often than not, boys and girls have different tastes in toys."[44] Even the White House struggles with this reality. In April of 2016, it hosted a major summit on "gender stereotypes in toys."[45]

But do kids actually have gender preferences in toys?

A recent study on toy preferences in babies as young as nine months found the answer to be a clear "yes." Researchers at the City, University of London gave babies a choice of "gender-specific" toys like a cooking pot, doll, ball, and truck and studied what each sex gravitated toward and how long they played with the toy. Their findings were unsurprising: the girls on average opted for things associated with girls, and vice versa. In their words, "Our findings of sex differences in toy choice in the 9 to 17 months age group add some weight to the suggestion that such preferences appear prior to extensive socialization and do not depend on gender category knowledge but are reflections of our biological heritage."[46]

The study was consistent with Lego's experience in making sets tailored to girls. But activists for gender neutrality were unimpressed. The girls' line even inspired a Change.org petition from a group called SPARK, which stands for Sexualization Protest: Action, Resistance, Knowledge. The petition accused Lego of reinforcing gender stereotypes and demanded more options for girls, like "things blowing up": "[I]f you keep on excluding [girls] from your marketing vision, soon [girls] will start to believe that they would rather have hot tubs and little plastic boobs."[47] Even so, the company said that the proportion of Lego sets purchased for girls had tripled following the release of Lego Friends.[48]

Lego demonstrated that the way to engage more girls in constructive play is not to make their toys gender-neutral or ban boys from playing with them, but to make them *different*, to tailor them to the things that make girls different from boys: their relationality, their femininity, and their distinctly less violent sense of adventure. Nobody was forcing Lego Friends on anyone; girls wanted the toys because corporate executives designed them based on *what girls said they wanted* in a toy. If you were to call in the folks at Harvard Business School for a case study on gender and Legos, their analysis would be pretty plain: if you want a more equal number of girls and boys playing with Legos, you have to make them different.

But society is pressing on in the opposite direction, in the misguided hope that if we can stamp out a clear distinction between girls and boys we will have achieved gender equity. But as the evolution of girls' sports makes clear, gender blindness is not gender fairness. It took a law that treated women and men differently in the athletic arena to empower female athletes. Policies and curricula that deny sexual difference threaten to undo those gains and rob girls and women of the chance to compete and flourish, in all tracks of life.

CHAPTER 2

DENYING THE DIFFERENCE

==

Language exerts hidden power,
like the moon on the tides.

—Rita Mae Brown

"**W**hat's in a name?"
So asked one doomed young lady by the name of
Juliet. The question was a rhetorical one, but 420 years
later, it's still relevant.

An essential part of understanding today's insanity about sex is
understanding the language of the debate. To see how sex became scandalous, we need to back up and ask what "sex" is. And how did "gender"
elbow its way into the debate? Why are they increasingly used interchangeably? Should they be?

As it turns out, "sex" has been around for a long time. "Gender" is
a much newer player on the scene. Despite the fact that pundits, celebrities, and bureaucrats often use the words interchangeably, "sex" still has
a concrete meaning accepted by medical and linguistic experts—at least
for now.

When you go to the doctor, fill out a government form, or buy a
plane ticket, you indicate your "sex." But what exactly is "gender"?

According to the American Medical Association's style guide, *AMA Manual of Style*,

> Sex refers to the biological characteristics of males and females.[1]

The AMA manual is designed for writers and editors, so if you are writing about human beings and want to be scientifically accurate according to the largest group of doctors in the country, "sex" has a meaning, and it's quite definite.

ASK THE DOCTOR

The American Psychological Association (APA), the nation's largest professional organization of certified psychologists, offers a slightly longer definition:

> *Sex* refers to a person's biological status and is typically categorized as male, female, or intersex (i.e., atypical combinations of features that usually distinguish male from female). There are a number of indicators of biological sex, including sex chromosomes, gonads, internal reproductive organs, and external genitalia.[2]

As some will eagerly point out, there are human beings whose genitalia are more ambiguous; that's what "intersex" refers to. But this situation is exceedingly rare. So rare that even a clinical geneticist who has helped to pioneer research on this front referred to a real-life example as "science-fiction material."[3]

The medical community's treatment of the word "gender" is much more open-ended. The APA specifies,

> *Gender* refers to the attitudes, feelings, and behaviors that a given culture associates with a person's biological sex.

Behavior that is compatible with cultural expectations is referred to as gender-normative; behaviors that are viewed as incompatible with these expectations constitute gender non-conformity.

According to the AMA style manual:

Gender includes more than sex and serves as a cultural indicator of a person's personal and social identity.

The AMA places "sex" on par with "age," another objective and biologically rigid factor, and makes clear that "sex" is still a relevant factor for doctors. "Sex" is a straightforward scientific marker. Gender is a broader, changing sociological term. Particularly noteworthy is that both the AMA and the APA define "gender" in terms of "sex," while "sex" stands on its own. "Gender" is not included in either definition of "sex." But neither scientific organization is able to define "gender" without using "sex" as a reference point.

The World Health Organization (WHO) also differentiates between "sex" and "gender"; the distinction is important enough to merit its own explanation page:

What do we mean by "sex" and "gender"?
Sometimes it is hard to understand exactly what is meant by the term "gender," and how it differs from the closely related term "sex".

"Sex" refers to the biological and physiological characteristics that define men and women.

"Gender" refers to the socially constructed roles, behaviours, activities, and attributes that a given society considers appropriate for men and women.

To put it another way:

"Male" and "female" are sex categories, while "masculine" and "feminine" are gender categories.

Aspects of sex will not vary substantially between different human societies, while aspects of gender may vary greatly.

Some examples of sex characteristics:
- Women menstruate while men do not
- Men have testicles while women do not
- Women have developed breasts that are usually capable of lactating, while men have not
- Men generally have more massive bones than women

Some examples of gender characteristics:
- In the United States (and most other countries), women earn significantly less money than men for similar work
- In Viet Nam, many more men than women smoke, as female smoking has not traditionally been considered appropriate
- In Saudi Arabia men are allowed to drive cars while women are not
- In most of the world, women do more housework than men[4]

The fact is, the medical world has a lot to say about sex versus gender, and that has not changed despite recent shifts in the political landscape.

The Mayo Clinic, perhaps the premier medical institution in the country, recently held what it called a "first of its kind summit" to create "a road-map for integration of sex and gender-based evidence into medical and inter-professional education."[5] Of the need for the summit, the director of the Women's Health Research Center at Mayo said, "As we enter the world of precision medicine, medical research about basic sex differences between men and women must be incorporated into curriculum for physicians and all health care providers for it to be translated into better outcomes for patients."[6]

Translation: good medicine *requires* sexual difference as a baseline, because women have very different health risks and symptoms from men in a host of categories, from breast cancer to bone density to the signs of a heart attack. So understanding sexual difference drives medical and scientific advances, to make us all healthier.

A closer look at the Mayo summit goals makes it clear that better understanding the "unique needs of the female patient" was an important impetus for the event. That conference built on the work begun by a 2013 workshop Mayo Clinic had held in conjunction with major governmental bodies such as the National Institutes of Health and the Canadian Institute of Health and Gender. The opening line of the abstract summarizing the earlier workshop's findings defines "sex" as a "biological variable" and "gender" as a "cultural variable."[7] The summary paper cites a major study published in 2001 by the Institute of Medicine, which posed the question, "Does Sex Matter?" That study found that "sex, that is being male or female, is an important basic human variable that should be considered when designing and analyzing studies in all areas and at all levels of biomedical and health related hazard research"—a variable that remains relevant from "womb to tomb."[8]

More than a decade later, the 2013 Mayo summit demonstrated that a consensus of the medical community still holds that "sex is a narrowly defined term defining living things as male and female based on the complement of sex chromosomes and the presence of reproductive organs" whereas "gender refers to a complex psychosocial construct that takes into account biology but also the influences of society and environment." "The terms are distinct, not synonymous," the workshop attendees agreed, and confusion or conflation of the terms is a "barrier to developing sex-and-gender-based material for health professional educations."[9]

Attendees at the 2015 Mayo summit treated gender as important, but on par with other external factors such as "socio-economic status and culture" in making medical evaluations.

It is mainly women in the medical field who drive conferences and workshops such as these, because sex-based medicine is increasingly recognized as especially important for women. Up until a couple of hundred years ago, doctors and scientists did not have a sophisticated concept of sexual difference.

BACK TO THE FUTURE

We take chromosomes, DNA, hormones, and other important biological markers for granted, because we've all grown up in a time when they're all (relatively) well understood. But for most of human history, medicine treated men and women as identical, save for their reproductive organs. Until the eighteenth century, the female body was viewed as a flawed version of the male body, as essentially a male body with the reproductive organs inside out. To quote the fourth-century Greek philosopher Nemesius, "theirs are inside the body and not outside it."

For millennia, there weren't even unique terms for female reproductive organs; instead, they were primarily referred to with the male term for the comparable organ and the modifier "female." Ovaries, for example, were frequently called "female testes." In the eighteenth century, however, there was a major shift in science and medicine toward viewing the female body as entirely distinct, not just as a flawed version of the male body.

In *Making Sex: Body and Gender from the Greeks to Freud*, historian Thomas Laqueur writes extensively about this shift. Medical terminology for female reproductive organs did not really emerge until the 1700s, when there was a "more radical...reinterpretation of the female body in relation to the male." Of this period Laqueur writes, "Thus the old model, in which men and women were arrayed according to their degree of metaphysical perfection...along an axis whose telos was male, gave way by the late eighteenth century to a new model of radical dimorphism, of biological divergence. An anatomy and physiology of incommensurability replaced a metaphysics of hierarchy in the representation of woman in relation to man."

Incommensurability is defined as "having no standard of comparison." Prior to the 1700s, there was literally no standard for comparing male and female physiognomy other than the most obvious distinctions.

"Language," Laqueur points out, "marks this view of sexual difference." In other words, changes in language mirrored changes in thought, the departure from the notion that sexuality existed on a spectrum that pointed toward the alpha male as the ideal and away from the female, who was devalued as inherently flawed.

Even so, medicine largely persisted in overlooking the many unique aspects of the female anatomy and physiology well into the twentieth century, when women began demanding a more individualized approach based on sexual difference. In the 1980s, the National Institutes of Health (NIH) established a task force to better address these demands, and it concluded that "little was known about the unique needs of the female patient." A government report released in the early nineties found that half of NIH's proposed medical studies did not even include women. As a result, the NIH created an entire division devoted exclusively to women's health issues, and Congress demanded that research and clinical trials on medicine and procedures be designed to study the effects on *both* men and women.[10]

Even today, women are calling for medicine to put more emphasis on sex, pointing out, for example, "Many medications have been withdrawn from the market due to adverse side effects in women compared with men, and safety devices might be less than adequate because they were modeled and tested only for one sex."

The fact is, "sex" and the differences it demarcates are at the heart of the evolution of modern science. The word has a narrow meaning, but recognizing its significance is especially important to women—thus the continuing push coming from activists for women's health for more focus on the differences between the sexes in medicine, not less.

THE GENESIS OF GENDER

It's not just doctors and health professionals who affirm that pesky male-female binary. So do the professional linguists.

According to the *Oxford English Dictionary,* "sex" refers to "either of the two main categories (male and female) into which humans and many other living things are divided on the basis of their reproductive functions." The word, "(denoting the two categories, male and female)" comes from the "Old French *sexe* or Latin *sexus.*"[11] "Gender," on the other hand, while still denoting "the state of being male or female," according to the dictionary, is "typically used with reference to social and cultural differences rather than the biological ones.... Although the words **gender** and **sex** both have the sense 'the state of being male or female,' they are typically used in slightly different ways: **sex** tends to refer to biological differences, while **gender** refers to cultural or social ones."[12]

The *American Heritage Dictionary* (5th edition) defines sex in essentially the same way:

2.

a. Either of the two divisions, designated female and male, by which most organisms are classified on the basis of their reproductive organs and functions: *How do you determine the sex of a lobster?*

b. The fact or condition of existing in these two divisions, especially the collection of characteristics that distinguish female and male: *the evolution of sex in plants; a study that takes sex into account.*

3. Females or males considered as a group: *dormitories that house only one sex.*

4. One's identity as either female or male.[13]

The word "sex" to demarcate men and women has been in use for centuries. It is derived from the Latin *sexus,* "a sex, state of being either male or female." According to the Online Etymology Dictionary, it is "commonly taken with *seco* as division or 'half' of the race" and connected to *secare,* which means to "divide or cut."[14]

"Sex" didn't become associated with the birds and the bees until the 1900s, a change attributed to D. H. Lawrence, whose most famous book, *Lady Chatterly's Lover*, was so sexually explicit that it was banned in many places until the late 1950s. Before that, the word "sex" was used exclusively to differentiate between men and women.

"Gender" has been in use for a long time, too, though not remotely in the sense it is used today. The word can be traced back to the 1300s and comes from the old French *gendre* or *genre*, meaning "kind, sort, class, character, species," and ultimately from the Latin *genus*, meaning "race, stock, family, kind, order."[15] It mostly came up in the context of grammar, particularly the grammar of languages that divide all their nouns into masculine, feminine, and neuter, such as Latin and French. But once "sex" came to mean *sexual intercourse*, "gender" came into wider usage as a euphemism for *sex differences*—that is, for "sex" as traditionally and scientifically understood.

"Gender" as applied to people rather than to nouns and adjectives was little more than a euphemism, though, until the 1960s, when it began to take on a highly politicized meaning of its own.[16] From the Online Etymology Dictionary: "The 'male-or-female sex' sense is attested in English from early 15c. As *sex* (n.) took on erotic qualities in 20c., *gender* came to be the usual English word for 'sex of a human being,' in which use it was at first regarded as colloquial or humorous. Later often in feminist writing with reference to social attributes as much as biological qualities; this sense first attested 1963."

The chart on the following page tracks how frequently "sex" and "gender" have been used in books from 1800 to 2008. The word "gender" took off in the 60s and exploded in the 80s, right around the time that something called "gender theory" was laying down roots in academic institutions and feminist circles nationwide.

"Gender theory" is about as expansive and imprecise as it sounds. A Google search on the term yields close to 100 million results, with everyone from Pope Francis to pop psychology magazines to heads of academic departments taking a crack at defining it. Gender theory itself has spawned

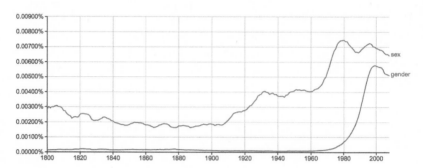

Google Books Ngram Viewer http://books.google.com/ngrams

an entire subset of offshoots such as "gender schema theory," "gender prediction theory," or "gendering theory." It's so broad that Amazon lists "Gender Studies" among such sweeping categories as "Politics & Government," "Ethics & Morality," and "Popular Culture."[17]

Fifty years after the birth of gender theory, we still don't know exactly what it is.

Even Wikipedia can't really pin gender theory down.

The online encyclopedia automatically redirects from "gender theory" to a "gender studies" page, which explains that "'gender' should be used to refer to the social and cultural constructions of masculinities and femininities and not to the state of being male or female in its entirety." But then it adds, "However, this view is not held by all gender theorists."

Wikipedia says that gender studies spans just about every major discipline, but then points out that those "disciplines sometimes differ in their approaches to how and why gender is studied." Then it offers the following point of clarification: "For instance in anthropology, sociology and psychology, gender is often studied as a practice, whereas in cultural studies representations of gender are more often examined. In politics, gender can be viewed as a foundational discourse that political actors employ in order to position themselves on a variety of issues."

In a final attempt at clarity, the online encyclopedia's introduction to the subject explains, "Gender can also be broken into three categories, gender identity, gender expression, and biological sex.... These three categories are another way of breaking down gender into the different social, biological, and cultural constructions. These constructions focus on how femininity and masculinity are fluid entities and how their meaning is able to fluctuate depending on the various constraints surrounding them."

"Fluid entities." "Able to fluctuate." Gender theory is hard to pin down. But the basic idea is that being a man or a woman doesn't follow from being born male or female. Gender is fluid, fluctuating. Gender theory is all about divorcing "gender" from biological "sex." To the gender theorists, masculine and feminine aren't realities of nature, they're artificial categories—"social constructs." *Oppressive* social constructs, which prop up "the patriarchy" and "subordinate" women. The "gender binary"—that is, the division of the human race into men and women—is a straitjacket from which we must be liberated.

As Simone de Beauvoir, a leading second-wave feminist, famously wrote in *The Second Sex*, "One is not born, but rather becomes, a woman." To Beauvoir, being a "woman" was a societal invention, made up of stereotypes about what female human beings are and how they should behave.

In an oft-cited 1986 article, gender theorist Judith Butler explained the significance of Beauvoir's line:

> "One is not born, but rather becomes, a woman"—Simone de Beauvoir's formulation distinguishes sex from gender and suggests that gender is an aspect of identity gradually acquired. The distinction between sex and gender has been crucial to the long-standing feminist effort to debunk the claim that anatomy is destiny; *sex* is understood to be the invariant, anatomically distinct, and factic aspects of the female body, whereas *gender* is the cultural meaning and form that that body acquires, the variable modes of that body's acculturation. With the distinction intact, it is no longer possible to attribute the values or social functions of women to biological necessity, and neither can we refer mean-

ingfully to natural or unnatural gendered behavior: all gender is, by definition, unnatural. Moreover, if the distinction is consistently applied, it becomes unclear whether being a given sex has any necessary consequence for becoming a given gender. The presumption of a causal or mimetic relation between sex and gender is undermined...[18]

Feminists in the 1960s and 70s argued that men and women are not inherently different. The many apparent differences between the sexes— beyond the undeniable anatomical ones—are simply the result of gender roles people are taught to fulfill, not of their natures as men or women.[19] This was the era when parents were told that their daughters would be just as happy playing with toy trucks as with dolls—and that making the switch would help end sexism and liberate girls for a better future. Women sought to detach themselves from the aspects of womanhood they found limiting, especially their fertility.

BURNING DOWN THE GENDER BINARY

The final frontier in the gender revolution is the complete abolition of gender distinctions in any way tied to the two biological sexes. This is something gender radicals readily admit. Rebecca Reilly-Cooper, a British professor of political philosophy focusing on sex, gender, and identity, summed up the position in an article for *Aeon*:

> Humans of both sexes would be liberated if we recognised that while gender is indeed an internal, innate, essential facet of our identities, there are more genders than just "woman" or "man" to choose from. And the next step on the path to liberation is the recognition of a new range of gender identities: so we now have people referring to themselves as "genderqueer" or "non-binary" or "pangender" or "polygender" or "agender" or "demiboy" or "demigirl" or "neutrois" or "aporagender" or "lunagender" or "quantumgender"...I

could go on. An oft-repeated mantra among proponents of this view is that "gender is not a binary; it's a spectrum". What follows from this view is not that we need to tear down the pink and the blue boxes; rather, we simply need to recognise that there are many more boxes than just these two.[20]

Activist Riki Wilchins put it more succinctly in a piece for the hard-left *Advocate*, writing that the ultimate goal is to demolish "the entire underlying hetero-binary structuring of the world."[21] "This," Wilchins writes, "is the real struggle." Wilchins is the author of the forthcoming book, *Burn Down the Binary*.

But what happens to women when the binary burns down? How do the members of the physically weaker sex, who bear a disproportionate share of the burden for reproduction, defend ourselves in a world where gender distinctions are a matter of individual interpretation, with no anchor in physical reality? How does a woman prove she is suffering any kind of sex-based abuse if identifying as a woman is just one choice among many? Even Reilly-Cooper warns that replacing the "gender binary" with a "gender spectrum" will "obscure the reality of female oppression."

It doesn't just obscure that reality. It invalidates every claim of abuse, discrimination, or violence on the basis of sex by robbing women of the right to claim their biologically determined gender as a valid category.

That's not just my prediction about where "gender theory" is taking us. It has already happened, in an American courtroom, when the successful young singer songwriter Kesha sued her producer in 2014 for abusing her for more than a decade "sexually, verbally, physically, and emotionally"—according to her lawsuit, he drugged and raped her, and she "woke up naked the next day in his bed," as the Daily Beast put it, "sore and sick, with no memory of how she got there."[22] The (female) judge decided to toss Kesha's entire case on this basis: "Although Gottwald's alleged actions were directed to Ke$ha, who is female," the claims "do not allege that Gottwald harbored animus toward women or was motivated by gender animus when he allegedly behaved violently toward Ke$ha," the judge explained. "Every rape is not a gender-motivated hate crime."[23]

We'll look more closely at the details of this court case in chapter five, but we should be worried by the argument that rape, an act in which a man uses his superior physical strength and aggressiveness to take advantage of a woman, is not considered to be inherently "gender-motivated." It makes a strange kind of sense, though—if gender is only a "construct."

And "gender theory" just keeps driving our society even further from reality. As Professor Reilly-Cooper explains, "Once we assert that the problem with gender is that we currently recognise only two of them, the obvious question to ask is: how many genders would we have to recognise in order not to be oppressive? Just how many possible gender identities are there? The only consistent answer to this is: 7 billion, give or take. There are as many possible gender identities as there are humans on the planet.... your gender can be frost or the Sun or music or the sea or Jupiter or pure darkness. Your gender can be pizza."[24]

How is it compatible with women's dignity, happiness, or even safety for "woman" to be put on an equal footing with "pizza"?

The effort to detach the human person from the body may have seemed newfangled when "gender theory" was invented in the twentieth century. But in fact it was a throwback. It harks back to Gnosticism, an ancient belief system whose adherents viewed matter as evil and saw the rejection of the body as the path to freedom. The Gnostics cooked up the concept of having an identity that mismatched the body a couple of millennia before the gender theorists.[25]

But despite the Gnostics and their present-day heirs in gender theory, the differences between the genders or the sexes, whichever you prefer to call them, remain stubbornly persistent today.

VIVE LA DIFFÉRENCE

In 1992, amid the gender theory ferment, family therapist John Gray published *Men Are from Mars, Women Are from Venus*. The book's premise was simple: men and women are different, and understanding those differences, not living in denial of them, is the key to relationship success. The book's popularity exploded. It became not just a bestselling book of its decade,[26] but one of the bestselling books of all time.[27]

It was pop psychology, but it hit a social nerve. Despite the push to build a gender-neutral society, it seemed people were still desperate to understand their differences. Paradoxically, the dawn of gender theory was also the period when social scientists and doctors began to make the most progress in understanding sexual difference and the delicate physiological interplay between men and women.

Major advances in neurobiology, for example, unveiled just how differently men and women respond physically to intimacy. During intercourse, the female releases more oxytocin than the male. Oxytocin is the hormone that facilitates bonding between human beings, in particular between mothers and new babies and between heterosexual partners. It's colloquially referred to as "the love hormone," "the hug hormone," the "cuddle chemical," the "moral molecule," and the "bliss hormone,"[28] and is especially noted for the different roles it plays in female reproduction.[29]

According to the American Psychological Association, "New studies are adding to a body of literature that shows oxytocin plays a key role in maternal bonding and social affiliation—what [social psychologist Shelley] Taylor has labeled the 'tend and befriend' response, as opposed to the 'fight or flight' response."[30]

Oxytocin, researchers discovered, makes a woman more vulnerable and attached to the man with whom she is having sex. Men release a small amount of oxytocin during intercourse, too, but they release an even bigger amount of testosterone, which has the effect of *suppressing* the oxytocin.[31]

So science has a basic explanation for why women will stare at their phone after casual sex, hoping their partner will contact them, while men do not. As one woman wrote in a piece for Elite Daily, "The Truth Behind Why Women Find It Harder to Have Casual Sex than Men Do," the phenomenon of oxytocin offers "a scientific explanation as to why after sex, women are left wondering if and when she will hear from a guy. All the while, guys are scrolling through Tinder on their couch, wondering if that chicken parm they ordered an hour ago is actually on its way."[32] "Women," she writes, "are programmed to become emotionally attached" in a way that men are not.

But men have their own physiological process for bonding and emotional attachment. They are affected by oxytocin, too, but in a different way.

A study conducted in 2013 found that men who had been intimate and fallen in love with a woman, then inhaled oxytocin as a nasal spray and looked at pictures of different women, including strangers, experienced brain activity in the region that regulates "pleasure and desire" only when they saw the photo of their female partner.

A summary of the findings in *Time* explained that inhaling the oxytocin had the effect of enhancing the attractiveness of a man's partner as compared to other females: "[O]xytocin can create unconscious biases in favor of a partner, possibly providing part of the biological mechanism behind monogamy. A prior study by the same researchers, in fact, found that men in monogamous relationships who were given oxytocin actually kept a greater physical distance from an attractive research associate, compared with single men."[33]

As the *Atlantic* put it, oxytocin, which can be stimulated by something as simple as hand-holding or hugging, "promotes monogamy by preventing men from 'signaling romantic interest' to other women."[34]

One little hormone can help women to fall in love and men to stay in love.

A woman also triggers physiological changes in her male partner when she becomes pregnant. Her body produces pheromones that he breathes in, causing him to produce different hormones, such as prolactin, that make him more sympathetic to the baby and his or her needs. And his testosterone level dips by as much as a third.

There is a seemingly unending litany of ways that men and women are different, many of them still unexplained.

As Harvard professor Harvey Mansfield notes in *Manliness*, his treatise on manhood, data show that women are friendlier. Two-thirds of people who are more inclined toward smiling are women.

Women are also more communicative. Multiple studies have found that women, on average, say more words than men in a given day, with one estimate putting the difference at approximately 20,000 to 7,000. The difference in verbal facility between males and females is a phenomenon that begins early, as any parent who's had children of both sexes can attest to.

My daughter, for example, said her first word at nine months: a clear and crisp "book!," which I captured on video. At nineteen months, my son has one word and one word only, and it's hardly a word: "ay-ya!," much like what you'd hear in a martial arts film. I'm just one mom, but when I tell that story, listeners, including my pediatrician, immediately reply, "Well, we all know girls are much more verbal than boys." Of course there's plenty of variation within each sex, too, but there are a lot more stories like my family's than the other way around.

That difference persists into adulthood, and scientists now ascribe it in part to higher levels of the protein FOXP2 in the female brain. As one researcher who studies sex differences at Michigan State put it, "Higher levels of FOXP2 expression are found in the more communicative sex in each species."[35] According to another scientist at the Society for Neuroscience, the FOXP2 link "raise[s] the possibility that sex differences in brain and behavior are more pervasive and established earlier than previously appreciated."[36]

On the other hand, there was the study released in 2015, based on MRI images, finding no evidence that there is such a thing as a "male" or "female" brain. In the words of one science journal, "The majority of the brains were a mosaic of male and female structures."[37] As was to be expected, gender theorists promptly declared victory in the debate about sexual difference. "There is no such thing as the 'male brain' or 'female brain,' and scientists have the scans to prove it," exclaimed the *Los Angeles Times*, and about one million other news outlets.[38]

But as Louann Brizendine, an Ivy-educated neuropsychiatrist and author of *The Male Brain* and *The Female Brain*, summarized the science of sex differences in a piece for CNN.com, "Our brains are mostly alike.

We are the same species, after all. But the differences can sometimes make it seem like we are worlds apart."[39] Or to some, planets apart.

Medical phenomena continue to point to stark differences between the male and female brains.

Men, for instance, are significantly more likely to have reading disorders, something that has been attributed to, among other things, "differences in brain functioning."[40] And reading disorders may arise differently in men and women. According to a Georgetown University Medical Center study, "Brain anatomy of dyslexia is not the same in men and women, boys and girls."

The study's lead author explained, "There is sex-specific variance in brain anatomy and females tend to use both hemispheres for language tasks, while males just the left. It is also known that sex hormones are related to brain anatomy and that female sex hormones such as estrogen can be protective after brain injury, suggesting another avenue that might lead to the sex-specific findings reported in this study."[41]

Men are also more likely to stutter, something the Stuttering Foundation readily points out. Indeed, an expert quoted on its website states that "gender is one of the strongest predisposing factors for stuttering." He reports that scientists "have long suspected that underlying the gender ratio in stuttering are genetic factors (likely affecting brain structures associated with speech-language processes)."[42]

Women, on other hand, are more prone to insomnia and need more sleep than men, and scientists researching sleep are increasingly focusing on differences between the male and female brain.[43]

The world of science and medicine is trending toward greater, not lesser, understanding of the importance of what makes us different.

Have what we call "gender roles" changed over time? Sure. Women did a lot more manual work and spent a lot more time outside the home in the hunter-gatherer era than they did in suburban America in the 1950s. As one *Daily Mail* headline put it, "Our Ancestors Were FEMINISTS."

Pink wasn't always a girly color. Long before Disney and Mattel made it the go-to hue for little girls, plenty of men, from the court of King

Louis XVI to Robert Redford in the movie of *The Great Gatsby*, have been known to wear pink.[44] I find my own husband rather dashing in a pink button-down with khaki slacks. And even slacks weren't always fashionable for the male sex. In some cultures today, they still aren't.

Does great variety exist within the sexes? Of course. Some men are poets, some men are soldiers. Some women are trial lawyers, while others write books. Some men vacuum. Some women don't cook.

And yet, despite historical changes in fashion preferences, domestic arrangements, professional inclinations, and so much more, certain aspects of nature stubbornly persist. Shifts in who wears pink have not changed the fact that women, and only women, can conceive, gestate, and give birth to a new member of the human species. Men are, on the whole, the physically stronger sex. Culture may imbue gender with certain random characteristics, but science is not walking away from sex as a key feature of humanity.

Culture may change, but reality doesn't.

BRAVE NEW WORLD

In 2014, Facebook launched a feature that allowed users to choose from as many as seventy-one different ways of identifying their gender. Whereas previously users could only select "male" or "female" or choose to keep that information private, the new feature added options like "Androgyne," "Gender Fluid," "Neutrois," "Non-binary," "Pangender," and "Two-Spirit," among many others. The move caused media pandemonium, with some outlets even producing glossaries for all the new label choices.[45]

But seventy-one choices apparently weren't enough. One year later, the Facebook Diversity page announced that it would be expanding that feature to include a "free form field."

In their words: "Now, if you do not identify with the pre-populated list of gender identities, you are able to add your own. As before, you can add up to ten gender terms and also have the ability to control the audience with whom you would like to share your custom gender. We recognize that some people face challenges sharing their true gender identity with others, and this setting gives people the ability to express themselves in an authentic way."[46]

One would have expected jubilation from gender activists. Instead, the comment section was full of angry rants that not enough had yet been done, for Facebook continued to insist that users provide their true legal names.

One commenter by the name of "Bootblack Marta" wrote,

> Your "Authentic Name" policy makes those who are ALREADY expressing themselves in an authentic way and who are very invested in the friend networks that they have built through this site vulnerable to attack.
>
> We are leatherfolk, LGBTQIA people, drag performers, burlesquers, pagans, Native people, activists, abuse survivors, and your policy empowers anonymous people to target us, forcing arbitrary name changes and automatic account suspensions that take interminable lengths of time to resolve.
>
> You, Facebook, enable this hate.
>
> Dozens upon dozens of MY leather community members and extended family have been reported in just the last two weeks. We are interconnected, we are authentic, and we deserve to, as you say here, use our own words to describe ourselves.
>
> Please investigate the source of these recent reports. Please reconsider allowing anyone to report our accounts.
>
> You, Facebook. can be doing better.
>
> Like · Reply · 29 · February 26, 2015 at 11:25am · Edited

To which one commenter added, "The authentic name police is super terrible and favors those with the privilege and safety of preferring/using their legal name. Can we please stop that now?"

Others demanded expanding the "Interested In" feature, which only allows users to select "men" or "women." One commenter proposed "allowing polyamorous people to list multiple romantic relationships. I've been in situations when I just have to say I'm single because I don't want to pick one and leave out the others."

Still others asked for more pronoun options. As *Cosmopolitan* magazine complained, "pronouns sometimes used, but not offered on Facebook, are Zie/Zir or Xe/Xyr."[47]

That same year, the American Dialect Society proclaimed "they" as its word of the year. The linguistics group, which is more than a century old, announced that "'They' was recognised by the society for its emerging use as a pronoun to refer to a known person, often as a conscious choice by a person rejecting the traditional gender binary of 'he' and 'she.'"

As a lengthy piece for the BBC commenting on the decision noted, "[G]rammar is at the vanguard of a gender revolution. In the new gender revolution, there are no pyres of charred bras or prison hunger strikes. Instead, key battlegrounds are dictionaries, and the choice of weapon includes linguistics."[48]

And that brings us back to Juliet. What's in a name?

Everything.

When the word "sex" became scandalous, the door was cracked open to use "gender" as a euphemism. But "sex" meant something specific and—as evidenced by Facebook—"gender" can mean anything to anyone.

Half a century after "gender" replaced "sex," major data amalgamator Wikipedia doesn't even know how to explain all its meanings. When you unhinge identity from sex, the result is a sort of gender anarchy. Either sex means something, or nothing means anything.

One German politician unwittingly illustrated the insanity of it all by addressing sixty different genders, including "bi-gender," "inter*Females" and "two-spirit third genders," in his introduction to a vote on a gender diversity bill. After more than a minute had passed, the presiding member tried to interrupt him, to which he replied with a frank, "I'm not done with my introduction yet, Mr. President." The visibly irritated members couldn't help but laugh. But the observer is left wondering, where does it end?[49]

Meanwhile, society has split away from science on the issue of sexual difference. Scientists are finding more and more reasons to incorporate innate sexual differences into their research, practice, and instruction, and more and more reasons to believe that sexual difference sheds a great deal of light on why people are the way they are. Anatomy may not be destiny, but it's not nothing.

As Professor Mansfield predicted in *Manliness*, "When you hear the word gender, you don't know whether it means sex in the sense of what is fixed or in the sense of what is changeable. You only know that it represents the aspirations of the gender-neutral society to declare that everything concerned with what used to be called sex can be remade. Deborah Tannen says, 'Gender is a category that won't go away.' But the name for the category has changed or become confused, and perhaps that won't go away either."

Certainly not, when the world's largest social network can't even put a seventy-one-word boundary down around the word "gender."

These days we hear about "climate change deniers." But the full-blown denial of something much more obvious—a reality that both science and our lived experience make plain—which started in the sixties has now reached critical mass. At their best, sex deniers sought to understand the complexities within the sexes. But they have completely overshot and now deny the very real differences that define us.

CHAPTER 3

PASSED-OUT GIRLS IN SHOPPING CARTS

That's right, the women are smarter.

—The Grateful Dead

eturning to my dorm room at Tufts University one evening, I heard the sound of rusty metal wheels swerving across pavement, punctuated by a guttural laugh. The sounds grew louder, until four large intoxicated college men came careening around the corner, laughing and pushing a shopping cart. I hid behind a column, terrified. I was alone, and Tufts was in the middle of a sexual assault epidemic.

I squinted in the dark, trying to make out the oddly shaped mass in the cart.

It was a female student.

Passed out, she lay slumped in a limp ball, her legs dangling over the rim of the shopping cart, her Tory Burch shoes clanging against the metal. It was around 1:30, the wee hours of Sunday morning. The men had a wild look in their eyes; they were panting little, steaming clouds into the frigid winter air with their laughter.

I briefly envisioned myself stepping out from behind the column and yelling, "Hey you sick, drunk freaks, back away from the cart and the girl and go vomit yourselves to sleep!" I pictured myself straining to push her the half mile to the campus health center, where someone would nurse her to health and ensure that she made it home safely in the morning with a pixie cup with Tylenol and some apple juice. At least then she wouldn't wake up in the filthy sheets of one of those creeps, wondering how she'd gotten there and what she'd done. I imagined the men stumbling away in fear of being caught with their prey.

After calculating the odds on the basis of my approximately one hundred pounds to their collective almost eight hundred, I wised up and hurried back to my dorm.

HOOKUP HELL AND RAPE UNCERTAINTY

A few weeks after the incident, I opened the Tufts homepage for students and noticed a small hyperlink in the corner that read, "Unsure if you have been raped?" I thought of the drunk girl in the shopping cart, and wondered if she was wondering that herself. Not only did Tufts experience a spate of incidents involving date-rape drugs in drinks at fraternities during my time there, but the school was grappling with the latest frontier in the sexual liberation movement, supposedly so empowering to women: rape uncertainty.

No one was willing to blame the hookup culture, but based on my time at Tufts, the connection was obvious.

Tufts was a debaucherous hookup hell.

There was the annual Naked Quad Run, held during the study week before exams, in which hundreds of students would get rip-roaring drunk and run laps around the quad. The university played its part by enlisting the campus police to stand guard and setting out cider and doughnuts for the nude athletes. Students would "pre-game" by getting naked and drunk at parties beforehand. I attended as an observer my freshman year, and before the race had even begun, a female friend with me was attacked by a drunk and naked pirate wearing only a cape, tri-corn hat, and an eye-patch. He left her bleeding.

Then there was the annual Sex Fair, held on Valentine's Day in the student center, hosted by Planned Parenthood affiliate "Tufts Vox" and sponsored by the Women's Center. Students could enjoy vagina cupcakes or check out the latest sex toy. There wasn't a whiff of romance, or even so much as a pamphlet about sexual assault.

When I wrote a connect-the-dots piece for the student paper pointing out that celebrating the most pornographic vision of human sexuality on Valentine's Day, one completely detached from any moral boundaries, was facilitating the rape crisis that Tufts was experiencing, the student groups predictably freaked.

And yet when I ventured back to the Tufts student publications ten years later to see what had become of the Sex Fair, I found (surprise!) an article about the women's group's response to concerns that the sex fair was sending a "sex compulsory" message to women. An article in one student paper said "some have worried that Vox often blurs the lines between being sex-positive and sex-compulsory."[1]

The story quoted one student leader of the Planned Parenthood Affiliate as saying, "Often in trying to promote sex positive attitudes, people can wind up pushing people into spaces where they're not comfortable with the kinds of conversations about sex or talking about sex at all. In a way, being sex positive is about empowering others to choose their conversations about sex and being sex compulsory actually takes that power away."

Do tell.

But Vox is also responding to criticism that's not so grounded in reality. Apparently the Planned Parenthood affiliate is too "gender rigid." In addition to the concern about promoting a rapey culture, critics also worry that "the group creates a less-than-inclusive space, catering mostly to heterosexual, white, cisgendered women." The Vox president takes this concern seriously: "Reproductive injustice is the love child of the white supremacist heteropatriarchy and all other systems of oppression...So it is impossible to effectively combat this oppression while simultaneously ignoring the plurality of identities that affect our reproductive health." Later in the article she asks, "What does access to abortion mean for uterus owners who don't identify as a woman?"

"Uterus owners"? I thought the female body wasn't property?

STRANGE BEDFELLOWS: WOMEN'S STUDIES AND PROSTITUTION

Even without the help of the white supremacist heteropatriarchy, the Women's Studies departments at colleges and universities the nation over have been doing an awesome job of promoting the objectification of the female body for profit.

One star in the Women's Studies department at Duke University was Miriam Weeks, also known as Belle Knox, colloquially known as the "Duke porn star." Duke University was thrown for a loop in 2014 when word began to spread that a freshman student had been recognized in a porn movie making the rounds. Knox, who specialized in what she called "rough kink," became an overnight sensation when, rather than denying the allegations, she leaned into them, arguing that her porn "career" was an empowering way to pay for her degree.

She penned a mind-bending piece for *xoJane* in which she defends pornography that involves violence against women as "feminist": "Whatever choice a woman is making and she is the one deciding to do—reclaiming the agency behind the decision to do, even if it is a degrading sexual act—is absolutely feminism." Weeks argues that her "critics are missing the bigger picture of feminism—perhaps the most important, where women support other women, even the ones who enjoy mascara-smeared, on-your-knees fellatio."[2]

To be a feminist, she explains, "is simply to say that you should not feel pressure to adhere to canonized ideas of gender. People attack feminism by saying a feminist who enjoys submission—even degradation—in the bedroom is upholding patriarchy, but if she likes 'dominance' then she is trying to be like a man."

"I am not going to apologize for getting turned on by embracing an archetypal submissive role during sex," Weeks declares. "The same way that a powerful CEO businessman likes to visit a dominatrix in his off hours, I am not ashamed to admit that I enjoy the pleasure derived from these rough scenes. It provides a cavewoman-like epiphany that no intro to feminist studies ever will."

The Duke porn star believes that "Life is neither black nor white when it comes to sex."

In a *Rolling Stone* interview, Miriam Weeks revealed that she first started watching porn at age twelve, got heavily involved in the hookup culture in high school—during which time she was sexually assaulted at a house party—and began performing in porn by age sixteen. (Which may suggest that her porn career has something to do with what the sponsors of the Tufts Sex Fair call "sex compulsory" situations.) She added that she was headed to an interview for a "coveted internship" with Duke's Women's Center.[3]

Weeks is not the only Women's Studies major to come up with creative ways to sell sex for money. One young woman with a B.A. in Women's Studies from Sacramento State, going by the name Natalie Dylan, decided to auction off her virginity and write about it for the Daily Beast. She was trying to raise cash for grad school. Like Weeks, Dylan framed her move as empowering in a world where she authored her own value system:

This all started long before September. In fact, it started in college, where my eyes were opened by my Women's Studies professors and fellow classmates. I came to understand the role of "woman" spanning culture and time. At the university level, I was given permission to think differently and form a moral code of my own design. College opened my eyes. Like most little girls, I was raised to believe that virginity is a sacred gift a woman should reserve for just the right man. But college taught me that this concept is just a tool to keep the status quo intact. Deflowering is historically oppressive—

early European marriages began with a dowry, in which a father would sell his virginal daughter to the man whose family could offer the most agricultural wealth. Dads were basically their daughters' pimps.

And so she decided to become her own pimp. Dylan succeeded in fetching a cool $3.8 million and praise for her "entrepreneurial gumption" from a Fortune 500 CEO. The idea, she wrote, began as her senior thesis.

"These days," she claimed, "more and more women my age are profiting directly from their sex appeal."[4]

WILL HAVE SEX FOR TUITION

She is more right than she probably knows. Female students from elite colleges fill the ranks of the women available as escorts on the website SeekingArrangement.com, which connects wealthy older men known as "sugar daddies" with "sugar babies," meaning young women available for sex. The site, which *Vanity Fair* writes is helping to create a "new prostitution economy" for elite young women,[5] advertises that nearly half of its sugar babies are in college, as most of the daddies are looking for a woman who is intelligent enough to handle herself in a roomful of say, Wall Street bankers. Student sugar babies get a free membership.

Caroline Kitchener, a Princeton graduate, wrote of the popularity of the site among elite college women in a piece for the *Atlantic* entitled, "How Sugar Daddies Are Financing College Education." Kitchener, a Gender and Sexuality Studies major, cites a friend who told her "tons of girls at Columbia and NYU had profiles to help pay tuition bills. This made the website seem safer, and less like prostitution."[6] As one woman interviewed for *Vanity Fair* put it, "People don't call it 'prostitution' anymore. That sounds like slut-shaming. Some girls get very rigid about it, like 'This is a woman's choice.'"[7]

The sugar babies operate under the same assumption as Dylan, namely that selling the female body for sex can be justified and even empowering once you decide to invent your own moral code. As Dylan wrote, "You should develop your own personal belief system—that's exactly my point! For me, valuing virginity as sacred is simply not a concept I could embrace. But valuing virginity monetarily—now that's a concept I could definitely get behind. I no longer view the selling of sex as wrong or immoral—my time at college showed me that I had too blindly accepted such arbitrary norms."[8]

Setting aside the deep irony that all of these women made money off of their bodies because of the sexual appeal rooted in sexual difference, there are two ideas tying all these stories together: one, that anything can be justified sexually when one is the author of one's own moral code, and two, that women somehow regain power from men by making money off sex.

Dylan describes auctioning off her virginity as a decision to "flip the equation" and use sex "to gain power and opportunity from men."[9] She sounds like Ariana, another woman selling her virginity to pay for college tuition, who told the *Daily Mail* of the ethics behind her decision, "I am also an independent woman and can do just what I want."[10] If men can pay for sex, then gosh darn it, women can sell it.

But somehow in their attempt to establish equality with men, whether through deconstructing sexual difference in a Women's Studies class or replacing men as their own pimps, today's college women have found themselves caught in a world of rampant rape and prostitution.

Or having pro-rape slogans shouted at them, as happened at Yale University in the fall of 2010. A group of fraternity pledges marched through a residential section that housed many of the school's female freshmen shouting slogans like "No Means Yes, Yes Means Anal."[11] This was just one in a series of misogynistic incidents at Yale. In 2008, male students stood outside the Women's Center wearing t-shirts that read "We love Yale sluts," and in 2009 a leaked "preseason scouting report" ranked women according to the number of drinks the men who ranked them would need to down before having sex with them.[12] The rape chant kerfuffle and the alleged mishandling of sexual assault cases led to a Title IX complaint by students charging that Yale had created an environment that was hostile to women, thereby denying them equal access to education on the basis of their sex.[13]

It became quickly apparent that the hostile environment was not isolated to Yale, when the list of schools that came under investigation for similar complaints grew to over one hundred.

As one Harvard student wrote for the student paper, the *Crimson*, "No matter how much we like to deny it, Harvard and Yale are very similar....

"It is easy to view the 'no means yes' chants as an isolated instance conceived of by impulsive, misguided, and possibly intoxicated frat brothers," she said. "However, the Yale community's reaction to the DKE incident belies this convenient dismissal. In fact, on Oct. 18, the *Yale Daily News* published an editorial calling the Yale Women's Center's response an 'overreaction.' It proclaimed that 'feminists at Yale should remember that, on a campus as progressive as ours, most of their battles are already won: All of us agree on gender equality.'"[14]

Memo to the women of Yale et al.: You are overreacting! Because, gender equality.

BRAVE NEW LANGUAGE

But what exactly does gender equality mean, when gender doesn't mean anything?

Colleges are hard at work putting out an entirely new version of the English language that makes recognizing sexual difference as difficult as possible.

Wesleyan University, for example, offers students and faculty a helpful chart breaking down pronouns according to traditional masculine and feminine—he, she, his, hers, and so on—and then encourages all to use gender-neutral options such as "they" or "ze" or "hir."

Traditional Masculine	He laughed	I called him	His eyes gleam	That is his	He likes himself
Traditional Feminine	She laughed	I called her	Her eyes gleam	That is hers	She likes herself
Gender Neutral (Singular They)	They laughed	I called them	Their eyes gleam	That is theirs	They like themself
Gender Neutral (Ze)	Ze laughed (pronounced: "zee" as in the letter 'z')	I called hir (pronounced: "here")	Hir eyes gleam (pronounced: "here")	That is hirs (pronounced: "here's")	Ze likes hirself (pronounced: "hereself")

"We suggest avoiding assumptions, and asking others about their preferred pronouns. Alternatively, you might use gender neutral pronouns," Wesleyan's website reads.[15]

The University of Wisconsin at Milwaukee has an even fancier chart, with offerings such as "eirself," "sie," "vers," "sim," and "zerself."[16]

1	2	3	4	5
e/ey	em	eir	eirs	eirself
he	him	his	his	himself
[name]	[name]	[name]'s	[name]'s	[name]'s self
per	per	pers	pers	perself
she	her	her	hers	herself
sie	sir	hir	hirs	hirself
they	them	their	theirs	themself
ve	ver	vis	vers	verself
zie	zim	zir	zirs	zirself

The lingo has gotten so confusing that even the *New York Times* can't keep it straight. A recent piece about colleges' many different gender-neutral offerings concluded with the following equally confusing correction:

Correction: February 8, 2015

A chart on Page 20 this weekend with an article about gender identity at the University of Vermont renders four gender-neutral pronouns incorrectly. The pronouns are zirs and zirself, not zis and zieself (for his/hers and himself/herself); sir, not sie (for him/her); and eirself, not emself (for himself/herself).[17]

One can't help but notice that, in attempting to clarify its own inaccuracy about the non-gendered pronouns, the *Times* is forced to refer back to gendered language as the anchoring framework.

Wesleyan also offers a gender-inclusive housing option, LGBTTQQFAGPBDSM housing, which stands for—take a deep breath—"lesbian, gay, bisexual, transgender, transsexual, queer, questioning, flexual, asexual, genderf**k, polyamorous, bondage/discipline, dominance/submission, sadism/masochism." According to the university's website, the housing strives to "be a welcoming space for non-normative sexuality and gender minorities, acknowledging this task is one of perpetual motion and action" and is a place "for people of sexually or gender dissident communities."[18]

Universities are in a spectacular display of one-upmanship on the question of who can do the most to enforce "non-gendered language" on campus. As the *New York Times* reports, the University of Vermont spent $80,000 to create a software patch to wipe out all gendered pronouns. And "Activists on campuses as diverse as Penn State, University at Albany, University of Chicago, University of Wisconsin, Milwaukee, and University of California, Riverside" are hard at work, "[i]n hopes of raising consciousness of the biases built into social structures and into the language we use to discuss them...pressing administrations to make changes that validate, in language, the existence of a gender outside the binary."[19]

And it's not just on college campuses that fighting the "gender binary" means upending grammar. The *Washington Post*'s "Civilities" columnist got a letter asking how to square a young woman's desire to be referred to by the plural but genderless "they": "...maybe I'm old school, because I find it odd and grammatically incorrect to say something like, 'Oh, they went to the movies this afternoon,' in reference to one singular person. What is the right thing to do, and say, in this circumstance?"

The response from the *Post*'s Steven Petrow: "My first reaction is: Wow, this is complicated. But really, it's not. Language is about respect, and we should all do our best to recognize how people wish to be identified, whether it is using their preferred name or a pronoun spelled any which way. In other words, do your best to adjust to changing times and terms, and address people the way they ask you."

Petrow does admit that "this latest evolution of the English language has felt awkward to me as well, as I have witnessed my inner Strunk and White struggle with what I first saw as 'political correctness.'

"Clearly, there's change afoot in the language to refer to gender identity, and this clashes for some people with strong feelings about established rules of English. On my Facebook page, when asked for input about this question, many expressed views along these lines: 'The letter writer needs to follow the rules of grammar and pick a singular. You can't just toss the rules on a whim.'" But Mr. Civilities attended a seminar at Duke University's Center for Sexual and Gender Diversity, where he learned to become more comfortable about throwing grammar out the window in the name of "respect."[20]

The writing center at the University of North Carolina at Chapel Hill offers a pamphlet on this very topic. It argues,

Words matter, and our language choices have consequences.
If we believe that women and men deserve social equality,

then we should think seriously about how to reflect that belief in our language use.

If you're reading this handout, you're probably already aware that tackling gender sensitivity in your writing is no small task, especially since there isn't yet (and there may never be) a set of concrete guidelines on which to base your decisions. Fortunately, there are a number of different strategies the gender-savvy writer can use to express gender relationships with precision. This handout will provide you with an overview of some of those strategies so that you can "mix and match" as necessary when you write.[21]

The first strategy is to use "they" as a catch-all, despite the fact that that option is admittedly "currently much debated by grammar experts." Aren't *university writing centers* supposed to be bastions of grammar expertise? The UNC center says, "In order to use 'they' to express accurately gender relationships, you'll need to understand that 'they' is traditionally used only to refer to a plural noun." But use it anyway, they say, because language is evolving and because "there is a relationship between our language use and our social reality."[22] Yes, there is. And currently, language is being drafted into the attempt to deny certain aspects of reality—and to transform society.

A viral video showed just how far down this path colleges are leading their students. In the video a five-foot, nine-inch white man interviews students on the campus of the University of Washington. He cannot find a single one who will deny his assertion that he is a six-foot, five-inch seven-year-old Chinese girl.

The interviewer tests whether, in the gender-neutral—and apparently reality-optional—climate on campus, it's possible to be wrong at all, about anything related to identity.

At one point, the man asks a female student, "So if I told you I was a woman, what would you say?" Her reply?

"Good for you, okay, like, [giggles] yea."

When asked the same question, one slightly more discriminating student pauses and says, "I'd ask you how you came to that conclusion."

When the interviewer presses the point and asks how the first student would respond if he told her he was Chinese, she hesitates, apparently unsure whether it's racist to say "cool, no problem" or racist not to, and then replies, "I mean, I might be a little surprised, but I'd say good for you, like yea, be who you are."

When he asks her what she would say if he told her he was seven years old, she pauses, and then says, "If you feel seven at heart, then so be it, yeah, good for you." She can't even say no when he asks if he should be allowed to enroll in a first-grade class: "If that's where you feel, like, mentally you need to be…"

The video only goes further down the rabbit hole, with students unable to deny the interviewer's assertion that he is six feet, five inches tall.

Says one student, "I feel like that's not my place, as like, another human to say someone is wrong or to draw lines or boundaries."

Lines and boundaries. Those pesky things.

CEOS AND OFFICE HOES

When Harvard's first female president decided to effectively ban single-sex clubs on campus on grounds of gender equality and in the hope of reducing campus rape, she wasn't expecting to cause uproar among the students she was purporting to help: women.

The university was already a bit sensitive about the gender issue. Its previous president, Larry Summers, had found himself embroiled in controversy after daring to suggest there are inherent differences between the sexes. He pointed out obvious realities about men and women's differing representation in fields such as science and banking, attributing the gender gap in science primarily to the principal factor behind such gaps in similarly demanding "high-powered" professions: the statistically documented desire of most women to work fewer hours than men, which affects their ability to advance to higher levels and greater degrees of success and prominence in those fields.

Summers noted that high-level women in most professions are "disproportionately either unmarried or without children.

".... It is a fact about our society that [working long hours] is a level of commitment that a much higher fraction of married men have been historically prepared to make than of married women." (For decades, the Pew Research Center has consistently found that the vast majority of women with children under the age of eighteen do in fact prefer to work part-time or not at all.) Summers questioned whether employers were asking too much of employees, making it hard for women in particular to advance in their fields.

Unaware that what he was saying would soon be leaked by disgruntled feminist faculty to one of the biggest newspapers in the country, Summers went on about the differences between the sexes. At times he got personal, referring to his own experience as a parent and saying, "there is reasonably strong evidence of taste differences between little girls and little boys that are not easy to attribute to socialization."[23]

Summers was pressured into releasing the transcript of his remarks, raked over the coals for weeks by a rabid national media, and finally fired from his role as head of the university. His replacement was Drew Gilpin Faust, a woman labeled by the *New York Times* as a "Rebellious Daughter."[24]

Rebellious against what? Among other things, against her mother's "requirements of what she usually called femininity." According to Faust, her mother frequently told her, "It's a man's world, sweetie, and the sooner you learn that the better off you'll be." As her friend, fellow Harvard professor–turned–U.S. Senator Elizabeth Warren, said of Faust, "She was raised to be a rich man's wife. Instead she becomes the president of the most powerful university in the world."

To her credit, Faust had blazed trails at a time when few women were advancing in academia, eventually landing a prestigious role as a professor at the University of Pennsylvania. During her time there, she served for four years as the director of the Women's Studies Program, among other roles. She eventually made her way to Harvard, where she was tasked by Summers after his gender slip-up to advise him and the university on how better to advance women faculty. When Summers was fired, she landed his job.

When asked whether "her appointment signified the end of sex inequities at the university," she answered, "Of course not. There is a lot of work still to be done, especially in the sciences."

Faust immediately set off on a gender equity campaign. First she completely reshaped the business school, installing stenographers in classrooms to remind professors they were being watched for gender bias and providing faculty with software that checked their patterns of grading male versus female students, and of calling on them in class.[25]

Eventually she turned her eye to Harvard's single-sex clubs, which she all but banned in the spring of 2016. In a campus-wide email, she announced that students who are involved in Harvard's unregistered single-sex "final clubs" as well as those involved in Greek life through fraternities and sororities would be barred from leadership positions in student groups and captaincies of sports teams, as well as ineligible for school endorsement and scholarships such as the Rhodes Scholarship:[26] "Although the fraternities, sororities, and final clubs are not formally recognized by the College, they play an unmistakable and growing role in student life, in many cases enacting forms of privilege and exclusion at odds with our deepest values. The College cannot ignore these organizations if it is to advance our shared commitment to broadening opportunity and making Harvard a campus for all of its students."

The school's dean tag-teamed with his own email about the move, writing, "[T]he discriminatory membership policies of these organizations have led to the perpetuation of spaces that are rife with power imbalances. The most entrenched of these spaces send an unambiguous message that they are the exclusive preserves of men. In their recruitment practices and through their extensive resources and access to networks of power, these organizations propagate exclusionary values that undermine those of the larger Harvard College community."[27]

I see where they're coming from. At Tufts, frat-sponsored parties with themes like "Secretaries and Bosses" were common—and widely attended by female students who were self-styled feminists by day, saucy secretaries by night. A catchier variation on this common fraternity party theme is what the website "College Party Guru" calls "CEOs and Office Hoes." According to the site, "with a CEOs & Office Hoes party...all the guys dress up in suits and nice business attire while the girls get to dress up like slutty office secretaries."

The site advises students on dress code for such parties, suggesting that men "need to dress in their nicest clothes. No CEO would show up for work in jeans and a t-shirt. You need to wear black dress pants, a tie, and an overcoat if you have one. The overcoat is what sets you apart from the rest of the guys there. It shows you are the real CEO."

"Ladies need to dress classy but still show some skin," the page continues. "Girls have a lot more options on this one than the guys, so be creative. You can be as risque as you are comfortable with."[28]

I guess the guys at Tufts never saw this website, because I overheard two female students at breakfast one morning talking angrily about being turned away from a Secretaries and Bosses party because they weren't showing enough skin.

In a hazing incident, other women at Tufts were told to strip to their undergarments in front of male students, who then marked their physical flaws with Sharpies—something that has apparently been done at other schools as well. Pledges at one school in Georgia were forced to sit on top of a running washing machine naked so that "any body part that jiggled" could be circled with a Sharpie.[29]

One can see how Faust would find it hard to encourage future female CEOs at Harvard's business school while fraternities host parties for "CEOs and Office Hoes." But not all Harvard women were enthusiastic about the attempt to stop men and women from freely deciding to associate in organizations limited to their own sex. As one recent Harvard alumna said of her threatened single-sex club, "We're scared we're going to die...."

"We're trying to think how we can go co-ed in a safe, effective way. It's hard to figure out how this will help women or improve the social experience."[30]

Maybe requiring that men and women socialize as if there were no differences between them is not the way to solve sexual assault, male boorishness, and discrimination.

"GO WHERE THE RAPES ARE"

Another push for gender equity on campus seems similarly misguided: the demand that sororities should be given the same options as fraternities when it comes to partying.

Sororities have traditionally been barred from serving alcohol at parties, which makes them less than ideal locations for ragers. The movement to change this, premised on the idea that it might reduce sexual assault if women hosted parties on their own turf, garnered enough traction as to merit an op-ed in the *New York Times* by Juliet Lapidos, who argued, "The decision to strike at frats makes sense: They're hubs for binge drinking and hooking up, sometimes consensual and sometimes not. But instead of only regulating fraternities, administrators might want to consider a more free-market approach to changing the campus party scene. Specifically, they could rattle the virtual monopoly that frats often have on large parties by encouraging other, possibly more responsible groups to throw parties that are less dangerous for women. Who could compete with fraternities and bring more party choice to universities? Sororities."[31]

Lapidos quoted Julie Johnson, an officer of the National Panhellenic Conference, who pointed out that the sorority drinking ban is to "ensure safety." Which makes a lot of sense. How exactly does encouraging sororities to function just like fraternities—which are cesspools of rape and "unwanted sexual contact" (the euphemistic term for consent-hazy drunken hookups), make women safer? Do we really expect the sorority parties to stay rape-free once they start wheeling in kegs and inviting the frat boys over?

The same questions should be asked of Harvard's forced sex integration of social clubs. As Harvard grad Naomi Riley points out in a piece for the *New York Post*, "Newsflash: Even if women were in 'positions of power,' drunken sexual encounters and even sexual assault would still be a problem at these clubs." The article is pointedly entitled, "Harvard Tells Its Women: Go Where the Rapes Are."[32]

Riley cites Caitlin Flanagan, who wrote a lengthy exposé for the *Atlantic* entitled "The Dark Power of Fraternities." Flanagan argues that "college women are no longer a civilizing force. They drink really heavily and they love to prove that they are just as gross as the guys.

"…. if [Harvard's all-male social clubs] are actually such centers of sexual assault, why in God's name would the university recommend that its female students join one of them? 'Women get raped at this location. We must send more women to this location.' What's next? Sending women students to areas with a high murder rate?"[33]

Riley points out that Middlebury College has already experimented with forcing frats into becoming coed "social houses." "At one, I recall," she wrote, "when Madonna's 'Like A Virgin' started playing at any of its parties, all the women in the room would spontaneously remove their shirts. The patriarchy didn't make them do it.

"…. If these task force members really believed that women were being regularly raped at Final Clubs, the university president would be on the phone with local police. Harvard men would be escorted out in handcuffs."[34]

A RETURN TO PRIVACY?

While Harvard was theoretically hoping to stop rapes by plunging into the wave of gender neutrality sweeping the nation's campuses, one university was going against the tide—re-instituting same-sex housing.

Coed dorms have long been the norm: approximately ninety percent of colleges and universities have coed dorms, often mixed by floor, and more than 150 schools have coed bathrooms (including showers).[35] A significant and rising number of schools allow coed rooms—38, by one recent count.[36] That these rooms are "gender neutral" doesn't make them safe. Several schools offering them—including Harvard, Brown, and Dartmouth—are among the 124 colleges and universities being investigated by the Department of Education's Office for Civil Rights for mishandling sexual assault cases.

CNBC recently labeled college "one of the most dangerous places for women in America."[37] And a woman's dorm room mattress might just be the most dangerous spot on campus. According to data reported by universities and colleges in accordance with federal law and published by the government, in 2014, for example, seventy-four percent of all reported rapes of college students, eighty-two percent of reported on-campus rapes, and fifty-three percent of what they termed "on-campus fondlings" happened in student housing.[38]

While that data didn't differentiate between dorms and other student housing such as fraternities, another extensive study conducted over the course of a decade on rape and sexual assault in colleges in Massachusetts found that eighty-one percent of reported rapes and sexual assaults took place in a dorm, versus nine percent in houses and apartments and a stunningly low four percent in fraternities.[39]

One college president decided to do something practical about this problem—and a host of others exacerbated by campus housing arrangements that try to pretend men and women aren't different. In a 2011 piece for the *Wall Street Journal*, Catholic University's president, John Garvey, announced that the school would try a "slightly old-fashioned remedy" to address the binge drinking and hooking up in coed dorms that was connected to problems ranging from sexual assault, to depression, to deaths on college campuses: single-sex dorms.[40]

Garvey cited studies indicating that students in coed dorms were more than twice as likely to binge drink and more than twice as likely to have three or more sexual partners, and research showing that such risky behavior harms women in particular. As many as twenty percent of women who have had two or more sexual partners in a year, for example, are depressed, nearly double the rate of women who had none.

As the college president wrote, "the point about sex is no surprise. The point about drinking is. I would have thought that young women would have a civilizing influence on young men. Yet the causal arrow seems to run the other way. Young women are trying to keep up—and young men are encouraging them (maybe because it facilitates hooking up)." In other words, today's colleges, in practically forcing the sexes to cohabit, wind up creating an environment where women are pressured into risky and promiscuous behavior that leaves them vulnerable to sexual assault.

Naturally Garvey and the school got blowback. There was even an undercover report in the *Washingtonian* alleging that, *surprise*, male and female students still sneak into each other's rooms.[41]

And yet when I spoke to President Garvey about his perspective on the decision five years later, he said that the feedback he has gotten from both students and R.A.s has been positive. Having same-sex privacy has encouraged a greater cultivation of friendship, among women in particular, he noted, and facilitated more same-sex programming that puts students at ease. "Cultivating those friendships," he said, "is a healthy thing in forming their own sense of identity; it makes their own lives happier."

Garvey cited his own children as the impetus for returning Catholic University to same-sex housing. In raising kids, he learned firsthand "how important it is that young men and women, as they mature, be entitled to some privacy when they are sleeping and bathing and getting dressed." Learning to respect another's natural sense of privacy was something he believes can only happen when members of one sex are afforded some basic privacy from the other.[42]

SHUTTING DOWN SAFE SPACES FOR WOMEN

Meanwhile, Harvard's President Faust is taking the first steps toward eliminating the few remaining sex-segregated spaces on campus. (Never mind, as the *Wall Street Journal* noted, that there are as many female final clubs as male clubs, as well as two coed options, and never mind that seventy-five percent of assaults happen in Harvard-run housing.)[43]

To the university's surprise, women responded angrily. Many of Harvard's women viewed the change as an attempt to shut down places where they felt safe. Just days after the announcement, women marched through campus shouting, "What do we want? Safe spaces! When do we want them? Now!"[44] Women in crimson t-shirts and backpacks carried banners with slogans like "Women's Groups Keep Women Safe" and "Assault Is Not Our Fault" and rallied online under the Twitter hashtag #HearHerHarvard.

One female student interviewed by the *Washington Post* said, "The most important message that we do want to share is the value that we put on women's spaces. We're looking to improve the environment on campus for women, and we feel it's important that we have space for women on campus."

Another woman student said,

My first semester at Harvard, I lost my voice and sense of self at such a competitive school. Joining a women's organization helped me find my place at Harvard. I finally had a home at school. My women's organization has been more than a social organization. It has been a mental health respite, a place to discuss sexual assaults, Harvard's failure in expelling rapists, where I became a feminist, and where I re-found my voice. My women's organization taught me how to be a leader. It taught me when I could take the initiative and when to ask for help. And my women's organization has given me the voice to protest when Harvard shows their continued disdain and ignorance of women's voices on campus.

But Harvard dug in its heels. A university spokeswoman compared the female protestors to the men who opposed admitting women to Harvard in the first place, stating that while "past steps to remove gender barriers at Harvard" were met with opposition, "few today would reverse those then-controversial decisions. We continue to believe that gender discrimination has no place on Harvard's campus."[45]

Like their counterparts at Yale, Harvard's upset women were dismissed as reactionaries who just need to realize that everyone here agrees on gender equity, so it's no big deal. Welcome to the modern elite university, where a woman who says she is being discriminated against when robbed of her distinct space and privacy is accused of discriminating... against her own sex.

Perhaps nothing exemplifies the way that denying sexual difference shortchanges women better than rationale behind the decision of Mount Holyoke, an all-women's college, to cancel its annual performance of *The Vagina Monologues*. The play, all about women's sexuality, is designed to raise awareness about sexual violence against women and funds for abuse victims.

The reason for the cancellation?

There was no role for biological men, who are obviously lacking the titular organ. An email from the student group behind the decision explained, "At its core, the show offers an extremely narrow perspective on what it means to be a woman.... Gender is a wide and varied experience, one that cannot simply be reduced to biological or anatomical distinctions, and many of us who have participated in the show have grown increasingly uncomfortable presenting material that is inherently reductionist and exclusive."

And so you have it. Elite institutions have created their own safe space and gender equity Catch-22s. Women's Studies departments have been quietly at work for decades, dismantling the meaning of sex and gender and pushing a form of feminism premised on a denial of woman's distinct nature, especially her capacity for procreation. But that project ultimately required the denial of all reality. It gave birth to a new world in which a short white man is a tall Chinese elementary-aged girl, in which performing as a victim of male violence in porn is empowering, in which prostituting oneself to a Wall Street banker is not a win for the patriarchy, but a perfectly fine way to pay for college.

The project has turned universities into enforcers of an invented vocabulary too confusing for even the *New York Times* to explain. It has rendered universities unable to take the most basic steps toward reducing sexual assault, because sex-segregated spaces are considered anathema. Even when they make women safer, they are sexist.

And when women persist in asking for respect and for a safe space—whether it's an all-female club, a house for women, or a room to put on a play about sexual violence against women—it is they who are the enemies of gender equity.

Universities and colleges have become the primary engines behind making sexual difference scandalous. And now the scandal is on them.

CHAPTER 4

FEMMES FATALES

War is the domain of physical exertion and suffering. If one is not to be overcome by these features, he must possess a certain physical and mental strength, native or acquired, which makes him indifferent to them.

—Carl von Clausewitz, *On War*

I n February 2010, then Secretary of Defense Robert Gates announced that the Navy would lift its longstanding ban on female sailors serving aboard submarines. Women had been permitted to serve aboard surface ships for more than a decade, but submarines presented unique challenges to the Navy's ongoing integration efforts: very cramped quarters, minimal privacy, and tours as long as three months at sea.[1] The Navy was worried that locking up a group of men and women in a small metal tube underwater for three straight months might cause less than ideal things to transpire between the sexes.

That's exactly what happened.

The USS *Wyoming* was one of the first submarines to bring women sailors on board and was one of the first two submarines to see a woman receive her "dolphins" and become a submarine officer. Dozens more women followed suit, and the Navy proudly announced that sex integration aboard subs was smooth sailing.[2]

SCANDAL OF THE SUBMARINES

But in 2014, a rumor began circulating about the USS *Wyoming*. Word on the nearby USS *West Virginia* was that lewd videos were being filmed aboard the *Wyoming*. A formal investigation confirmed the appalling truth: a ring of male sailors had been collaborating for more than a year to film female sailors in the showers and share those videos with fellow shipmen. This was not just a one-time prank that went viral. This was a calculated and collaborative effort that implicated dozens of men who stood guard and covered for one another while they used banned electronic devices like iPods to film women as they undressed and bathed.[3]

On one three-month patrol, reports later revealed, every single woman aboard the USS *Wyoming* was filmed naked every single time she took a shower.

The incident should have been a shocking wake-up call for senior military officials. Women were systematically victimized for months on end because a policy agenda built on blindness to sexual difference tore down longstanding barriers designed to protect both women and the integrity of the Navy.

But rather than hit the pause button, the Navy gave the perpetrators a slap on the wrist and pressed toward its next goal, integrating nuclear-powered *Virginia*-class attack subs and eventually all the enlisted ranks on submarines.[4] This despite the fact that one of the Navy's own officials charged with investigating the USS *Wyoming* incident had said, "No amount of barriers will be able to prevent all illegal attempts to record personnel.... the upholding of standards and holding personnel accountable is the best method to prevent reoccurrence."[5]

Aside from the barrier, of course, that had been in place since the inception of the Navy's submarine program, the barrier that took into account the fact that the average submarine has just fifteen square feet of space per sailor and virtually no privacy except in the captain's quarters.

But the Navy's press release announcing that it would begin allowing women to serve on submarines made no reference to privacy or concerns.

Rather, it read like a page out of a college university's P.C. handbook, with a litany of quotes from the Navy's highest-ranked officers touting the talents and drive of women.

Secretary of the Navy Ray Mabus said, "There are extremely capable women in the Navy who have the talent and desire to succeed in the submarine force. Enabling them to serve in the submarine community is best for the submarine force and our Navy."

Admiral Gary Roughead, Chief of Naval Operations, praised the "great enthusiasm" of "young women," and the commander of Naval Submarine Forces, referring to the fact that women earn half of science and engineering degrees, said, "There are capable women who have the interest, talent, and desire to succeed in the submarine force."

The press release made no mention whatsoever of security concerns, either, just a passing reference to the fact that integration had previously been considered "cost prohibitive."[6]

Something to do with the single set of showers, perhaps?

The scandal embodied the reality that an initiative to pursue gender equality, even if noble and premised on the talents of women and their desire to serve their country, will fail if it is pursued in denial of sexual difference. What the male perpetrators on the USS *Wyoming* did was deplorable. But the scandal made it clear that sex integration in the military is not as simple as throwing men and women together and hoping it all works out. And yet this seems to be the new *modus operandi* for our armed forces, as they push toward complete integration of the sexes in every last corner of military service.

WOMEN TO THE FRONT LINES

Around the same time that the USS *Wyoming* scandal became headline news, the military dropped another bombshell. Defense Secretary Ashton Carter announced that the Pentagon would be opening combat roles in the United States military to women.[7] Every single branch, elite forces included, would be required to open every single combat role to women. The process had to begin in just thirty days.

Even more stunning, Secretary Carter referred to gender integration on submarines as an example of previous success in this department. He didn't mention the ongoing media fallout about the shower-spying.

Secretary Carter's move was actually a follow-up on a decision by his predecessor, Leon Panetta, three years before. On his way out the door, Panetta gave the Pentagon a three-year deadline for lifting the ban on women in combat and dumped responsibility for the actual implementation on his successor. If a branch of the military felt like a particular combat role should not be opened to women, they had to ask for an exemption.[8]

Every branch of the military went along without pushback, except the Marines.

After Panetta issued his directive, the Marines spent millions of dollars conducting a year-long test to study the effects of mixed-sex units on combat readiness. They wanted to investigate whether the Marines could implement this policy change while maintaining, in their own words, "the clear recognition that the brutal and extremely physical nature of direct ground combat, often marked by close, interpersonal violence, remains largely unchanged throughout centuries of warfare, despite technological advances."[9]

The Marines emphasized that their starting point in conducting the study was combat readiness—not exactly a standard they made up. It was a standard that the 1992 Presidential Commission on the Assignment of Women in the Armed Forces—the last thorough investigation of the effects of sex integration in the military—made clear was the most important benchmark against which to measure any policy change in the military. The Commission's formal report had said, "A military unit at maximum combat effectiveness is a military unit least likely to suffer casualties. Winning in war is often only a matter of inches, and unnecessary distraction or any dilution of the combat effectiveness puts the mission and lives in jeopardy. Risking the lives of a military unit in combat to provide career opportunities or accommodate the personal desires or interests of an individual, or group of individuals, is more than bad military judgment. It is morally wrong."[10]

The findings of the Marines' new study were devastating for proponents of sex integration. Mixed-gender units performed worse than all-male ones by significant margins in every single metric. Overall, male units fared better sixty-nine percent of the time. In the area of speed, which the Marines consider one of the two most important metrics for combat readiness, all-male squadrons were faster than mixed-sex squadrons in every single tactical movement. All-male units were noticeably more accurate in their aim with every single weapons system. The male units engaged targets more quickly and scored more hits than the mixed-gender ones. The study even found that male infantry with no formal rifle training performed with greater accuracy than women who *had* received formal training.

But the study went beyond measuring speed and accuracy and considered the physical impact of placing women into combat roles alongside men. Those findings were equally devastating. Women in the study suffered injuries at a staggering six times the rate of their male counterparts. Not only were women more likely to develop an injury related to the grueling work, but they were also slower at getting an injured Marine off the battlefield—an especially concerning result.

One female Marine pointed out the high stakes involved, "No one questions why there aren't any females in the NFL, NBA, MLB, NHL, etc. Olympic athletes are the elite of the elite. No one questions why the women compete against women and men against men. Those are great sports and achievements. But lives and missions aren't on the line. In our world, if you move slower one day, you don't get bumped off the medal stand, you could die or get someone else killed."[11]

Former Marine Tom Neven put it more bluntly: "The only possible outcome of this policy is more dead Marines."[12]

Unsurprisingly, the progressive vanguard was not about to just accept the facts. Within a few weeks, a barrage of articles from left-wing sources such as NPR and *Jezebel* accused the study of "flaws"—the standard liberal response to any study whose results they don't like. You can read dozens of articles about the "flawed" nature of the study without learning what exactly its flaws are supposed to be, but the most popular

canard seems to be the accusation that the study focused on average
female performance instead of highlighting stand-out female Marines of
exceptional physical ability.[13]

The secretary of the Navy himself took up this line of attack against
the study, saying, "I mean, in terms of the women that volunteered,
[there] probably should've been a higher bar to cross to get into the
experiment."

Ouch.

Even more outrageously, Secretary Mabus charged that the Marines
had rigged the study's results.[14] In an interview with NPR, he accused
the Marines of sexism, saying, "[The study] started out with a fairly large
component of the men thinking 'This is not a good idea' and 'Women
will never be able to do this.'... When you start out with that mindset,
you're almost presupposing the outcome."[15]

Despite Mabus's claim that the study was biased and had relied on
average women Marines when it should have focused on the strongest
outliers, the Marines had in fact chosen female outliers.

The study itself included clear measurements of the physical abilities
of the men and women who participated, as recorded by objective third-
party medical professionals at the University of Pittsburgh's Neuromus-
cular Research Laboratory. The female participants in the study
outstripped average women in strength and physical ability far more
dramatically than male participants outstripped average men.[16]

Some of the female participants in the study were angered by Secretary Mabus's suggestion that the men running and participating in the
study were sexist and the women "average." Sergeant Danielle Beck, a
female anti-armor gunner involved in the study, commented, "Our secretary of the Navy completely rolled the Marine Corps and the entire
staff that was involved in putting this [study] in place under the bus."
"Everyone that was involved," she said, "did the job and completed the
mission to the best of their abilities." She called Mabus's remarks a "slap
in the face."[17]

Another participant in the study, Navy Cross recipient Sergeant
Major Justin LeHew, posted on Facebook, "The Secretary of the Navy

is way off base on this and to say the things he is saying is...flat out counter to the interests of national security and is unfair to the women who participated in this study.... No one went into this with the mentality that we did not want this to succeed. No Marine, regardless of gender would do that." (LeHew later deleted his post.)[18]

Yet another Marine pointed out, "If you were to look at our training plan and how we progressed from October to February, you're not going to find any evidence of institutional bias or some way we built this for females to fail."[19]

None of this seemed to matter to Secretary Mabus, who, before the Marines had even had the chance to formally present the study's findings and ask for exceptions to the new women-in-combat policy, said in a press conference that he saw no reason to grant the Marines any exceptions.[20] When, days later, Marine Commandant General Joseph Dunford did send a memo to Defense Secretary Carter recommending that women continue to be prohibited from serving in certain infantry and reconnaissance positions, Carter didn't seem to care much about the findings, either. When Carter gave a press conference a few months later, his decision was unambiguous: "There will be no exceptions." Dunford, who was on his way to becoming the chair of the Joint Chiefs of Staff, was conspicuously absent.[21]

DOWN WITH STANDARDS

Just weeks after Carter's sex-integration shocker, Secretary Mabus came back to the Marines with even more demands. The first was to make its infamously difficult boot camp coed. And he gave them just two weeks to figure out how to do it.[22]

The Marines were sent reeling yet again. They had long maintained sex-segregated training for numerous reasons—privacy concerns, the prevention of sexual misconduct, and the reality that most women, even the strongest, could not meet the same physical requirements for graduation as men.[23] The Marines have different sets of physical standards for men and women. Men, for example, must be able to do three pull-ups in order to graduate from boot camp and must continue to be able to do them in their annual test for physical strength and combat readiness. When the Marines experimented with holding women to that same standard, more than half of female Marines failed.[24]

The story behind the sex difference in pull-up ability is purely physical: Men have an advantage because testosterone makes for more lean muscle mass, whereas women have more body fat. For pull-ups, muscle in the back, biceps, triceps, and pectorals—where men tend to carry much of their strength—is essential.

As one *Washington Post* reporter put it, "Putting physiology, social policy, behavioral theory and military doctrine aside, it appears that for reasons known only to the Maker (in whatever form you may visualize Him or Her), men and women are different."[25]

The pull-up is not a random requirement. Upper-body strength is absolutely crucial in combat. Anyone lacking in it puts fellow fighters at risk. The summary of the Marines' sex-integration study touched on this point, noting two "basic combat tasks"—evacuating casualties and negotiating obstacles—for which upper body strength is essential. Their report found that "when negotiating the wall obstacle, male Marines threw their packs to the top of the wall, whereas female Marines required regular assistance in getting their packs to the top. During casualty evacuation assessments, there were notable differences in execution times between all-male and gender-integrated groups, except in the case where teams conducted a casualty evacuation as a one-Marine fireman's carry of another (in which case it was most often a male Marine who "evacuated" the casualty)." Unsurprisingly, the study found that "all-male squads, teams and crews and gender-integrated squads, teams, and crews had a noticeable difference in their performance" of these tasks.[26]

Add some enemy fire to the mix, and suddenly the inability to do a pull-up has life-and-death consequences.

Nevertheless, female Marines have long been permitted to do a flex-arm hang instead of a pull-up in order to pass the Physical Fitness Test (PFT). They have also been allowed three extra minutes to complete the three-mile run.[27] In holding women to lower physical standards, the

Marines are only following the other branches of the military. When West Point went coed, nearly two-thirds of female plebes failed the standard physical test, versus five percent of men. And so they created lower standards for women. The same happened at the Air Force Academy.[28]

But in July of 2016, in the wake of the policy changes to put women in combat and make boot camp coed, the standards were revised down even further. Only this time, instead of simply allowing a lower bar for women, the standard was lowered for everyone. So integrating women into every aspect of the military without any regard for the very real differences between the sexes is not just lowering the standards for women. It's also dragging down the standards for men.

In the biggest change to the PFT in four decades, Military.com reported, the Marine Corps is "solving the problem of requiring pull-ups for women by adding a push-ups option for all troops on the physical fitness test." Previously, push-ups were not even a part of the fitness standards.[29]

Even as the Marines rolled out what Commandant General Robert Neller called "the biggest changes to the PFT since 1972," Neller admitted that pull-ups are a better measure of the strength Marines actually need to do their job.[30] "Push-ups become an option on the PFT," he said, "but Marines are incentivized toward pull-ups, as these are a better test of functional, dynamic upper body strength and correlate stronger to physically demanding tasks."[31]

The lower standards did not come as a surprise to everyone. One senior commander had seen the writing on the wall and, in a highly atypical move, spoken bluntly on the matter.

Marine General John Kelly, then the outgoing head of the Southern Command, stunned a room full of reporters in January of 2016 when he said he absolutely expected pressure "from the agenda-driven people here in Washington" to lower standards across the board in order to accommodate women in combat roles. General Kelly, whose own son died in combat in Afghanistan, said, "They're saying we are not going to change any standards. There will be great pressure, whether it's 12 months from now, four years from now, because the question will be asked whether we've let women into these other roles, why aren't they staying in those other roles? Why aren't they advancing as infantry people...?"[32]

As it turned out, it was just seven months after his remarks that the Marines announced the new changes to the PFT.

Interestingly, even the new lower standards are still different for men and women; women can pass the test by doing thirty-three percent fewer push-ups: "Notably, all of the new standards will keep in place a gender-normed scoring system, which scores men and women differently on the same exercises in acknowledgment of different physical ability thresholds."[33] So even as the U.S. military denies any difference between men and women that would justify different roles or training for the two sexes, its physical fitness standards for men and women testify to the reality of that difference.

The end of single-sex boot camp creates other problems as well. As many realists have pointed out, coed military training gives rise to all sorts of sexually-charged issues, from sexual harassment of females by male superiors to false allegations of harassment by women and an ensuing litany of lawsuits, to just the natural distraction that occurs when the sexes are mingled. As a former female Marine put it, "Harassment? That's boot camp: you can't train young kids to attack and defend without some touching. A drill instructor's simple correction or instruction can be construed as harassment when done by the opposite sex. Having separate boot camps allowed the Marines to postpone or at least greatly minimize the opportunity for all these problems until after recruits had finished their training and earned the title."[34]

The Marines had insisted on single-sex training not just to maintain physical standards but also to preserve certain moral standards. In their eyes, placing members of the opposite sex into an intensely physical environment where pressures run high was not an ideal way to prevent misconduct and a host of other unintended consequences of integration that could tarnish the reputation of the Marine Corps and the character of its soldiers.

Secretary Mabus's insistence on a twenty-five percent quota for female Marines raises the question of what changes are yet to come.[35]

One boot camp drill sergeant wondered, "The thing is how much more integrated can we get? We already train with females. What do they want? Them to live in the same squad bay? Cause that ain't going to happen."[36]

In fact it very well may. Just ask the women on submarines how that worked out for them.

SEX AND SELECTIVE SERVICE

Lost in the media frenzy of excitement about women in combat was one minor detail: women in all sectors of the military have lost any say over whether they will serve in combat roles. NPR ran the headline "Pentagon Says Women Can Now Serve in Front-Line Ground Combat Positions."[37] But a different and equally accurate headline would have been "Pentagon Says Women Now *Must* Serve in Front-Line Ground Combat Positions." Defense Secretary Carter confirmed this explicitly in a press conference. When asked whether women deemed fit for combat would have a choice about whether they would serve in such a role, he gave a resounding no. The lack of "absolute choice," he said, was a part of military life.

Further, the change meant that the military could become a part of life for every woman. The national debate about women in combat slid down the slippery slope fast. Almost immediately, we were talking about drafting women. As soon as Secretary Carter announced that every branch of the military must place women in combat roles, people began asking why only men must register for Selective Service when they turn eighteen. (Men who violate this requirement can be denied all sorts of benefits, including financial aid for college.)

Until recently, the idea of forcing women to register for the draft seemed barbaric, something only the most extremist of liberal feminists and boorish of men would suggest. But Secretary Carter did not rule it out. In fact, when announcing the new policy about women in combat roles, he acknowledged it was a viable possibility, saying the issue of forcing women to register for Selective Service "is a matter of legal dispute right now."

It's been a matter of legal dispute before. In the 1980s, the Supreme Court took up the question of whether conscripting only men violated the equal protection clause. The Court ruled in *Rostker v. Goldberg* that it did not, because the Selective Service's stated purpose related only to combat troops, and women were then barred from serving in combat. Secretary Carter's new policy flings that door wide open again.[38]

But President Obama had beat him to the punch long ago, when he endorsed the idea of conscripting women on the campaign trail. He said, "I think that if women are registered for the service...I think it will help to send a message to my two daughters that they've got obligations to this great country as well as boys do."[39]

In a 2016 presidential primary event, Republican presidential candidate Ted Cruz invoked his own daughters but from a completely different perspective, calling the idea of drafting women "nuts," "dangerous," and "immoral." He said, "We have had enough with political correctness—especially in the military. Political correctness is dangerous, and the idea that we would draft our daughters, to forcibly bring them into the military and put them in close contact—I think is wrong, it is immoral, and if I am president, we ain't doing it. I'm the father of two little girls. I love those girls with all my heart. They are capable of doing anything in their hearts' desire, but the idea that their government would forcibly put them in the foxhole with a 220-pound psychopath trying to kill them, doesn't make any sense at all."[40]

All the while, top military officials pointed to the seeming inevitability of women's being required to register for Selective Service. In a meeting with the Association of the U.S. Army at the Walter E. Washington convention center in Washington, D.C., Army Secretary John McHugh said, "If your objective is true and pure equality then you have to look at all aspects" of women in the military, which he said most certainly includes registering for the draft. It "will be one of those things. That will have to be considered." McHugh was reiterating similar positions staked out by other high-ranking military officials who had discussed this topic at the 2015 Aspen National Security forum in Colorado. On one panel discussion, a former commander of the SEALs and Navy Special Operations Command said that if women are allowed to serve in combat, they should have to register for the draft. In a different panel discussion, Deborah James, secretary of the Air Force, showed no concern at the idea of requiring women to register.[41]

Even the Selective Service took note of the changing tides, and updated its website with the following clarification, which left the door open for coming change:

> FEMALES & REGISTRATION: While there has been talk recently about women in combat, there has been NO decision to require females to register with Selective Service, or be subject to a future military draft. Selective Service continues to register only men, ages 18 through 25.[42]

Almost overnight, women in America woke up to the very real prospect that they could be forced into the military. That prospect came one step closer to reality when in June of 2016, the Senate voted to require women to register for the draft as a part of a military policy bill. The requirement, as the *New York Times* noted, had "surprisingly broad support among Republican leaders and women in both parties."[43]

As Senator John McCain, chairman of the Armed Services Committee, put it, "every single leader in this country, both men and women, members of the military leadership, believe that it's fair since we opened up all aspects of the military to women that they would also be registering for Selective Services."

And so the "longings of yesteryear's feminists," to use a phrase of Mary Eberstadt's, have come full circle. One feminist principle—complete gender-blind equality—has come into direct conflict with two others—bodily autonomy and choice. Today's young women face the possibility of being forced into military service, including every last form of physical combat, whether they like it or not.

NO SKIRTS ALLOWED

When I struck up a conversation with a physical therapist helping me recover from surgery, I learned that she was in the Navy Reserve. As women are wont to do, I asked if she had any kids. Five-year-old twins, she told me. We kept talking, and she revealed that she had been deployed for more than a year, beginning when they were two and a half years old. When she left, they were not yet three; she returned after their fourth birthday. She had absolutely no choice in the matter.

Later I told this to a fellow mom, whose eyes widened. Her only response was a sympathetic but shocked, "There's just something so wrong with that picture."

It's the politically incorrect response, but a natural one among mothers who innately know that we are hardwired to be with our children in a different way from men.

Men have been leaving their families behind to fight to defend them since the dawn of humanity. But forcibly sending women, including mothers of young children, into harm's way is a thoroughly modern development—a harsh sacrifice to the reality-denying belief that men and women are the same, that true equality is only achieved when every last vestige of difference is eradicated. And it has become anathema to question the practice, even when the fall-out is obvious. As Mary Eberstadt wrote years before the push to abolish sex difference in the military picked up velocity:

> The facts are these. With the obvious assent of the American people, as well as most of our political and military and other leaders, the United States military now routinely recruits mothers or soon-to-be mothers of babies and young children—and often puts them in harm's way more or less as it does every other soldier. This is a practice so morally questionable, and in virtue of that fact so fraught with policy difficulties, that both its persistence and its apparent lack of controversy fairly beg for explanation....

One reason why those mothers have gone off to Iraq and Afghanistan without so much as a murmur is this: It has become nearly impossible, against the backdrop of two wars involving large numbers of deployed servicewomen, to raise questions about the wisdom of their service without risking public wrath.[44]

Indeed, whereas once it would have been considered scandalous to send a woman into harm's way, or to conscript a woman into military service against her will, today it has become a scandal to raise even the most practical of questions about how to integrate women into the military, let alone to ask whether women should be sent into combat. To ask these questions is infantilizing, condescending, and sexist.

When I spoke to Aaron MacLean, a combat Marine veteran who has written extensively on the subject, he said that certain defense leaders and politicians today are "dedicated to achieving a certain outcome, regardless of whether it's a good idea." The goal, he said, is to override a perceived "toxic masculinity" and replace it with "a genderless military." In the eyes of those aggressively pressing forward with gender neutrality in the military, sexual difference is viewed as a "biological accident aggravated by toxic uses of power. They have stopped asking the question, 'What's more important, the individual rights of service members or the effectiveness of the unit?' and whether those two things are even rightly considered to be in conflict with one another."[45]

No one doubts the courage and patriotism of the women who serve in our armed forces, nor denies the fact that some women have the ability to perform the military's most arduous tasks. Further, many men and women in the military will readily acknowledge that exclusion from certain combat roles has kept women from advancing to higher ranks. But rather than build a modern military that takes into account the very real differences between the sexes that persist, the current approach is to try to stamp out the differences wherever they might appear—even as the differences in the military's own physical requirements for men and women betray the ineradicable reality of those differences.

The result is a false equality. It is premised on sameness, but produces differences that harm women in particular. As the Marines' own study found, women may now have an equal opportunity to fight on every front line, but an unequal chance of surviving.

Under this false equality, accommodations that promise to help advance women do not empower women as they are. Instead they have the effect of requiring women to be more like men. For example, the military's solution to the highly inconvenient reality that women in the prime of their physical strength are also in the prime of their fertility is to cover the cost of harvesting and freezing eggs so that female service members will, as the *New York Times* says, "have the flexibility to remain deployed overseas or otherwise pursue their careers and put off having children."[46] In other words, to make their bodies function reproductively more like men's.

The program was launched in early 2016. According to the *Times*, it is intended, among other things, "to encourage women to stay in the military during their 20s and 30s, a time when many leave after giving birth." The *Times* cites Secretary Carter as saying that women who have been in the military for ten years are in their "peak years for starting a family" and so, unsurprisingly, leave military service at rates thirty percent higher than men during those same years. The egg-freezing benefit, ironically, came in tandem with slashes in maternity leave for the Navy and the Marines.

Not even the vocabulary of the military has escaped the campaign for gender neutrality. Every branch has been ordered to review its ranks and titles and change all those that indicate a particular sex to a unisex alternative. So women in the military can rejoice that they may no longer be called "artillerymen." But young women everywhere face the very real prospect of having to register for the draft when they turn eighteen. And a young woman in the military who wants to start a family will have to explain why she chose to have children when she could have just frozen her eggs and risen in the ranks first.

In reality, a gender-neutral military offers women false choices. Their only real "choice" is to squeeze themselves into the masculine mold. Perhaps nothing better embodies this than the Naval Academy's 2016 decision, for the first time in its history, to ban female midshipmen from wearing their skirts at graduation.[47] The only choice for female graduates was the same trousers the male midshipmen wear. As the Navy spokesman Commander John Schofield told the press, the new dress code was meant to reinforce the concept of "shipmate before self."

Even, apparently, before one's own sex.

CHAPTER 5

FIGHTING FIRE
WITH FEMALES

I don't mind living in a man's world as long as I can be a woman in it.

—Marilyn Monroe

t was a 2016 spring training game between the Atlanta Braves and the Pittsburgh Pirates, when a hitter lost control of his bat. It went hurtling into the stands, straight toward the head of an unsuspecting child. A freeze-frame viewed all around America for the following week captured the image of the bat mere seconds before it would have smashed the boy's face. Three men are frozen with their arms out, trying to stop the bat. The two women in the frame are crouching down, shielding themselves.

One man in particular stands out. In the picture, his brawny arm is extended into the one or two inches between the bat and the boy's face. His face is calm. It turned out that the man, who saved his son from major injury and potentially death, was a firefighter.[1]

Like military combat, firefighting is a profession that requires physical strength and a quick reaction time in life-and-death scenarios. Unsurprisingly, it remains a predominantly male profession: as of 2011, only 4.5 percent of all employed firefighters were female.[2] Of the nearly three hundred fire departments in cities and major metropolitan areas around the country, more than half have no female firefighters whatsoever.[3] But lawsuits filed by aspiring female firefighters and the Equal Employment Opportunity Commission (EEOC) have been slowly changing that, mostly by changing the way fire departments screen applicants for physical fitness. The standards have been gradually revised downward—and are now beginning to disappear altogether.

WHAT IT TAKES TO DO THE JOB

After a landmark 1982 ruling that New York City's Fire Department's physical standards discriminated against women,[4] fire departments everywhere altered their requirements. Instead of directly testing for strength, endurance, and general fitness, they began to assess applicants with simulations of the tasks firefighters perform.[5] To pass the widely used Candidate Physical Ability Test (CPAT) developed by firefighters' unions and several large fire departments in the late 1990s, for instance, applicants must climb stairs carrying an extra seventy-five pounds and, wearing a fifty-pound vest, drag a hose, carry equipment from one point to another, penetrate a locked door, and complete similar tasks within ten minutes and twenty seconds. Although time is of the essence in fighting fires, the International Association of Fire Fighters (IAFF) does not permit departments to use CPAT completion times to rank candidates; the time threshold is simply a pass/fail cut-off.[6]

The limited available data now indicate that departments using the CPAT to screen candidates' physical fitness report higher pass rates for women than departments that use other tools.[7] But by 2002 it was clear that women—unsurprisingly—pass the test at lower rates than men. The EEOC sprang into action, accusing the CPAT of discriminating against women. The resulting conciliation agreement with the IAFF, formalized in 2006, amended the CPAT testing process to provide prospective firefighters with training, tips, and practice runs in advance of their test date.[8] The explicit goal, according to IAFF

President Harold Schaitberger, was "to increase the rate at which female firefighter candidates pass the test."[9]

Indeed, says the IAFF's 2007 manual on the screening tool, "the CPAT cannot be separated from the department's broader goal of attaining a properly trained and physically capable workforce whose members reflect the diversity of the community." The manual implicitly warns departments that failing to recruit a diverse workforce—"made up of both genders to include all races and ethnic backgrounds"—will result in "lawsuits, court orders, and consent decrees" that "[take] control of the recruitment and hiring process out of the fire department's hands."[10]

But will concerted recruiting efforts make up for the greater difficulty women have in passing the CPAT[11] and meeting the challenges that await them as trainees? The experience of the Los Angeles Fire Department suggests the answer is no. In 2008, the *LA Weekly* reported that despite millions of dollars devoted to recruiting and accommodating female firefighters over the past few decades, women who worked on the fire line (as opposed to working as paramedics or at desks in the fire department) numbered only 27—out of 3,940 people in the department. And that's after some women (but not the men in their recruiting class) "were given special pay for months by the city...to undergo extra preparation before facing the academy," preparation labeled "a complete failure" by an academy instructor.

Few of the hundreds of women whose interest the Los Angeles Fire Department attracted in 2006 managed to pass the CPAT. And even for those who did, the subsequent academy training for new hires proved incredibly difficult. Reporter Christine Pelisek describes one female recruit who flew through the CPAT without trouble but still found academy training too tough on her body—and not because of male supervisors who wanted her to fail. She emphasized to Pelisek that at the academy, "everyone was treated the same.... The staff [there] was very professional and I never felt a sexual bias whatsoever." Similarly, Angela Vesey, a former Air Force officer determined to re-enroll in the academy after failing the first time, said of the men who trained her, "I respected them. I wanted to be on their crew. The people at the tower [academy] were phenomenal. They really wanted you to learn."

The positive experiences these women report are heartening—no one wants aspiring female firefighters to suffer bias or harassment—but Pelisek also revealed many problems created by the LAFD's aggressive push to hire more women. For one thing, it's expensive. Sending just one recruit through the training academy costs upward of $80,000 (and another $80,000 every time a failed recruit is given another try). Sixteen of ninety-nine women in the Los Angeles department (including those with desk jobs) were drawing disability pay for work-related injuries.[12]

Some fire departments, then, made the calculation that it was cheaper, and less of a legal hassle, to just go ahead and graduate women who couldn't pass the physical test.

In New York, for example, Choeurlyne Doirin-Holder thrice failed her physical fitness test to become a firefighter. The Fire Department graduated her anyway, because she is considered a "priority hire." Ten days into the job, she injured herself, fracturing her foot during a routine equipment check. Because she was injured on the job, she qualifies for the department's handsome disability benefits.[13]

And then there are the sexual harassment and discrimination lawsuits. Often involving "back-and-forth finger-pointing between women and men," these suits cost taxpayers millions.

And the lawsuits skew heavily female: an audit of the Los Angeles personnel department revealed that in one year alone, though women accounted for fewer than three percent of firefighters, fire paramedics, fire administrators, and fire investigators, they were behind more than half of the city's many millions of dollars worth of lawsuits against its fire department.

Pressure to increase women's representation has not only created double standards for male and female applicants, according to some firefighters. It has also driven potentially harmful changes in on-the-ground operations. Some fire chiefs in Los Angeles were accused of passing unqualified women through the academy, which naturally enraged firefighters and stoked fears that recruiting efforts were endangering them and the public alike. After one female firefighter dropped a ladder on herself, it was ordered that three rather than two firefighters be assigned to carry the thirty-five-foot ladder, which means one less person to handle other vital tasks in high-pressure situations.

As one firefighter said about the change, "It basically took a third member, handcuffed them, and delayed other vital operations on the ground, like forcible entry, shutting off utilities and shutting off gas. They are kind of little things, but they are big things. Why go out and drill with this 35[-foot ladder]? It is a valuable tool, but no one wants the [internal] repercussions if someone can't do it."

His bigger concern, however, was about going into danger alongside someone unable to perform a basic task of the job. "It is hard to go in a fire with someone when you know from drilling she can't lift the ladder.... If you can't do it in a perfect environment in a drill tower or academy, there is no way you can do it in a life-threatening situation."[14]

Nevertheless, some fire departments are simply tossing standards to the wind. In 2015, Rebecca Wax became the first woman to graduate from the FDNY's fire academy, despite failing the physical fitness test.

"We're being asked to go into a fire with someone who isn't 100 percent qualified," an anonymous firefighter told the *New York Post* of the unprecedented move by the FDNY. "Our job is a team effort. If there's a weak link in the chain, either civilians or our members can die."[15]

Following right on Wax's heels was Wendy Tapia, allowed to graduate despite failing the physical fitness test not once, or twice, but six times.[16]

As one woman wrote for the *New York Post*, "If you're ever trapped in a burning building, just pray the firefighter climbing up to rescue you isn't Rebecca Wax. Or someone like her, who's been given an EZ-Pass through firefighting training for the sake of gender equity."[17]

Physical fitness standards for firefighters are becoming untenable—women can graduate without meeting them, or sue. Bending over backward to recruit and train women is expensive and not necessarily effective. It's going to be a lot harder for firefighters to fight fires when their own basic safety and fitness standards are going up in flames.

LADY COP

There are a lot more women policing America's streets than fighting its fires—and with good reason—though the percentage is still quite low. As of 2013, thirteen percent of police officers nationwide were female.[18] Unlike firefighting, whose extreme demands are almost entirely physical, policing requires a broader range of abilities, as well as a certain emotional equanimity, where women might actually have an advantage.

Women have a longer history in police departments than in firefighting forces. In the mid-nineteenth century, larger police departments frequently hired women as "police matrons" in charge of incarcerated and institutionalized women and children. Though they worked in cooperation with the police, police matrons' roles were often more similar to those of social workers. Lola Baldwin, the woman often considered America's first policewoman, joined Portland's police department in 1908 and had the authority to make arrests; but she acted "as a surrogate parent to protect women and girls from the moral dangers and temptations of urban life" and her unit was housed in a local YWCA.[19] Through most of the twentieth century, women accounted for only two percent or less of police officers and sheriffs' deputies.[20]

It was only in the late 1960s—and especially the 1970s, following the Equal Opportunity Act of 1972 and the Crime Control Act of 1973—that female police began taking on the same roles as policemen. Soon, lawsuits began to "[contest] departments' entrance requirements related to education, age, height, weight, and arrest records; their selection criteria, including written examinations, agility tests, and veterans' preference; and discriminatory assignment and promotion procedures." In response, "almost all [police] agencies eliminated or altered height and weight requirements and modified physical agility tests that disproportionately eliminated women and Hispanic and Asian men." As in firefighting, some departments shifted the focus of screening tests away from upper-body strength and toward general health and fitness.[21]

Despite these broad trends, the physical fitness standards of police departments continue to vary from one place to another,[22] and a small minority of agencies administer no fitness test at all. The most common measures of fitness include a timed run (often of 1.5 miles) as well as sit-ups and push-ups.[23] These may sound like reasonable objective measures of general fitness applicable to everyone, but in many departments all three requirements are different, depending on the applicant's age and gender.[24] That is, standards are significantly lower for women and for older applicants than for young men.

Before entering a police academy in the state of Michigan, for example, aspiring officers must pass the physical fitness test of the Michigan Commission on Law Enforcement Standards.[25] The test consists of a vertical jump, sit-ups, push-ups, and a shuttle run. Men ages 18 to 29 must jump 17.5 inches, perform 32 sit-ups and 30 push-ups (each in one minute), and finish the half-mile shuttle run (doing laps around markers roughly 90 feet apart) in 4 minutes and 29.6 seconds. Women in the same age bracket must jump 11 inches, perform 28 sit-ups and just 7 push-ups, and complete the shuttle run within 5 minutes and 35.4 seconds. Standards are somewhat lower for older members of each sex, but the age-related differences are dwarfed by those linked to gender. The push-up requirement, for example, is the same across all ages for women, and varies by just two for men of different ages. But prospective male police officers are required to do, on average, more than 300 percent more push-ups than women in order to pass.[26]

Like the double standards that now prevail in the military and the FBI,[27] those in some police departments raise serious questions. Just how much strength do police really need to have to do their jobs—enough to do 7 push-ups in a minute, or 30? And how fast must they be able to run? Must we hope that criminals pursued by female police officers will run more slowly and fight less aggressively to accommodate them? Complaints that fitness tests for firefighters and police are not predictive of on-the-job performance will probably never cease, but setting different standards for applicants of different genders makes a mockery of the very idea of screening for job-related skills.

And as lawsuits over fitness tests pile up, it's probably safe to assume that gender-specific standards will become more widespread. In 2014, the Department of Justice sued the Pennsylvania State Police over its gender-neutral fitness test, which male applicants passed at higher rates than their female counterparts. (Specifically, 94 percent of men and 71 percent of women passed the version of the test used from 2003 to 2008, and 98 percent of men versus 72 percent of women passed a similar test between 2009 and 2012.) According to the DOJ, this disparity indicated employment discrimination.[28] It couldn't possibly indicate basic differences between the male and female body.

Nope, in their eyes, the test was just an "artificial barrier" designed to "keep qualified women out of public safety work."[29]

State Police Commissioner Frank Noonan fired back, arguing that lowering the fitness standards "would be insulting to those men and women who already strove to achieve those standards and, more importantly, would endanger current and future troopers, the residents of Pennsylvania and all individuals served by the distinguished men and women of the Pennsylvania State Police."[30]

Meanwhile, in Colorado Springs, Police Chief Pete Carey instituted a gender- and age-neutral physical fitness test involving running, push-ups, and sit-ups in December 2013. According to one news story, his goals included "creating a 'culture of fitness,'" "reducing work related injuries," and "increasing officer longevity in the police force."[31] In a later statement, Carey noted that "To ensure officer success, [the department] called upon many resources in our community, including local healthcare and sports facilities, to provide personal training sessions and design exercise plans." Notwithstanding these efforts, when twelve female police officers over the age of forty failed the test and were transferred to desk jobs, they filed a civil suit alleging gender and age discrimination. Though Carey defended use of the test, he agreed to suspend it and return the twelve officers to their regular duties until the issue was settled in court.[32]

When the DOJ came for the city of Corpus Christi, Texas, over its police department's one-sex-standard fitness test for officers, the city folded entirely, paying $700,000 in back pay to female officers who had sued when they couldn't pass the test, and hiring them as "priority hires" with retroactive seniority and benefits. Eighty-two percent of men passed the test, compared with thirty-three percent of women. According to the federal government's lawyers, "The city failed to show any criteria or evidence supporting its use of the test and its cut-off scores." (Because apparently government bureaucrats know best how to test for physical fitness for law enforcement personnel.) Like in a good Orwell novel, the principal deputy assistant attorney general for the DOJ's Civil Rights Division had the same thing to say about Corpus Christi's police department as it did about the state of Pennsylvania's: their physical fitness standards were "artificial barriers that keep qualified women out of public safety work."[33]

The male advantage in physical strength is a stubborn biological reality. Since it won't change, today's gender ideology demands that fitness standards for first responders change instead, whatever the potential negative consequences. Taxpayers around America get to pony up to settle lawsuits, the results of which make them less safe, as well as signal to women that being less qualified for the job is essentially inherent in being a woman. All of which suggests the question: Who exactly is being treated equally here?

IT'S BIOLOGY, STUPID

Law enforcement, as we have seen is different from firefighting: it is not a job that always requires brute strength in life-and-death scenarios. To the contrary, much of police work is about interfacing with people, de-escalating tense situations, and quick thinking. And studies are increasingly finding that the presence of *more* women may actually benefit police departments.

Incidents of police brutality, protests, and riots swept the country in 2015 and 2016. Ferguson, the Baltimore riots, and the Dallas sniper incident were just a handful of tumultuous events brought about by incidents of police brutality, many of which were captured on video and involved male police officers unnecessarily and unjustly beating, shooting, and killing American citizens. The number of police shootings had reached a record high by 2015, and 2016 was no better.[34] Americans wondered what could be done to end the destabilizing standoff between citizens and the uniformed officers tasked with protecting them.

While most focused on resources for communities most impacted by police violence or better protection and training for police, a few people offered a counter-intuitive suggestion in response to the violence and chaos: bring in the females.

Female police, as it turns out, are significantly less likely to use excessive force and instead are much more likely to use their female prowess to de-escalate potentially violent situations and calm down would-be assailants.

One significant study entitled "Men, Women, and Excessive Police Force: A Tale of Two Genders" told markedly different stories of the two sexes when it comes to law enforcement: While women accounted for just under thirteen percent of police officers nationally, they accounted for only five percent of citizen complaints against officers for excessive force and just two percent of sustained allegations in large departments. The study found that on average, male police officers were almost ten times as likely as females to use excessive force on the job and three times more likely to be named in a citizen complaint for inappropriate behavior.[35]

When I spoke with Matthew Bucholz, who is both a former police officer in Alexandria, Virginia, and a retired lieutenant colonel in the Marines, he said he was "not surprised" to learn of these statistics. His own experience very much confirmed them. Women, he said, "make fantastic police officers." He said a typical scenario in which a male police officer places another male under arrest might go something like this:

Officer: "You're under arrest."

Citizen: "Oh, yea? F*** you!"

From there, he said, the situation would frequently escalate. With male officers, he said, the norm is, "As soon as you meet any kind of resistance, it's right to the mattresses." Bucholz told me that he would marvel at the way that a female cop "could often talk a guy into handcuffs, rather than fight him into them." The female officers he saw would say things like, "C'mon, you're a big guy, and I'm a woman. Your mom's right there. You don't want anyone to see this. You want your kids to see this?" and in doing so would talk men down and away from getting themselves into further trouble and potentially harming more people, including the officer herself.

"I had one female colleague," he told me, "who, man, she would charge right into a risky situation and control it. "Sit down!" She would yell. "Pull your pants up!" "She would immediately show command through the way she spoke, which diffused tension. It was amazing."[36]

Former Houston Mayor Anise Parker told *Time* magazine about female officers: "What women never think is: 'Can I wrestle this guy to the ground?' She's more likely to control the situation with voice and presence than any kind of physical tool."[37]

Bucholz pointed out that policing is still a very physical job. But "there are only two ways to deal with a situation as an officer," he pointed out. "Reason or use force." Women, he says, are "simply better at reasoning than men. But having a gun is a force equalizer, and having a radio is a force multiplier." "Bad guys can't outrun a radio." Because of that, he argued that law enforcement is a whole different ball game from firefighting, in that women bring distinct skills to the table, and can be equipped so that they are on par with a 250-pound bad guy, with reinforcements almost always close by.[38]

The female propensity for communication instead of excessive force saves taxpayers money, too. The "Tale of Two Genders" study found that only six percent of legal fees paid in excessive force cases involved offenses by female officers, meaning that male officers cost "somewhere between two and a half and five and a half times more than the average female officer in excessive force liability lawsuit payouts."[39]

In a piece making the case for more female officers to reduce police violence, *New York* magazine cites the example of Los Angeles, which in one decade paid out $63.4 million in lawsuits for excessive force and other violent incidents involving male officers compared to just $2.8 million for legal settlements involving female officers, none of which involved excessive force.[40] In that same decade, according to *Time*, settlement costs for cases of male brutality were twenty-three times that for similar cases involving female police officers, killings by male police were forty-three times that by female police, and assault and battery by male officers was thirty-two times that by women.[41]

In a strange foray away from political correctness, New York magazine chalked the difference up to sexual differences that can be seen as early as infancy, noting a 2007 study that found toddler boys are more likely than toddler girls to bite or kick, a finding, the author wrote, that "makes you think that the male disposition to violence is not wholly a matter of socialization to traditional gender roles, or, more bluntly, acculturation to toxic masculinity. Even more astounding, there's evidence that humans aren't the only one with gender disparities in aggression." The study points out, "Males are the more belligerent sex in virtually all mammalian species that biologists have studied." The differing propensities toward aggression and violence, the author says, "may be in our very biology."[42]

When, God forbid, we allow ourselves to acknowledge sex difference, suddenly we see that men and women bring different things to the civic table—different but equally important contributions.

As another writer put it, in Time magazine:

"Women have a long history of social work and community outreach, and female police officers tend to excel at community building. Ever since women started serving on the police force, they have focused on community outreach. The first female police officers—Lola Baldwin in Portland, Oregon, in 1908 and Alice Stebbins in Los Angeles in 1910—were former social workers, and most early female officers dealt almost exclusively with women and children. Study after study show[s] that the tools of social work—an overwhelmingly female occupation—[are] critical in modern policing, and that women's softer skills may counter the escalation of conflicts."

There are plenty who would call that statement a sexist reinforcement of gender stereotypes. And yet the studies and numbers make it clear that female officers on the whole approach law enforcement differently from men in critical ways—just as, on the whole, we are not as strong as men and generally not going to be as well-suited for some jobs, like running up seven flights of stairs carrying a ladder and back down carrying a deadweight two-hundred-pound man. To push first responder agencies into accepting unqualified women into these roles endangers both society and women, as well as affirming the notion that the male norm of brute strength is the ideal. Instead, we should be putting resources into identifying how women's unique capacities can benefit everyone.

As Matthew Bucholz put it, "You don't have to be kicking in a door to be deemed critical."[43]

CHAPTER 6

VALLEY OF THE DOLLS

*Humanity requires both men and women, and we
are equally important and need one another.*

—Beyoncé Knowles Carter

When R&B singer John Legend and his wife, the model Chrissy Teigen, announced she was pregnant, they opened up about their fertility struggles. Not only had they used in vitro fertilization to conceive, they had used reproductive technology to choose their baby's sex.

In an interview with *People* magazine, a grinning Teigen, pictured in a clingy white maternity dress noshing on a bowl of strawberries, said, "I've made this decision. Not only am I having a girl, but I picked the girl from her little embryo. I picked her and was like, 'Let's put in the girl.' ... I think I was most excited and allured by the fact that John would be the best father to a little girl. That excited me. It excited me to see...just the thought of seeing him with a little girl. I think he deserves a little girl. I think he deserves that bond. A boy will come along. We'll get there too, so it's not like we really have to pick. But he definitely is very lucky to have a little girl. And this girl is going to be so completely lucky to have John as her papa—it's crazy!"[1]

As *People* goes on to explain, "Teigen, 30, thinks that something magical happens to guys when they become a dad to a daughter: 'How soft they get, how mushy, and excited they get. It's so cute,' she says."

Sex selection is considered a form of eugenics and condemned by international entities such as the United Nations and the World Health Organization, which points out that the practice "raises serious moral, legal, and social issues." It results, the WHO says, in "the distortion of the natural sex ratio leading to a gender imbalance" and reinforces "discriminatory and sexist stereotypes towards women by devaluing females."[2] Sex selection through abortion has also been used to eliminate more than 100 million girls from the world.[3] But it's still legal in a few countries like Thailand—and the United States.[4]

Never mind all that, though. Teigen got her fair share of criticism about the ethics of her choice,[5] but most people hardly noticed that she accidentally affirmed the "gender binary" in daring to acknowledge the differences between the sexes that mean mothers and fathers have different relationships with their daughters and their sons. And nobody complained about Chrissy Teigen and John Legend prematurely "assigning" their child a gender instead of letting the child choose a gender for zerself.

THE KATE EFFECT

When the "Royal Couple," Prince William and Duchess Kate, had their second baby, their announcement became a flashpoint in the gender debate. An official Twitter account for the royal family sent out the following notice: "Her Royal Highness the Duchess of Cambridge was safely delivered of a daughter at 8.34am."[6]

The public response to the birth of Princess Charlotte was primarily one of jubilation, but partially one of quasi-satire about the audacity of identifying the baby by her sex.

One viral tweet read, "Please stop calling the #RoyalBaby a girl. We don't know what the baby's gender is until it is old enough to decide for itself."

One Reddit post read: "Remember to stop gendering and speciating the Royal baby. Xe may be a girl, but could also be a boy. For all we know, xe is a demiboy, or may not even be a baby but a fox, a ghost, or a sycamore. It is up to xe to decide this, not us." The poster was appropriately named "daretobesane."[7]

It was hard to tell satire from seriousness, when the folks at *Slate* were calling the identification of newborns by sex "child abuse" and a pregnant woman in my own Facebook feed, a fellow graduate of Tufts, wrote that same week of taking offense when someone asked her if she was having a boy or a girl, because, in her words, "a fetus can't have a gender."[8]

The Royal Couple's fetus, like Teigen and Legend's, most certainly had a sex, though; both were girls. And despite the mini-gender debate that followed the birth of Princess Charlotte, the fact is that a major part of the appeal of the Royal Couple is their striking sexual difference and complementarity.

Prince William is almost always seen in crisp military uniform or a neatly tailored suit. Duchess Kate is one of the most feminine and fashionable figures in the world. Their wedding was one of the most watched events in world history, with tens of millions of viewers on television[9] and another 72 million on YouTube in 188 countries. As the official blog for YouTube wrote of its Royal Wedding viewers, "You old romantics you."[10]

The wedding was Cinderellaeqsue, she in a traditional lace gown reminiscent of Grace Kelly and a tiara, he in full military regalia of a striking red hue. As they rode a carriage through the streets, he frequently held a white-gloved hand in salute as she respectfully and demurely lowered her eyes. According to YouTube, their "highly-anticipated kiss" on the palace balcony resulted in an additional ten thousand viewing requests per second on top of the 101 million viewers already tuned in.

People are starved for traditional romance, and the Royal Couple just keeps delivering it. In the six years since their wedding, Kate in particular has become a media focal point, not just because of her fashion sense but because of how she's blossomed very naturally into her role as wife and mother. She is considered to be the most talked-about woman in the world, and a YouGov survey found that ninety-eight percent of respondents hold a positive view of her.[11]

But not everyone has something nice to say about her. Indeed, Kate Middleton has become the subject of a feminist tug-of-war. The argument is over whether she deserves admiration, considering the traditional trajectory of her life.

Germain Greer, dubbed the "queen of British feminist thinking" in a cover story on the Duchess for *Newsweek*, said, "Kate is not even allowed to decorate her own houses. Even the wives of the American presidents get to do that. The whole thing is a mad anachronism. The 'firm' tell us that the first born will now become the monarch regardless of sex. Well, big f*cking deal! Kate is not allowed to have an interest in modern culture, even in art—to collect, to attend openings. She is made to appear absolutely anodyne. She cannot do or say anything spontaneous. She has learned what she has to do and say and how to do and say it in the approved way. Spontaneity will get her in trouble."

In a 2013 podcast for the *London Review of Books*, author Hilary Mantel, another feminist—she has said, "I think for a woman to say 'I'm not a feminist' is [like] a lamb joining the slaughterers' guild. It's just empty-headed and stupid,"[12] and admitted to fantasizing about killing Margaret Thatcher, whom she described as a "psychological transvestite"[13]—called Middleton "a jointed doll on which certain rags are hung": "In those days [before her first pregnancy] she was a shop-window mannequin, with no personality of her own, entirely defined by what she wore. These days she is a mother-to-be, and draped in another set of threadbare attributions. Once she gets over being sick, the press will find that she is radiant. They will find that this young woman's life until now was nothing, her only point and purpose being to give birth."[14]

Mantel calls Middleton "machine-made" with a "perfect plastic smile and the spindles of her limbs hand-turned and gloss-varnished."

But second-wave feminist hate hasn't stifled the duchess's appeal, even among a rising generation of self-styled feminists. As Charlotte Alter wrote for *Time*,

I love Kate against all the odds. I am a feminist, she is a poster child for marriage and motherhood. I work, she waves. I love talking, she hates talking. You might call us star-crossed. As implausible as it seems for an empowered American millennial woman to love Kate, I'm not alone. The feminist blog Jezebel posts regular updates on Princess Shinylocks' every move. Breathless coverage of the royal wedding and birth dominated U.S. news outlets.... There are many theories about why we love Kate...[none] explain why some modern American girls are mesmerized by a woman who stands for everything we disavow; beauty as value, marriage as achievement, procreation as purpose.[15]

Might it be that we love her because she embodies a certain womanly paradigm, one that today's women are taught to hate and deny, and she does so without the slightest suggestion of misgivings? Because she represents feminine grace, maternal instincts, elegance, poise, and intelligence, and appears to be adored by a handsome man (who also happens to be a prince) all the while?

She *is* a poster child—a particularly glamorous one, at that—for marriage and motherhood, two things that, study after study finds, women very much want (men, too, still desire marriage and fatherhood). Eighty-five percent of female college students in the U.S. still want to get married by thirty[16] (the Duchess tied the knot at age twenty-nine), and all but a very small slice of the population still want to have children.[17]

But never mind all that, we aren't supposed to like Kate, because, as *Newsweek*'s Ed Docx put it, "Kate's story thus far has been the very antithesis of a feminist narrative; quite literally that old pernicious fairytale: wait for a prince, become a princess and then cede all authority to the man while assuming the subservient role of mother and wife."[18]

Memo to my fellow female adorers of Duchess Kate: we are backward betrayers of feminism and our own sex!

FOAM FINGER FEMINISM

So what is pop culture's vision of the empowered woman? It's hardly an attractive alternative to all things Kate. As Charlotte Alter puts it, "Our own tawdry celebrities have to feign masturbation with a foam finger to get our attention."[19]

Or sit naked on a toilet eating cake for the entire world to see, as Hollywood's poster child for women's rights, Lena Dunham, infamously did in the opening sketch for the 2012 Emmy Awards. The creator of the HBO soft-porn series *Girls* gets naked a lot. So often that there are articles devoted just to her nudity sessions.

Lena Dunham has positioned herself as a feminist mentor of sorts for Hollywood's young starlets, but her credentials when it comes to empowering women are highly questionable. Her show *Girls*, when it came out, got an atypically candid and despondent review in the *New York Times*:

> One reason that "Girls" is unsettling is that it is an acerbic, deadpan reminder that human nature doesn't change.... For all the talk of equality, sexual liberation and independence, the love lives of these young women are not much more satisfying than those of their grandmothers. Their professional expectations are, if anything, even lower.
>
> And that is the baseline joke of "Girls."
>
> "Sex and the City" served up romantic failure wrapped in the trappings of success. "Girls" offers romantic failure wrapped in the trappings of failure.[20]

Dunham made her name and fortune off of a show that almost revels in today's sexual objectification of women, and their professional flounderings.

Even so, she's been crowned the spokeswoman for my generation when it comes to gender. As Heather Wilhelm points out, Dunham has been dubbed "the voice of a generation of women" by *Rolling Stone* and "the voice of a generation" full-stop by *Harper's Bazaar*; she is said by

Vanity Fair to have "captured her generation's story" and has been called "a generation's gutsy, ambitious voice" by *Time*.[21]

In her own voice, Dunham said in an interview with *Vanity Fair* that feminism means, "You believe you deserve all the same things that people who were born, uh, not of your gender deserve. If you care about equality, it's really simple and hard to negate."

That sounds benign enough. But she goes on to add, "Part of feminism is the freedom to let other women make choices you don't necessarily understand." Her first example: "So while you may not want to walk out with, like, tape, like, X's on your nipples, and booty shorts, that may be the strong feminist choice for another woman, and if you can't imagine yourself in her shoes, part of your job as a feminist is just to support her."

Naturally, then, as Dunham explains, "I have no feminist issue with the Kardashians. It's not my place to judge the Kardashians, it's my place to enjoy the beauty that they're bringing to the table."[22]

Dunham's feminist bona fides include telling a story about sexually abusing her sister, cracking an abortion joke about Kate Middleton's pregnancy,[23] and dressing as a Planned Parenthood abortionist for Halloween. Planned Parenthood gave her a shout-out in return, calling her a "tireless champion for women."[24] Dunham returned the love by attending a Planned Parenthood gala clad in what *US Weekly* called "the world's most appropriate top: a sweater embroidered with a pink image of the female reproductive system."[25]

The magazine gushed, "Womb love! Lena Dunham spoke at the Planned Parenthood 'Champion of Choice' event.... The *Girls* creator and star...donned the girl-power burgundy sweater by Rachel Antonoff ($218, though now sold out!), teamed with a pleated leather skirt. She accessorized the ensemble with polka-dotted heels and an emerald statement necklace. She styled her hair into tousled waves and finished with a rose-hued lip."

Dunham's anything-goes approach to women's empowerment demonstrates how feminism degenerates into aggressive, masculine raunch when untethered to any specific principle—and actually strips women of choice by requiring adherence to certain controversial beliefs as entry-tickets to the club, which, as it turns out, is exceptionally small.

According to Dunham, "Women saying 'I'm not a feminist' is my greatest pet peeve."[26]

So in Lena Dunham's world, women shouldn't really have a choice about being feminists, and their "job" as a feminist is to "support" any "choice" a woman makes, even if that includes posting naked selfies, as the likes of Kim Kardashian are wont to do. And Dunham's hostage-style feminism is purported to represent an entire generation.

No wonder the overwhelming majority of Americans, women included, don't self-identify as feminist. In one poll conducted by Vox, only eighteen percent of respondents considered themselves feminist.[27] In Duchess Kate's kingdom, that number dips to a staggering seven percent.[28] Another poll found that less than one-fourth of American women accept the label "feminist."[29] Yet another revealed that nearly fifty percent reject the term, and of those women, half do so because they find modern feminism too extreme, and another quarter because they view it as too "anti-man."[30]

That's what Taylor Swift thought, until she met Lena Dunham. In an interview with the *Guardian*, Swift says that she used to have the wrong impression of feminism: "As a teenager, I didn't understand that saying you're a feminist is just saying that you hope women and men will have equal rights and equal opportunities. What it seemed to me, the way it was phrased in culture, society, was that you hate men.... For so long it's been made to seem like something where you'd picket against the opposite sex...."

But then the singer-songwriter struck up a Twitter friendship with Dunham that quickly blossomed into a full-on feminist lovefest and resulted in what Swift described as a "feminist awakening": "Becoming friends with Lena—without her preaching to me, but just seeing why she believes what she believes, why she says what she says, why she stands for what she stands for—has made me realize that I've been taking a feminist stance without actually saying so."[31]

Swift came out as a feminist right in the middle of a Hollywood girl-power burst that was entirely befuddling.

The most prominent member of feminism's new pop culture faithful was Beyoncé, who made a hairpin turn away from being the sexy and soulful woman who had spoken candidly about sleeping with only one man (the man who "put a ring on it," as she admonishes men to do for the women they love in one of her biggest hits);[32] broken Twitter records (besting the death of Osama bin Laden) at the 2011 MTV Video Music Awards when she stopped in the middle of a performance and tore off her jacket to reveal a baby bump; and basked in her new maternity, describing the sound of her baby's heartbeat on the sonogram as "the most beautiful music I ever heard in my life."[33]

Ever so briefly, Beyoncé was a rare Hollywood star who was, as I described her for *Acculturated*, "an incredibly talented, strong, and fearless woman who loves babies and marriage and isn't afraid to show it." Even President Obama had something to say about her role as a woman: "Beyoncé could not be a better role model for my girls because she carries herself with such class and poise and has so much talent."[34]

Sadly, it didn't last.

Barely a year after Obama spoke those words, a mostly nude Beyoncé was gyrating onstage in her husband's lap in a performance for the 2014 Grammys. As Naomi Schafer Riley wrote in a piece pointedly entitled, "Jay-Z a Poor Excuse for a Husband," "What do you call a man who stands there smiling and singing as his scantily clad wife straddles a chair and shakes her rear end for other men's titillation?"[35]

Riley could also have asked: What do you call a woman who uses her platform to degrade herself sexually for money, attention, and fame? Not a feminist, surely.

Nevertheless, Beyoncé became Hollywood's empowered woman du jour with something to say about gender. As a contributor to the Shriver Report, a self-described "nonpartisan initiative that raises awareness, ignites conversations and inspires impact around the defining issues and fundamental changes facing modern women," Beyoncé wrote in early

2014, "We need to stop buying into the myth about gender equality. It isn't a reality yet."[36]

That same year, Beyoncé was on the cover of *Time*'s 100 Most Influential People issue. Facebook COO Sheryl Sandberg, of feminist manifesto *Lean In* fame, penned the profile of Beyoncé, writing, "In the past year, Beyoncé has sold out the Mrs. Carter Show World Tour while being a full-time mother.... She raises her voice both on- and offstage to urge women to be independent and lead."[37]

Sandberg cited some of Beyoncé's PG lyrics, but omitted others, such as "He Monica Lewinsky-ed all over my gown" (from her album *Partition*). And she might have been less enthusiastic in her praise after Beyoncé's fifteen-minute MTV Video Music Awards performance a few months later. As the *Federalist*'s Mollie Hemingway detailed, that performance included "a stage full of back-up dancers in 'naked stripper' costumes gyrating on strip poles, one of the most amazing collections of derrières I have *ever* seen, songs about performing oral sex in the back of a limo, a song about having a guy 'tear that cherry out' (complete with the word 'cherry' in big letters as the backdrop), a song that tells women who don't respect Beyoncé sufficiently to 'Bow Down Bitches,' S&M themes, [and] intimate acquaintance with much of Bey's crotch...."

"The usual," Hemingway continued. "I mean, it wasn't totally usual in that Beyoncé's toddler child was in the audience to witness all this dry-humping and simulated getting-down, but other than that, your typical Beyoncé."[38]

Out with the old, somewhat more wholesome Beyoncé, in with the new, "feminist" Beyoncé. However lamentable, her evolution embodied Hollywood's approach to sex and gender: the "empowered" woman is as hyper-sexualized as the raunchiest teenage male and can do whatever she wants, even celebrate sexual violence against women. Don't forget that it's your feminist "job," as Lena Dunham put it, to respect any woman's "strong feminist choice."

Unless you are Sofía Vergara?

Less than twenty-four hours after Beyoncé's strip-tease before the block letters "FEMINIST," Bruce Rosenblum, the chair of the Academy of Television Arts & Sciences, asked *Modern Family* star Sofía Vergara to stand on a rotating pedestal so that all could admire her famous curves as he gave a speech at the 2014 Emmys.

Vergara was a lot more dressed than Beyoncé was at the VMAs, and she did little more than stand there, but because her performance involved a physical pedestal, feminists raked her over the coals for acquiescing to the whims of the patriarchy. The contrasting responses to Beyoncé's and Vergara's actions made it clear, in Hemingway's words, what an "incoherent mess of double standards" pop culture feminism has become.[39]

When Vergara was asked whether she considered herself a feminist, she didn't help her cause with the women she had vexed. Vergara spelled out plainly how many women see feminism as directly in conflict with...being a woman: "Umm...I'm in the middle ground. As a Latin woman, I love having a husband, someone to be there waiting for me, supporting me. I don't see anything bad with getting help from somebody that loves you and treats you well. That's an amazing job and a lot of effort to do it right. I think the beauty of a woman nowadays is that we can do everything. We have more options and we should do everything we can. But why not have support and love? And if somebody can help you in any way, why not take the help?"[40]

THE REAL FEMINISTS OF HOLLYWOOD

Hollywood's misogyny masked as feminism really became undeniable when, later that year, Emily Ratajkowski, the topless star of the music video of Robin Thicke's song "Blurred Lines," hitched herself to the "feminist" bandwagon. She graced the cover of *Cosmopolitan* magazine (little more these days than a digest on how to sexually please a man) and was featured in an article with the headline, "I Feel Lucky That I Can Wear What I Want, Sleep with Who I Want, and Dance How I Want, and Still Be a Feminist."

The Daily Beast's Tricia Romano called "Blurred Lines" "kind of rapey," and pointed out that the music video, which helped propel the song to the top of charts, was little more than "three models, Emily

Ratajkowski, Jessi M'Bengue, and Elle Evans, wearing nothing but shoes and nude-hued thongs, as they cavort and dance and flirt with Thicke, Pharrell, and T.I., who are all fully clothed," while occasional lines like "Robin Thicke has a big d***" flash across the screen.[41]

Another female author agreed that the song was "rapey," and defended the use of the term in a piece for the *Wall Street Journal*. "The word 'rapey' has become a popular word among young third-wave feminists," she wrote. "Some people have criticized the use of the word, claiming that it trivializes sexual assault. I disagree. I find the term very useful—I like to think of the word as the adjectival form of 'rape culture.'"[42]

It's hard to argue that "Blurred Lines," which achieved the longest run at number one on Billboard since the early 1990s,[43] does not have clear violent undertones. The lyrics include lines like:

> Tried to domesticate you
> But you're an animal

and

> Good girl!
> I know you want it

and

> I'll give you something big enough to tear your [expletive] in two

and

> He don't smack that [expletive] and pull your hair for you

Some music critics brushed the song off as one among many problematic pop songs with lyrics that degrade women and imply non-consensual or violent sex.[44] But most feminist writers and websites expressed outrage. One piece on *xoJane* featured pictures of rape victims holding up signs displaying words their rapists had said to them, some of them verbatim lines from Thicke's song.[45]

Feminists' reaction to Thicke's lyrics betrayed the fact that people, women especially, still intuit that, when it comes to sexuality, not every "choice" is okay.

So when "Blurred Lines" video star Ratajkowski called herself a feminist, she unleashed a liberal feminist panic. Over the course of decades, the word "feminism" had been stripped of any meaning, as it was used to justify even the most demeaning behavior—as long as choice was somehow, somewhere involved. This left today's feminists, as I said on *Acculturated*, "stuck between a rock and a stripper pole" when it came to stars of rapey, pornographic videos claiming the label.

The smash success of Thicke's song revealed the uglier side of Hollywood. Despite all the talk about empowering women and fostering gender equity, misogyny sells. And Hollywood's head honchos and stars—plenty of women included—aren't afraid to cash in.

Few episodes illustrate this better than the legal battle that developed between one of the music industry's most influential producers, Dr. Luke, and a young female singer who accused him of rape: Kesha.

Dr. Luke, or Lukasz Sebastian Gottwald, is a Grammy-nominated guitarist and producer behind many of today's biggest hits. He specializes in music for young women, with an ironic subspecialty in girl-power anthems like "Since U Been Gone" by Kelly Clarkson, "Circus" by Britney Spears, "Wrecking Ball" by Miley Cyrus, and "Roar" by Katy Perry.[46]

"Roar" was the campaign anthem for Alison Lundergan Grimes, whose attempt to unseat Republican Senate Majority Leader Mitch McConnell was a spectacular failure. Katy Perry repeatedly performed it on the campaign trail for Hillary Clinton (Clinton is a fan of Perry, and also considers Kim Kardashian to be "inspirational"); at one Iowa event, Perry wore multiple outfits with the Hillary for President logo and even sported Hillary-themed nails.[47] As it turned out, Hillary Clinton's campaign was also a spectacular failure.

But all the girl power in Hollywood was no help to Kesha, who, we have seen, filed a 2014 lawsuit against Dr. Luke, alleging he had drugged and raped her. Her description of waking up naked in his bed with no memory of how she got there is eerily reminiscent of lyrics that Dr. Luke himself wrote, from the song "Last Friday Night:"

> There's a stranger in my bed
> There's a pounding in my head
> ....
> Is this a hickey or a bruise?

The singer? Hillary Clinton's Hollywood liaison to women, Katy Perry.

Kesha's battle against Dr. Luke garnered major media attention and lots of support from other young women: fellow Sony star Adele dedicated her Brit Award to the embattled singer,[48] and Taylor Swift donated $250,000 for her legal bills.[49] As the hashtag "#FreeKesha" went viral, other female celebs like Lady Gaga offered their support over Twitter.

"There are people all over the world who love you @KeshaRose. And I can say truly I am in awe of your bravery," said Gaga, in a tweet liked by over one hundred thousand Twitter users.[50]

The way Kesha's legal drama unfolded horrified many.

Sony sided with Dr. Luke in the case, refusing to release Kesha from her contract and insisting that she continue to work under her alleged rapist, despite Kesha's claim that he had threatened to destroy her music career if she told anyone about the rape.

As one article for *Bust* magazine noted, the music industry gave Kesha the "cold shoulder," and in pushing the singer "out of the music world," sent a "warning to all young women in the music business to keep their mouths shut if they want to continue with their careers."[51] It was the ultimate blow to Hollywood's new claim to be feminist.

When Dr. Luke filed suit in New York claiming that Kesha had committed defamation and violated her contract, Kesha filed a counterclaim accusing him of gender-based hate crimes. But as we have already seen, the judge threw out her suit, explaining that rape is not always "a gender-motivated hate crime."[52] To get on with her contract, the judge wrote, was the "commercially reasonable thing to do."

A wave of starlets' stories of sexual abuse followed in the wake of Kesha's story. Thandie Newton revealed that early in her career, a major Hollywood director had sexually abused her in an audition. Years later, she was stunned to learn that the director had actually shown a film of the incident to friends at poker parties at his house.[53] Rose McGowan came out as having been raped by a Hollywood executive she was still too afraid to name.[54] All this while Hollywood was reeling from the revelations that "family man" Bill Cosby had been systematically raping women throughout his career.[55]

And so Hollywood's feminism comes full circle. Any "choices" women make (under who knows what kind of pressure from male producers and record label executives) must be afforded the feminist label—including giving voice to lyrics that downplay the seriousness of violent or potentially non-consensual sex. But the same women, the very stars who enrich the likes of Dr. Luke by performing music that raises serious ethical questions about the treatment of women, find themselves powerless—and are written off by those with actual power.

So women in "feminist" Hollywood have their own voice. Just as long as they are using it to sexify rape music.

Andi Zeisler summed the paradox up in a piece for the *Guardian* entitled "Music Business 'Feminism' Is Little More than Branding. Just Ask Kesha."

> Because while it's easy to throw the label "feminist" into a fizzy mix of other identifying descriptors, it's a lot harder to carve out a space for ongoing, norm-shifting progress in an industry that has been shaped by and steeped in inequality, stereotyping and ambient discrimination. A place where groundbreaking performers from Joni Mitchell to Kathleen Hanna to Nicki Minaj have been defined less by their musical or vocal skills than by their looks and whom they were sleeping with; a place

where female musicians have their work diminished by or in favor of their male collaborators; and, most definitely, a place where female musicians are expected to go along to get along....

Inspirational but over-broad statements about "empowerment" and "girl power" become exclusively personal, acts of independent saleswomanship that manifest as branding, rather than action.[56]

Despite all the power talk, Zeisler points out, few women are in actual positions of power in the music business. Women make up less than 5 percent of recognized record producers. According to the Huffington Post, "Creative & Cultural Skills report that the gender divide across all music industry related jobs is 67.8% male to 32.2% female. PRS for Music report that their membership of over 95,000 songwriters and composers is only 13 per cent female. AIM's 2012 membership survey revealed that only 15% of label members are majority-owned by women."[57]

Only fifteen people on the 2015 Billboard Power 100 list were female.[58] And a chart in *Time* magazine showed that the professional category of "musicians, singers, and related," had one of the lowest percentages of women in the field as compared with other professions, with less than one-fourth of the field being female. Only five industries were more male-dominated, examples including "dishwashers" and "cleaners of vehicles and equipment."[59]

Television and film have similar gender equity woes. The situation is so bad, in fact, that there have been recent calls for the ACLU to get involved and investigate sex discrimination throughout the industry.

To quote *Salon*, Hollywood is a "cesspool of misogyny and racism. Bring on the lawsuits."[60]

As one higher-up at the ACLU told the *New York Times*, "Women directors aren't working on an even playing field and aren't getting a fair opportunity to succeed. Gender discrimination is illegal. And, really, Hollywood doesn't get this free pass when it comes to civil rights and gender discrimination."[61]

The *Times* cites a number of studies finding that in the last twelve years, only four percent of the top-grossing movies were directed by women, and in 2013 and 2014, less than two percent were. In those same years, women directed only fourteen percent of television shows.

There is basically no end to the articles and exposés about misogyny in Hollywood.

"CASTING WHORES"

One of the ACLU's complaints about sexism in Hollywood is rampant and "overt sex stereotyping."

To take just one example, a casting agency for a film produced by Quentin Tarantino placed an ad on Facebook beginning "Casting Whores for Quentin Tarantino project." The ad was deleted, but not before it was captured in a screengrab:

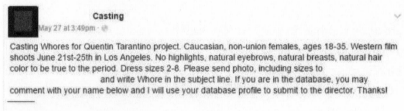

Casting
May 27 at 3:49pm ·

Casting Whores for Quentin Tarantino project. Caucasian, non-union females, ages 18-35. Western film shoots June 21st-25th in Los Angeles. No highlights, natural eyebrows, natural breasts, natural hair color to be true to the period. Dress sizes 2-8. Please send photo, including sizes to   and write Whore in the subject line. If you are in the database, you may comment with your name below and I will use your database profile to submit to the director. Thanks!

Unsurprisingly, Tarantino was widely slammed for the ad. To quote one feminist blog: "Putting a casting call out for, or including women in your script with the description of 'whores,' is not ok. Nor is asking actresses to submit their photos and information for consideration with the subject line 'Whore.' Aside from the fact that there are better words to use if one is looking to cast women who work in the sex industry, this description is actually a typical example of Hollywood sexism, particularly as it pertains to roles for women."[62]

Forget for a moment that referring to prostitution as "the sex industry" legitimizes using women. This ad is coming from the same industry that gave us *Pretty Woman*, the cult classic starring Julia Roberts and Richard Gere that glamorizes prostitution, making it look like a gateway to romance, replete with a happy ending and a "balcony-set reunion scene" straight out of *Romeo and Juliet*.

According to Mental Floss, *Pretty Woman* is the fourth-highest-grossing romantic comedy of all time. It's also categorized as a "Cinderella Complex" movie; in that category, it comes in number two, just behind *My Big Fat Greek Wedding*.[63] The term "Cinderella complex" was coined by feminist Collette Dowling in her 1981 book *The Cinderella Complex: Women's Hidden Fear of Independence*. Dowling, who boasts about leaving her husband, determined after much study of "the psychological differences between the sexes" that "Women are brought up to depend on a man and to feel naked and frightened without one. We have been taught to believe that as females we cannot stand alone, that we are too fragile, too delicate, too needful of protection. So that now, in these enlightened days, when so much has become possible, unresolved emotional issues often hold us back."

We are, apparently, plagued by an "unconscious desire to be taken care of by another."[64] Refer back to Exhibit A, Sofía Vergara, the traitor to her sex who horrified the feminists by standing on a pedestal and describing her husband as "supporting," and saying, "I don't see anything bad with getting help from somebody that loves you and treats you well."

I guess Julia Roberts should have stayed a prostitute.

DUMBING DADS DOWN

Not all of Hollywood's sex-based animosity is directed at women.

A study entitled "Daddies or Dummies?" conducted at Brigham Young University concluded that "the media may not only be portraying fathers negatively, but actually *teaching* youth to disrespect and disregard their dads." The study found that "40 percent of fatherly behavior" on popular tween shows could be labeled "buffoonery" and that half of "on-screen response[s] of children to their fathers" are negative behaviors like eye-rolling or walking away.[65]

As Naomi Schaefer Riley wrote, father humor is nothing new in movies and TV, but now it's happening at a time when a man's role in the home is more uncertain than ever. "Today's sitcoms," she writes, "...often show dads trying to act like mothers have traditionally—and failing miserably."[66]

And even though today's feminists go out of their way to claim that being a strong woman doesn't mean you have to hate men—as Lena Dunham put it, "feminism doesn't mean you want to like take a stake and kill all the men and create your own planet"[67]—masculinity is increasingly a source of scandal on screen.

Just take *Vanity Fair*'s reaction to the latest Captain America movie. Joanna Robinson opined in its pages that the "heterosexual virility" of the movie's male figures is the "one flaw" in the "otherwise great" flick.[68] *Captain America: Civil War* is a recent addition to the Avengers series, based on the Marvel comic books, which are basically muscles, violence, and masculine virility served up raw, cartoon-strip style.

Hyper-male superhero and action figure movies have long been a Hollywood specialty. The top ten–grossing film franchises of all time include the Marvel Cinematic Universe, Star Wars, Batman, James Bond, X-Men, Spiderman, and Shrek. Action heroes, super heroes, Luke Skywalker and Han Solo, more action heroes, and a giant green ogre.[69]

Calls for more female representation in the action figure universe ultimately began to materialize—but on-screen action heroines for the most part are highly sexualized and violent. Either they behave like men in peak moments of "heterosexual virility," or they look like the fulfillment of the most debased male fantasy.

Take, for example, Angelina Jolie in the 2005 blockbuster *Mr. and Mrs. Smith*, in which she doubled as blasé wife and sexy spy. She spends most of the movie violating Dunham's don't-kill-the-men principle by trying to kill her own husband, all while, to use Russell Scott Smith's phrasing for the *New York Post*, "exploiting her sexuality for shock value."[70]

Perhaps no one is as open about exploiting female sexuality as Axel Alonso, the editor-in-chief for Marvel Comics, whose movie empire takes the number-one spot on the list of highest-grossing franchises in history.

In a stunning interview with the *Telegraph*, Alonso says, "it's impossible not to sexualize [female] characters." When pressed about the fact that almost half of comic book readers are females, he responded, "We believe there's an audience of women out there who are hungry for this and we want to make sure they get it. This is affirmative action. This is capitalism."

And he insists that sexualizing female protagonists is essential:

> I won't say we won't do sexy female characters. That's preposterous and ridiculous...I want to make sure I have books like Ms Marvel and Black Widow that I'm proud about and could give to my daughter. But at the same time I don't want to be the PC police and say you can't be naughty; you can't be fun.

He openly affirms the obvious when he says, "I don't think men are as sexualised as women."

Although Alonso sounded like Hugh Hefner, his female interviewer closes the piece on a bland note: "Even though Marvel won't stop fully sexualising female characters, it's good news that they are still working on diversity."[71]

COVERBOY?

There is no denying Hollywood's influence in the cultural conversation. It has a lot to say, and gives us a lot to talk about, when it comes to sex difference and that ever-elusive quest for "gender equity." Girls today grow up on a steady diet of famous self-professed "feminists" like Miley Cyrus, Taylor Swift, and Queen Bey. Lena Dunham recently finished producing a documentary for HBO called *Suited*, which, according to *USA Today*, "explores the complexities of gender identity through the prism of Bindle & Keep, a Brooklyn tailor specializing in suits" designed for "gender-nonconforming clientele. The film documents the personal stories of people who have transitioned, are transitioning, or choose not to identify themselves by 'he' or 'she' pronouns, but share common desires for inclusivity and body confidence."[72]

But what about "body confidence" for the rest of us? Are we supposed to feel comfortable in our own skin as men and women? Not if you listen to Hollywood, where fathers are incompetent and ridiculous, masculinity is offensive, and feminine elegance and appreciation for men's contributions are pilloried—while hypersexualized women who celebrate domestic violence are supposed to be "empowered." Hollywood's ideal woman is forced into a mold cast by the most depraved male fantasy, and then slapped with the label "feminist." The architects of this ugly "feminism" then tell women everywhere it's their "job" to support it. We have an obligation to celebrate any "choice" women make—All hail Kim Kardashian, who practically invented the term "naked selfie"!—as long as it's not the choice to celebrate motherhood, traditional femininity, or any other authentic expression of our female selves.

To Hollywood, sex is only "real" when they want it to be. It's merely a construct when Bruce Jenner becomes Caitlyn and Miley Cyrus decides that she is neither boy nor girl.[73] It's up for debate when makeup line CoverGirl unveils that its newest model is a biological man. "Meet CoverGirl's First Cover Boy," read the CNN.com headline touting the cosmetics company's "bold move" of replacing a woman with a man for the first time, to advertise products for...women.[74]

But when Chrissy Teigen picks a female embryo out of a lab dish, sex is real and matters and we must all validate the significance of her choice.

And then again sex is just a plaything, as are the women who put their sexuality at the service of the entertainment industry. Even a cursory look at how it's all working out for Hollywood's women—and for the everyday women who consume what Hollywood produces—makes it clear that women have gotten the short end of Hollywood's "gender equity" stick.

CHAPTER 7

THE SEXUAL DEVOLUTION

Women's Liberation calls it enslavement but the real truth about the sexual revolution is that it has made of sex an almost chaotically limitless and therefore unmanageable realm in the life of women.

—Midge Dector

I t was one of the last weeks of my senior year at Tufts, and a group of us were standing in a circle talking. One female student, a friend of a friend, was staring at her feet as the rest of us chatted. I couldn't figure out what was wrong, but she seemed upset, her face slowly darkening to crimson. After a few minutes, a couple of the guys said good-bye and walked away. I leaned over and asked, "Are you okay?"

She looked up at me and glanced at the back of one of the guys. "I gave him [oral sex] last night," she replied, "and today he wouldn't even look at me."

I present to you: The Sexual Revolution.

The Sexual Revolution was like a hydrogen bomb taken to human sexuality. Though it was launched by the Americans coming of age in the 1950s and 60s, subsequent generations such as my own are still living in a cloud of nuclear fallout. Our moral landscape is like the bombed-out cities after the world wars, and we are like citizens left behind to sort through the debris.

To understand why we are where we are today—living in a world where suggesting the sexes are different is a national scandal, a world where the moral playbook that once held men accountable has been tossed, a world where educated girls are sent off to college to become sex toys for men, used and cast aside—you have to pull back the curtain.

PLAYBOY FEMINISM

You have to get back to where it all began. A very good starting point is with a prominent cultural figure who literally turned women into profitable playthings for men and called it empowering, a self-professed "feminist" who praises the Sexual Revolution and touts his own role in it: Hugh Hefner.

In an interview for *Esquire*, the founder of the Playboy enterprise said of the Sexual Revolution,

> Women were the major beneficiary of the sexual revolution. It permitted them to be natural sexual beings, as men are. That's where feminism should have been all along. Unfortunately, within feminism, there has been a puritan, prohibitionist element that is antisexual. *Playboy* is the antidote to puritanism. In the 1950s and '60s, there were still states that outlawed birth control, so I started funding court cases to challenge that. At the same time, I helped sponsor the lower-court cases that eventually led to *Roe* v. *Wade*. We were the amicus curiae in *Roe* v. *Wade*. I was a feminist before there was such a thing as feminism. That's a part of history very few people know.[1]

The common thinking is that the Sexual Revolution was primarily about liberating women from the constraints of traditional sexual morality, whose "double standard" discriminated against them. Second-wave feminists in the 1960s and '70s believed that once women were freed from the puritanical rules and taboos that repressed their sexual expression, they could enjoy sex just the way men do. Women only needed to be freed from oppressive expectations and institutions like modesty, chastity, and marriage; liberated from their bodies' fecundity; and released into a world where they could have sex on the same terms as men. In the words of Hugh Hefner—hardly a feminist, by anyone's definition—"It permitted them to be natural sexual beings, as men are."

Except women aren't exactly like men.

They're particularly unlike the kind of men whose sexuality seemed "natural" to Hugh Hefner—carefree libertines and heartless lechers.

The ideology that there are no significant differences between the sexes, which eventually became known as "gender equity," gave birth to the pantsuit, the Pill, and Planned Parenthood. All three had the effect of making women more like men—the stubborn paradigmatic ideal of the era.

As Harvey Mansfield put it, "Gender neutrality seems at first to disregard sexual differences, but it also wants women to be more independent, more like men. It assumes that what was until recently specific to men is actually common to both sexes." And yet there are elements of masculinity and femininity that don't overlap. As Mansfield puts it, "there remains an obstacle to gender neutrality—manliness—which does not seem easily removable, even in time."[2]

He points out the truth that many of today's feminists still won't look straight in the eye: "Men reject and resist the expectation that they should abandon their manliness." Women, on the other hand, abandoned a great portion of their femaleness in the Sexual Revolution in a mostly doomed attempt to establish equality (understood as being identical) with men.

The Sexual Revolution was premised on the long overdue empowerment of one sex, but it had the effect of erasing most of the distinctions that set it apart from the other. Femaleness was absorbed into maleness. And as female difference, a powerful check on the worst qualities of maleness, has been wiped out, women have gotten the short end of the stick. We've gotten a world where we are expected to perform emotionally, professionally, physically, and sexually just like men.

The Sexual Revolution, billed as progress for women, is actually just a Ponzi scheme for the patriarchy. When my generation of women comes to cash in on its promises, we're finding it bankrupt.

PAY ANY PRICE, BEAR ANY BURDEN

A 2016 article in *Cosmopolitan* magazine excitedly announced that "reversible, condomless birth control" for men is finally on the horizon and might be ready as soon as 2018. "This could be the answer to your male birth control prayers," the author breathlessly exclaimed. The woman who heads the organization trying to develop the male birth control—in what read like a desperate attempt to preempt men's horror at the thought of injecting a gel into their "ball sack" which will then "[block] sperm from leaving the vas deferens"—is quoted as saying, "There are so many men who want this so badly. The support is going to be there."[3]

An equally fevered headline in the *Telegraph* read "The Male Pill Is Coming—and It's Going to Change Everything."[4]

In fact, birth control options for men, including the exact injections described in the *Cosmo* piece, have been a viable option for decades. Trials on the drug found that it worked with almost perfect results and no serious side effects. The problem? Men don't actually want it.

Contraceptive injections for men were developed and patented nearly four decades ago, in the 1970s. And yet Arikia Millikan argues for *Vice* that the time for "reliable" male birth control is long overdue, because, "In present day 2015, the available options aren't great, and the burden still rests largely on women to mitigate the damages of our wanton impulses. Aside from the copper IUD, all the birth control devices and pharmaceuticals available to women alter our hormones with various weird side effects."[5] She is far from alone in expressing frustration that it is the women who wound up responsible for controlling their reproductive functions, despite all the talk about sexual equality and freedom.

There seems to be a major delay in developing artificial birth control for men that is as (relatively) convenient and effective as what's on the market for women. As one female writer sarcastically put it, the "Male Birth Control Pill Is Still 'Right Around the Corner,' like It Has Been For Years."[6]

Try decades, but that's basically accurate. WebMD will tell you there are plenty of drugs that have been in the pipeline that could disarm male fertility, much as the Pill alters ovulation and fertility in women. The problem, just about every article on male birth control argues, is "funding."[7] Despite the fact that the multi-billion-dollar pharmaceutical industry is one of the biggest drivers of the economy, apparently there is no funding for male birth control.

And not much interest. In 2016, excitement grew around the latest experiment in male birth control, but then men dropped out because they experienced side effects affecting their mood, libido, and skin "pretty similar to what women have suffered while taking the pill for years." "It takes two to tango," explained an article in Quartz, "but the burden of birth control falls largely on women."[8]

It couldn't possibly be that men don't want to give up an essential part of what makes them men: their fertility. Chemical birth control for men is branded as something that would give them control over their fertility—pretty much the same way the Pill was sold to women. In reality, it would be the ultimate surrender of something essential to who they are—the ultimate surrender of control. Somehow, in the wake of the Sexual Revolution, men have been able to see this—and to resist it—while women have not. So nearly six decades after the FDA approved the Pill as a contraceptive, women are still the ones stuck shutting down their fertility, suffering all the unwanted side effects, and, of course, dealing with the ramifications when birth control fails.

This shouldn't come as a surprise. From the get-go, the Sexual Revolution's plan for eliminating the "double standard" was not really to liberate women to be women. It was to make the female body just like the male body: barren.

In 1967, the National Organization for Women, a group founded by one of the Revolution's lady generals—Betty Friedan—inserted the "right of women to control their own reproductive lives" into its Bill of Rights for Women.[9]

The notion that female fertility was the problem underlying gender inequality pervaded the Sexual Revolution. Margaret Sanger, godmother of the Pill and founder of Planned Parenthood, defended the disproportionate burden of birth control on women, calling it "first of all a woman's problem":

> Many people who believe in Birth Control as the means of voluntary motherhood say that the propaganda of the movement is directed too much to women and too little to men. They contend that the appeal should be to men quite as much as to women and that a strong effort should be made to arouse the masculine half of humanity to its responsibilities in relation to the evils growing out of the enslavement of the reproductive function.
>
> It is true that the propaganda of the Birth Control movement in America has been addressed almost entirely to women. It has been couched in the terms of woman's experience. Its prime importance to her has been continuously and consistently stressed. The reason for this course is at once fundamental and practical.
>
> .... A free race cannot be born of slave mothers. A woman enchained cannot choose but give a measure of bondage to her sons and daughters. No woman can call herself free who does not own and control her body. No woman can call herself free until she can choose consciously whether she will or will not be a mother....
>
> Birth Control is a woman's problem. The quicker she accepts it as hers and hers alone, the quicker will society respect motherhood. The quicker, too, will the world be made a fit place for children to live.[10]

But the actual result was just the opposite. Birth control became "a woman's problem" all right. But respect for motherhood plummeted.

THE ULTIMATE FIX

The most obvious proof of this was—concurrent with the popular acceptance of birth control—the rise of abortion, which is the ultimate "fix" when the Pill and other contraceptives fail to make a woman's body work just like a man's.

Whereas early feminists were ardently opposed to abortion, viewing it as an assault on the female body, the Second Wave feminists of the Sexual Revolution made a major break with that thinking, arguing that full female freedom would only be attainable if abortion were made legal.

First Wave feminists saw abortion as exploitative of women. Suffragette and abolitionist Elizabeth Cady Stanton said of abortion, "when we consider that women are treated as property, it is degrading to women that we should treat our children as property to be disposed of as we see fit." The first woman to run for president, Victoria Woodhull, wrote, "Every woman knows that if she were free, she would never bear an unwished-for child, nor think of murdering one before its birth." And Elizabeth Blackwell, the first women to get a medical degree, called abortion "the gross perversion and destruction of motherhood" and said that it "filled me with indignation, and awakened active antagonism."[11]

These early activists for equality believed that women's rights could not be built on the rejection of an essential part of woman, her capacity for motherhood. Abortion is the ultimate rejection of motherhood, and in effect, a rejection of woman herself, including her body.

The Sexual Revolution saw a 180-degree pivot away from this appreciation for motherhood and the female body. Suddenly female fertility was a problem that had to be eradicated in order for women to achieve full equality with men.

Gloria Steinem, godmother of the Sexual Revolution, famously asserted that society treats women as mere "talking wombs." In an interview with the *Guardian* she said, "It took us awhile to figure it out, but patriarchy—or whatever you want to call it, the systems that say there's masculine and feminine and other [expletive]—is about controlling reproduction. Every economics course ought to start not with production but with reproduction. It is way more important."[12]

Steinem is famous for her maxim, "If men could get pregnant, abortion would be a sacrament." She dedicated her recent book to a man who helped her secure an illegal abortion when she was twenty-two, something he did on the condition "you will do what you want to do with your life."[13]

The perception driving much of the Sexual Revolution was that that was exactly what men did—they did whatever they wanted with their lives, including sexually—and a woman's only ticket to the same freedom was legal abortion. To the revolutionaries of the day, sexual difference was the source of inequality between men and women. Giving women control over their reproductive functions, at whatever moral cost, was feminists' top priority in the Sexual Revolution.

Somewhere, Hugh Hefner was smiling. And so was writer and pro-abortion activist Lawrence Lader.

While working on a biography of Planned Parenthood foundress Margaret Sanger, Lader had become an ardent proponent of abortion, gathering a group of likeminded activists in his Manhattan apartment to form what eventually became known as NARAL, a lobbying group devoted to the repeal of state abortion laws. Of Sanger, Lader told the *New York Times* that working on Sanger "completely convinced me that a woman's freedom in education, jobs, marriage, her whole life, could only be achieved when she gained control of her childbearing."[14]

Of abortion opponents, he said, "Basically, the opposition really hates women, which I think comes out of a woman's sexuality."

One of Lader's fellow NARAL founders, Dr. Bernard Nathanson, was an abortionist looking to expand and legitimize his business. Nathanson, who later in life changed his position, becoming an outspoken opponent of abortion, said that Lader once told him, "If we're going to move abortion out of the books and into the streets, we're going to have to recruit the feminists." Lader explicitly referred to another matriarch of the Revolution, Betty Friedan, saying, "Friedan has got to put her troops into this thing—while she still has control over them."[15]

Although Friedan had not even mentioned abortion in the first edition of *The Feminine Mystique*,[16] the infamous 1963 tome widely credited with launching the Second Wave feminism integral to the Sexual Revolution, Lader and Nathanson succeeded in making her their mouthpiece for abortion as a right. In a speech she delivered at the First National Conference for Repeal of Abortion Laws in Chicago in 1969, Friedan argued, "The basic personhood and dignity of woman is violated forever if she does not have the right to control her own reproductive process." To Friedan, "The right of woman to control her reproductive process must be established as a basic, inalienable civil right, not to be denied or abridged by the state."[17]

Nearly every women's rights advocate who followed in her wake made the same claims, and freedom and equality for women became inextricably intertwined with abortion.

A WOMAN'S PLACE

But the rejection of woman did not end with her perceived bodily imperfections. It was not just that women's rights became synonymous with the right to end maternity through the violent invasion of the womb. The Sexual Revolution also witnessed a devaluation of motherhood and home life that came in tandem with the demand for greater opportunities for women in the workforce.

Betty Friedan's *Feminine Mystique* was central to this change; she had likened unhappy housewives to "walking corpses" living in "comfortable concentration camps" in the book.

Friedan based a good deal of her writing on that of Margaret Mead, an anthropologist who studied tribal cultures. Because some tribes had less pronounced cultural differences between the sexes, Mead concluded that (in Friedan's words) there are an "infinite variety of sexual patterns" and an "enormous plasticity" to human nature. Friedan called Mead's work "a truly revolutionary vision of women finally free to realize their full capabilities in a society which replaced arbitrary sexual definitions with a recognition of genuine individual gifts as they occur in either sex."

Mead pivoted later in life toward a more Freudian approach that acknowledged distinct and mysterious differences between the sexes not attributable to random cultural influences, but Friedan dismissed her later work, saying that Mead "cut down her own vision of women by glorifying the mysterious miracle of femininity."[18]

Looking back, it would seem that the principal project of the Sexual Revolution was to wipe out that "mysterious miracle" under the mantle of ending oppression. To the warriors of the Sexual Revolution, women were only really living if they lived like men.

The leaders of the Sexual Revolution went beyond demanding that women have access to the same professional and educational opportunities as men; they outright rejected the notion that domestic work and raising children were acceptable ways for a liberated, modern, and empowered woman to spend her life. When Friedan dared to suggest to another revolutionary, Simone de Beauvoir, that women ought to at least have the *choice* as to whether or not to stay home and raise children, de Beauvoir replied, "No, we don't believe that any woman should have this choice. No woman should be authorized to stay at home to raise her children. Society should be totally different. Women should not have that choice, precisely because if there is such a choice, too many women will make that one."[19]

Sounds extreme, and yet decades later, in 2011, when the *Economist* held an online Oxford-style debate and poll on the statement "This house believes that a woman's place is at work," nearly half of respondents agreed with the statement.[20] The year before, Reuters had done its own survey, asking the opposite question, whether a "woman's place is in the home." Seventy-four percent disagreed.[21]

While the very idea that women have any one "place" where they belong would seem to be unnecessarily constricting, the litany of articles about female angst over feeling torn between their careers and their children and home makes it clear that the Sexual Revolution's devaluation of motherhood and domesticity thoroughly pervades modern culture.

SEX AND THE LAW

The Sexual Revolution upended centuries of policies built around sexual norms.

Not all the changes were bad. Thanks to a series of hard-fought legal challenges, women were afforded educational and employment opportunities they had previously been denied. The year *The Feminine Mystique* was published, for instance, President Kennedy signed the Equal Pay Act to remedy the "unconscionable" but at that time common "practice of paying female employees less wages than male employees for the same job."[22] The law banned compensating men and women unequally on the basis of sex for "equal work on jobs the performance of which requires equal skill, effort, and responsibility...under similar working conditions."[23]

The Civil Rights Act, passed just a year later, famously prohibited discrimination in hiring, firing, and other employment practices on the basis of sex, among other categories. "Sex" barely squeaked into the law, which had originally been written to bar discrimination on the basis of "race, color, religion, or national origin." But as the bill was being debated by Congress, segregationist Democrat Representative Howard W. Smith of Virginia proposed adding the term "sex" to Title VII of the bill—reportedly as a poison pill, to undermine its chances of passing. His proposal was met with laughs on the House floor. "I am serious," he said. "It is indisputable fact that all throughout industry women are discriminated against."[24]

Whatever his intent, "sex" made the final cut, and women were the better for it. The bill still passed, and with broad bipartisan support.

The Civil Rights Act also created the Equal Employment Opportunity Commission, which was tasked with, among other issues, fighting sex discrimination. Most notably, it created legal redress for women who were sexually harassed at work, on the grounds that such harassment constituted a form of sex discrimination.[25]

And then there was Title IX of the Education Amendments of 1972. Title IX may be best known for effectively giving birth to girls' sports, but its greater significance lies in the educational opportunities it opened to women. The law prohibits sex-based discrimination in schools receiving federal funding from the preschool level upward, and in programs and activities associated with those schools. As a result, many top universities and professional schools that had once capped the number of women they admitted, or refused to admit them at all, opened their doors to male and female applicants on an equal basis.

Private colleges and single-sex public colleges were exempt from the requirement to admit both sexes,[26] but by 1983 the formerly all-male Ivy League institutions had all gone coed amid a changing environment and mounting pressure to admit women.[27]

Following Title IX's enactment, women's enrollment in graduate and professional schools in particular skyrocketed. As one article on the law's legacy noted, "In 1970, women earned only 14 percent of doctoral degrees.... In 1971, just about 1 of 100 dental school graduates were women, while in 2005 that number grew nearly fortyfold. In medical schools the numbers jumped from less than 10 percent to nearly 50 percent, and law school numbers from about 7 percent to nearly 49 percent."[28]

Fast forward to today, and at every level of education, women today are earning more degrees than men.[29]

NO ONE'S FAULT

But not everything that was billed as sexual equality under the law worked out so equally for the two sexes. Take, for example, no-fault divorce, one of the final fruits of the Sexual Revolution. Initially viewed as the female ticket to liberation from the confining institution of marriage—"a comfortable concentration camp," according to Betty Friedan[30] and "the model for slavery law in this country," as Gloria Steinem labeled it,[31] the costs of no-fault divorce were disproportionately borne by women.

In 1970 California became the first state to implement no-fault divorce, and most states quickly followed its lead. As the name suggests, under the new regime couples did not have to prove that one spouse was at fault for the end of the marriage. Unsurprisingly, what followed was a notable spike in divorce rates.[32] Although the divorce rate has since fallen somewhat, even in the new millennium, more than four in ten couples marrying for the first time are expected to split.[33]

Divorce is terrible for women. Women are more likely than men to lose their health insurance after divorce, according to the University of Michigan,[34] and twice as likely as men to fall into poverty.[35] And no-fault divorce is even worse for women. In a no-fault divorce, only a third of women wind up keeping the family home, as opposed more than three-fourths in a fault divorce.[36] And even women who stay married are affected by no-fault divorce laws: a study at the University of Pennsylvania's Wharton School of Business found that people in states where unilateral no-fault divorce is permitted are less open to making financial sacrifices for their spouse's future.[37]

This and other female misfortunes, like the rise in single motherhood, have prompted some of the Sexual Revolution's icons to reconsider their position. "I think we made a mistake with no fault divorce," Betty Friedan admitted, acknowledging that it had led to "unintended consequences" for women.[38] In 2006, the then president of the New York chapter of the National Organization for Women wrote an article for the *New York Times* documenting the many ways that no-fault divorce hurts women in particular and pleading with state officials not to legalize it.[39] They did anyway.

THE RIGHT TO PRIVACY

Other policy upheavals affected American families in similarly dramatic ways. In 1965, five years after the FDA's approval of the birth control pill jump-started the Sexual Revolution, the Supreme Court in *Griswold v. Connecticut* overturned the many state laws forbidding the provision of contraception to married couples. Today, laws against birth control sound quaint, but the court's rationale—that such laws violate Americans' right to privacy, a right implicit (the Court said) within the

First, Third, Fourth, and Ninth Amendments to the Constitution[40]—set off a chain reaction of cases enshrining the notion that human sexuality was purely a matter of individual taste and recreation. By 1970, the federal government was actively promoting the use of contraception, particularly among low-income people, through Title X of the Public Health Service Act.[41]

Just three years later, in perhaps the most cataclysmic change of the era, the newfangled notion of a constitutional right to privacy was extended all the way to abortion. In *Roe v. Wade* the Supreme Court struck down most state limits on abortion and guaranteed every woman the right to terminate a pregnancy. The work of the Sexual Revolution was complete. Women were now equal with men; they had shed what society had declared to be their bodily limitations—the ways in which their sexuality was different from men's.

A few voices warned, however, that things were not that simple. One of the more prominent of these voices was Pope Paul VI's. He warned that the goals of the Sexual Revolution would backfire on the sex they purported to liberate: women. In 1968 he wrote: "[A] man who grows accustomed to the use of contraceptive methods may forget the reverence due to a woman, and, disregarding her physical and emotional equilibrium, reduce her to being a mere instrument for the satisfaction of his own desires, no longer considering her as his partner whom he should surround with care and affection."[42]

The pope's prognostications were widely dismissed at the time. But more than forty years later, a 2012 article in Business Insider under the rather unorthodox headline "Time to Admit It: The Church Has Always Been Right on Birth Control"[43] went viral. The authors pointed out that, think what you like about the pope, his predictions about what would happen if contraception became widely used—in chief, his warning about "the reduction of women to objects used to satisfy men"—were correct.

If you click on the article today, it has a little red flame next to the date, signifying its popularity, with over one million hits and counting. The piece recounts the staggering social costs not just of the Pill, but of legal abortion and the many other sweeping changes of the Sexual

Revolution. In short, as the economist George Akerloff and Fed chair Janet Yellen once wrote in *Slate*, "By making the birth of the child the *physical* choice of the mother, the sexual revolution has made marriage and child support a *social* choice of the father."[44]

All this brings me back to the Tufts quad, and the bright and beautiful young woman standing across from me with her head hung in humiliation. There was no way around it. She had been used as a sex object by a man, and he had walked away scot-free.

The "sex freak out"[45] of the 60s and 70s was supposed to de-scandalize sex and empower women. Instead, the inherent assumptions of the Sexual Revolution placed the scandal and its burdens squarely on their shoulders.

CHAPTER 8

DISPARATE IMPACT

Why can't a woman be more like a man?

—Professor Higgins, *My Fair Lady*

I t was Valentine's Day weekend in 2015, and millions of women across America were heading out on dates to see a newly released movie. But not a warm-hearted romance. It was a movie about torture sex. And it went on to be one of the biggest hits in cinema history.

Fifty Shades of Grey, adapted from E. L. James's hit tome, broke box office records as the highest-grossing movie to open on President's Day weekend and Universal Pictures' top-earning R-rated release ever.[1] The movie's premise was simple and sexist: a bookish young aspiring journalist is seduced by a corporate tycoon, who turns her into his pornographic plaything. He coaxes her into setting aside her reservations and becoming his sex slave in the twisted world of Bondage and Discipline, Dominance and Submission, Sadism and Masochism (BDSM).[2]

He is domineering and controlling, telling her, "I exercise control in all things" and "I don't do romance." That didn't stop women from lining the block; the movie's opening weekend audience was sixty-eight percent female. The smashing success of this "BDSM-filled romance flick," as *Cinema Blend* called it, was the death knell for chivalry.

One can draw a straight line back from the death of chivalry to the Sexual Revolution's Second Wave feminists, who demanded that women be treated exactly like men and slapped the "sexist" label on anyone who disagreed.

CHIVALRY IS DEAD

Emily Esfahani Smith opened a 2012 piece on chivalry for the *Atlantic* with a reference to the hundred-year anniversary of the sinking of the *Titanic*, in which chivalry was on full display despite the panic of those on board.[3] The vast majority of survivors were women; the overwhelming majority of those who perished were men. This was because chivalry taught men that women are owed preferential treatment—not just because we are the "weaker" sex, but because heroism and self-sacrifice are prized virtues in men.

But the Sexual Revolution enshrined the notion that this preferential treatment—meant to correct for physical inequities, quell the male propensity toward violence, and tame men's often-overwhelming sexual appetite—was little more than "benevolent sexism." That's according to a study published in the feminist journal *Psychology of Women Quarterly*, whose claims Esfahani Smith summarized: the concept of chivalry is rooted in the "'gendered premise' that women are weak and in need of protection while men are strong," and it perpetuates gender inequality.

So what's a world without chivalry like? Women are now more than willing to go see a movie that glamorizes a man's violent sexual abuse of a woman.

As one man explained in Elite Daily, "In the hookup culture we now live in, it's pretty obvious that chivalry is completely dead."

".... Dating is done. Seriously, who goes on dates anymore? It's all about hooking up, getting a number, grabbing a drink and getting down."

While maybe not a master of eloquence, he makes a good point: "The real problem here is that women, for one reason or another, have become complacent and allowed men to get away with adhering to the bare minimum." Until women "start asking for the things they deserve," he argues, "men are going to get away with putting in the bare minimum and receiving what we ultimately want anyway—sex. It's pretty obvious that women own the cards, and when they start acting like it, they'll finally start getting dinner from places that don't deliver."[4]

Men and women are eating the leftovers of the Sexual Revolution. We are taught that there is no difference between the sexes and that anyone who suggests otherwise is undermining women's equality with men. Advocates of chivalry are accused of infantilizing women—enforcing gender stereotypes that imply women are not capable of doing the same things as a man.

Yet without chivalry the worst masculine qualities run rampant, and women are expected to conform to them, rather than demand that men conform to higher standards. Nothing exemplifies this more than the hookup culture. Although it's billed as liberation for women and their long-repressed sexual appetites, a way that women can enjoy sex while delaying marriage and children for the sake their careers, women are the ones left feeling the negative consequences, whether it's sexually transmitted diseases that disproportionately affect women, unintended pregnancies, or just general anxiety.

In the fallout of the hookup culture, in which women are encouraged to explore their sexual appetites like the most base teenage boy, dating is nearly dead. The headlines tell the story: "Work It: Is Dating Worth the Effort?" in the *New Yorker*, "The End of Courtship" in the *New York Times*, or "All the Single Ladies" on the cover of the *Atlantic*, in which a forty-something single female journalist unconvincingly tries to persuade the next generation of women that we don't really need men after all.

What dating does still exist often begins in the electronic world, where men typically filter women by their looks. One study of online dating trends found that the most attractive women received eighty-three percent of all inquiries from male suitors, potentially more if their inboxes had not filled up.[5] A study on male versus female preferences in online dating revealed, "For men there is no amount of income that the woman in the bottom ten percent in terms of appearance can earn to make men prefer her over women in the top percent."[6]

Cohabitation represents the ultimate male triumph in a non-chivalrous world. Men get all the goods of marriage without any of the commitment. Women, meanwhile, face all the same risks as they do in sexually active dating, with no insurance against their partner simply deciding to move on to the next willing (and often younger) domestic partner.

"PREGNANCY IS NOT A PRIVILEGED CLASS"

But one needn't look into the bedroom to see what happens when society insists that men and women should be treated as if they are no different. A simple subway ride will do. Women who are nine months pregnant can routinely be spotted struggling to stand in a crowded train while able-bodied men look on. This happened to me more times than I can count on the metro in Washington, D.C. Once, days away from my due date, I was carrying two bags and could hardly reach the ceiling handle. When someone asked the eight able-bodied men sitting in the handicapped seats to give me a seat, they all refused.

My story is far from atypical. One pregnant woman recently found herself riding on the floor of the London tube after fellow passengers refused to give up their seats for her.[7] Another was ticketed on the New York City subway after switching cars mid-ride in search of a seat.[8]

A quick Google search yields countless stories like these, including other stories of men who outright refused to give up their seats. Perhaps the most alarming about these articles is the comments they inspire.

One commenter wondered why he or she should yield a seat to a pregnant woman: "Because you chose to get pregnant? Give me a break. Yes, there is a need for more civility in society, but rampant entitlement for choices made needs to come down a few notches."[9]

Other commenters echoed that sentiment:

"[Pregnant women] aren't disabled, they made a choice. When women stop whining that they are 'owed' because they are pregnant, then maybe people will give them a break. Everyone is sick and tired too. Deal with it; everyone else who has to ride a train has to also deal with it."

"Pregnancy is not a privileged class, although they'd like us to think otherwise."

But perhaps most illuminating were remarks along the lines of this comment, which takes us right back to the 1960s: "If we (men and women) are equal, then why would a man give up his seat to a woman?"[10]

And why would he pay for a date, or ask her out at all, when he can just page her for some "Netflix and chill"?

The problem with "gender equity," which entails the denial of sexual difference, is that it shuts down chivalry—which is built on *respect* for sexual difference—and women wind up with the short end of the stick. It is sexual difference that *activates* chivalry, and women are its primary beneficiaries. Chivalry is not exploitative; it is the force designed to prevent men from exploiting women, particularly when they are most in need of different treatment. Without it, women are reduced to bodies to be used for male pleasure, then denied the most basic courtesy when their bodies reflect the ramifications of sex in a way wholly different from the bodies of men. Pregnancy is their "choice" and they need to "deal with it."

Sounds like a raw deal to me.

SEX IN THE MODERN MARRIAGE

The attempt to stamp out sex difference has affected marriage, too.

It's no secret that marriage has evolved in radical ways over the past half century. Men and women meet romantic partners in different settings,[11] value different traits in prospective spouses,[12] and marry at significantly later ages than they did before the Sexual Revolution.[13] And while marriage in the U.S. once featured relatively rigid gender roles, and especially before the twentieth century gave husbands greater rights than wives,[14] married couples today typically share responsibility for earning money, keeping up their home, and raising their children.

Yet the extent to which men and women play the same roles in marriage is sometimes overstated,[15] presumably because many contemporary scholars and journalists are ideologically committed to a version of gender equality in which men and women are effectively identical. Even today, married American parents typically split up paid and domestic work along gendered lines—because that's what most of them want to do.

Consider, for example, how mothers and fathers spend their time. According to a Pew Research Center analysis of 2011 data from the American Time Use Survey, mothers of children under eighteen devote, on average, fourteen hours a week to child care, whereas fathers devote seven hours to it. Mothers spend eighteen hours a week doing housework, while fathers spend ten. And fathers engage in paid work thirty-seven hours a week, compared to twenty-one for women. In other words, fathers contribute roughly two-thirds of their household's hours of paid labor, and mothers shoulder roughly two-thirds of the housework and child care, making their total weekly work hours essentially equal.

Much has indeed changed since 1965, when mothers spent just eight hours a week performing paid work and fathers devoted a paltry 2.5 hours to the care of their children.[16] But little has changed in the past twenty years,[17] not because inequality between the sexes persists in marriage today, as many would have you believe, but because sex difference is stubborn. Most Americans still don't desire a marriage in which both spouses work full-time and all other tasks are divided on a fifty-fifty basis.

Despite unprecedented economic opportunities for women and equally unprecedented levels of domestic involvement among men, studies continue to find that we want different things out of marriage and family life.

A 2012 poll by the Pew Research Center reveals that the majority (fifty-three percent) of married mothers say their ideal situation would be to work part time. Other married mothers are as likely to prefer staying at home as they are to desire full-time work (twenty-three percent each). Fathers, in contrast, generally value full-time employment. Three-quarters say a full-time schedule is ideal for them, while only fifteen percent prefer part-time work and ten percent would like not to work at all.[18]

Of course, many if not most mothers—even those with employed husbands—are not able to achieve their ideal. One 2000 survey showed that only forty-nine percent of married mothers with college degrees and forty-four percent of those without college degrees were able to live out their labor force preference. Among those whose work schedule did not align with their ideal, more than seven in ten wanted to work less, not more.[19] As feminist psychologist Eleanor Maccoby concluded in *The Two Sexes: Growing Up Apart, Coming Together,* even in a society that seeks to minimize the penalty women pay in the workplace for becoming parents, "there is no reason to expect that men and women will want to make exactly the same choices about the way they invest their time."[20]

If dividing labor along gendered lines remains the societal norm and the average American couple's preference, might it also be linked to greater marital satisfaction and individual happiness? The scholarly literature does not provide a simple answer. As one 1998 study documented, "the relationship between wives' employment and marital satisfaction has changed over the last 30 years." Wives' employment predicted lower marital quality in the 1960s, but not in subsequent decades, and by the 1980s, some studies suggested working women were happier in their marriages.[21] Women's full-time employment may even be linked with lower divorce rates, according to another study,[22] or only increase the risk of divorce when a marriage is already unhappy.[23] A 2015 study using more recent survey data from thirty-two different countries, including the U.S., concluded that how couples with children divide paid and domestic work is unrelated to individuals' overall happiness in almost all regions of the world.[24]

On the other hand, a 2006 study using a large, nationally representative sample of Americans found, to quote a press release, that "women whose husbands earn the lion's share of income, who don't work outside the home, or who share a strong commitment to lifelong marriage with their husbands report the highest levels of marital happiness."[25]

Perhaps the most natural way to make sense of these contradictory findings is a commonsense hypothesis: different couples prefer different work-family arrangements, so their happiness may depend more on whether they can fulfill their personal ideal than on the precise division of their labor. Researchers have marshaled some support for this theory. For example, in a 2013 analysis, W. Bradford Wilcox and Jeffrey Dew found that "no one work-family strategy is linked to higher reports of marital happiness—that is, reporting that one is 'very happy' in one's marriage—among married mothers with children under eighteen." The fulfillment of individual preferences, however, mattered quite a bit: "Wives who are working full-time *or* who are at home in violation of their preferences are, respectively, 46 percent less likely and 39 percent less likely to be very happy in their marriages, compared to stay-at-home wives who prefer to be at home." Whether wives' preferences are fulfilled also affects their husbands' satisfaction.[26]

An earlier study on the same topic arrived at similar conclusions. The effects of the division of labor on both spouses' marital satisfaction "are largely explained by the mediating variables of perceived unfairness and perceived empathy," the researchers concluded. And "personal preferences regarding the division of both domestic and paid work significantly influence marital satisfaction for both wives and husbands."[27] The actual division of labor appears to matter less than dividing it the way a couple wants to—and that usually means the husband will take the lead in paid work and the wife in parenting and domestic labor.

While the question of how traditional versus gender-neutral arrangements affect couples' happiness does not have one clear answer, the research is more straightforward on cases where traditional gender roles are reversed. When a husband works fewer hours or earns less money than his wife, as is the case for about one in four dual-earner married couples today, [28] he is less happy and the marriage is more likely to dissolve. According to some studies, his wife's happiness also declines.

In Wilcox and Dew's study, the only work-family arrangement that predicted the marital satisfaction of men with children was working less than their wives. Married fathers whose wives worked more than they did were sixty-one percent less likely to be very happy in their marriage than men whose wives stayed home.[29] Even when the wives preferred this non-traditional arrangement, these husbands were less happy. Husbands whose wives worked more also showed a higher level of "divorce proneness"—a measure of "how far into the process of considering or pursuing a divorce [they] had ventured" that has proven to predict divorce likelihood—than other men.[30]

Drawing on some of the same survey data, other researchers recently looked at how men's and women's relative incomes affected various aspects of relationships. They found that aversion to wives' out-earning their husbands had widespread effects, impacting "marriage formation, the wife's labor force participation, the wife's income conditional on working, marriage satisfaction, likelihood of divorce, and the division of home production." Couples in which the wife's income was higher than the husband's were six percentage points less likely to say their marriage was happy, and six percentage points *more* likely to have discussed separating in the past year.[31] Other research has shown that in couples where women earn more money, and especially when they are the sole breadwinner, men are more likely but women are less likely to cheat.[32] A 2013 study of Danish couples even suggested that a counter-traditional balance of income undermines men's sexual performance and causes anxiety in women.[33]

Studies of employment and job loss likewise show that marriages in which the husband is not employed are more likely to end in divorce. One longitudinal study published in 2011 showed that when married men are not working, both they and their wives become more likely to initiate divorce. The authors attributed this finding in part to expectations about what marriage should look like. (Women's employment did not affect men's odds of seeking a divorce, and only made women more likely to seek divorce if they assessed their marriage negatively.)[34] A 2014 study incorporating recession-era data on job loss, and focusing solely on "involuntary displacement resulting from reduced business demand or firm closing" rather than terminations, indicated that job loss only produces a higher divorce risk if it is the husband rather than the wife who was displaced.[35] Seemingly, in the minds of both men and women, holding down a job is a crucial part of a husband's role, while labor force participation remains optional for wives.

DIVISION OF LABOR

The studies make clear that while there is no one-size-fits-all model that maximizes marital happiness for all couples, there are clear preferences that break down by sex. Ignoring those fault lines and exalting an androgynous vision of marriage undermines the supportive role that men clearly value and takes away the choice that women prize most.

And yet our culture is obsessed with enforcing uniformity in labor and the household, rather than respecting the differing preferences of the sexes. There is an unending litany of scholarly articles seeking to address the "gendered" division of labor, and feminists continue to wring their hands about the fact that men and women spend their time differently. They are particularly aggrieved—despite the profoundly different roles men and women have in bringing children into the world—by the fact that, since the dawn of humanity, women have spent more time with their children than men, and still seem to want to.

But this is not the only thing that differentiates the sexes when it comes to parenting. Even in our egalitarian society, men and women by and large treat their children in distinct ways that foster different and complementary strengths in them. One 2013 report summarizes the relevant research: "In numerous studies, fathers are noted to be the more physical, playful, surprising, challenging, and risk-oriented parent. The father's style of interaction seems geared to push children out of the nest. By contrast, mothers seem to be the more verbal, affectionate, predictable, comforting, and protective parent. Their style of interaction seems geared to make children feel at home in the nest. Taken together, these two diverse parenting styles supply children with a varied parenting diet."[36]

These differences emerge as early as the infant and toddler years,[37] and are especially evident in how parents play with their children. Mothers generally use toys and games as they are intended to be used, and often try to teach children through play.[38] Fathers are more apt to use toys unpredictably and to tickle and rough-house with their kids.[39] Rather than tilting the playing field in their children's favor, fathers compete with them.[40] Researchers are still working to devise ways to evaluate dads' interactions with kids, but the existing studies suggest that the rough-housing and risky exploration in which fathers specialize help children develop social skills down the road.[41]

We can also learn about the unique importance of fathers from the negative outcomes associated with their absence. In a recent review of rigorously designed studies on the causal effects of father absence, respected sociologists Sara McLanahan, Laura Tach, and Daniel Schneider concluded that a father's absence puts his sons and daughters at greater risk of dropping out of high school, using drugs and alcohol, and showing poor social-emotional adjustment, among other negative outcomes.[42] Other analyses show that a father's presence in the home, and especially a present father who has a good relationship with his children,[43] lower teen boys' likelihood of delinquent behavior,[44] teen girls' likelihood of becoming pregnant as teens,[45] and all teens' likelihood of suffering depression.[46]

Despite lingering skepticism about whether dads matter, few doubt the importance of having a loving, involved mother. Still, it's worth noting that mothers' central role in providing consistent comfort and affection and responding to children's distress promotes cognitive development[47] as well as healthy social and emotional adjustment.[48] According to Kathleen Kovner Kline and W. Brad Wilcox, mothers also "appear to be more adept at helping their children understand their own feelings and comprehend and attend to the feelings of others, in part by talking more about feelings and by encouraging their children to consider the feelings of others."[49]

Research on parenting and its effects on children is a complicated endeavor, and the study of fathers is still a young field.[50] But as Yale psychiatrist and author Dr. Kyle Pruett sums up the research, it's clear that "fathers don't mother and mothers don't father."[51] In parenting, as in much else, men and women have different strengths.

Yet so often, those different strengths are cast as qualities in competition. In particular, the female orientation toward domestic things is typically cast as a weakness, rather than a strength.

In a 2015 op-ed in the *New York Times*, Judith Shulevitz wondered why despite all of the changes in parents' responsibilities in recent decades it is still mom who is the "designated worrier." She writes, "I wish I could say that fathers and mothers worry in equal measure. But they don't. Disregard what your two-career couple friends say about going 50-50. Sociological studies of heterosexual couples from all strata of society confirm that, by and large, mothers draft the to-do lists while fathers pick and choose among the items. And whether a woman loves or hates worry work, it can scatter her focus on what she does for pay and knock her partway or clean off a career path. This distracting grind of apprehension and organization may be one of the least movable obstacles to women's equality in the workplace."

In a lengthy exhale of frustration, Shulevitz complains that because women tend to be more concerned about keeping home and family in order, they lose out on professional opportunities. She doesn't quite put it this bluntly, but she basically argues that if we could just beat woman's nature out of her, she could assign her husband more domestic things to worry about and spend more time advancing in the workplace. If she could just function more like her husband and less like herself, she could have a more successful career.[52]

Maybe she could. But would it make her any happier?

UNEQUAL RISKS

Efforts to establish a gender-neutral society have already led to very disparate impacts on the physical and mental health of men and women.

Just before Valentine's Day of 2013, researchers at the U.S. Centers for Disease Control and Prevention released a report calling the spread of sexually transmitted diseases (STDs) in America a "severe epidemic."[53] Human papillomavirus (HPV) was marked as the primary driver of an alarming uptick in STDs. The CDC now considers HPV the most common STD among sexually active adults.

While men and women alike get HPV, it takes a much harder toll on women. As the CDC states, "Most men who get HPV never develop symptoms and the infection usually goes away completely by itself."[54] Women are far more likely than men to see their HPV develop into cancer, 125 percent more likely, to be precise.[55] The female immune system appears to researchers to be less equipped to fight the disease; an *Oxford Journal of Infectious Diseases* review of the medical literature found that in all but one study, women infected with HPV had higher levels of the pathogen in their blood than men.[56]

HPV has basically spawned its own cancer that strikes only women: cervical cancer. In its booklet on cervical cancer, the American Cancer Society's information about its source is stunningly simple.

Q: "Do we know what causes cervical cancer?"

A: "Cervical cancer is caused by a virus called HPV."[57]

The female experience with HPV, the fastest-spreading STD in America, exposes the argument that women can experience casual sex just like men as a lie. And it's not just HPV. The STD crisis is a much bigger problem for women than for men—as plain language from the government makes clear. A CDC fact sheet entitled "10 Ways STDs Impact Women Differently from Men" states up front that "Sexually transmitted diseases (STDs) remain a major public health challenge in the U.S., especially among women, who disproportionately bear the long-term consequences of STDs." Those problems include infertility and infant death. The reality, as the fact sheet points out, is that "A woman's anatomy can place her at a unique risk for STD infection, compared to a man."

The ten differences the CDC lists are almost all ways in which STDs hurt women more than men, with the "good news" being that women go to the doctor more frequently than men and "there are resources available for women to learn more about actions they can take to protect themselves and their partners from STDs."[58]

So women are significantly more likely to become infertile, get cancer, and die from STDs than men. But there are resources that can tell them this. Therefore, we should all carry on believing that women can have sex just like men!

BODY INSECURITY

It's not just STDs taking a toll on the female body. Women are experiencing an epidemic of body insecurity. Our culture's insistence on wiping out sex difference in the name of sexual equality has done nothing to slow the tide of plastic surgery, something that tends to *enhance* sexual difference, which is on the rise, especially among teenage girls.

Teen starlet Chloë Grace Moretz talked about how she was tempted to have plastic surgery at just sixteen in an interview with *Elle* magazine. "When I was 16, I wanted a boob job. I wanted the fat pad under my chin to be removed. I wanted a butt reduction, or whatever," she said, until her mom talked her out of it. Now she is another of Hollywood's mouthpieces for women's rights; the magazine spread included a candid photo of the star with Hillary Clinton. When asked what she and the presidential candidate had discussed, Moretz answered, "Female empowerment, and how so many girls are afraid to be who they want to be. That's because of the underlying deep-rooted sexism that's been anchoring a big part of America."[59]

And yet decades of trying to root out sexism have failed to improve the self-confidence of the female sex. Indeed, those efforts have come in tandem with a *decline* in bodily self-confidence so severe that it has inspired a counter-movement: "body positivity." Experiencing their bodies no differently than men do was supposed to make women more confident. But today women need coaching on how not to hate their bodies. One study found that more than half of women are not happy with their bodies, and a mere glance in the mirror sparks a negative feeling for 80 percent of women.[60] Eating disorders have risen sharply in recent years, and plastic surgery rates have risen more than one hundred percent since 2000, with breast enhancements leading the way.[61]

But there are other even more troubling trends in plastic surgery, including a rise in teenage girls seeking what is called "genital cosmetic surgery." A *New York Times* piece on the phenomenon noted that the problem was alarming enough to have prompted new guidance from the American College of Obstetricians and Gynecologists' Committee on Adolescent Health, including the suggestion that doctors do more to screen teen girls "for a psychiatric disorder that causes obsession about perceived physical defects." As to why more and more teen girls were asking for genital plastic surgery, the committee chair told the *Times* that doctors are "sort of baffled" about what exactly is going on and why a girl would want a cosmetic surgery that could result in the "diminishment of sexual sensation after surgery, or numbness, or pain, or scarring."[62]

Slate pointed to porn and myths retailed by men on sites like Reddit with creating women's inaccurate assumptions about what their genitalia should look like.[63] Americans (rightfully) lament the genital mutilation that takes place in some parts of the world in the name of male dominance over women. And yet American girls are asking for it, to look better for the boys they seek to please.

Adding to the irony of increased female demand for plastic surgery is that it comes as women have succeeded in pressuring Mattel to give Barbie new, more androgynous body options, options that drew near universal acclaim for looking healthier and more realistic.[64]

So Barbie doll bodies are getting better, but real women's bodies are not.

MIND OVER MATTEL

A 2009 *Atlantic* headline asked a question that stumped pundits, pollsters, and political scientists alike. It asked, "Why Are Women Better Off, but Less Happy?"[65]

The article was one of countless responses to a study by two economists at the University of Pennsylvania's Wharton School of Business entitled "The Paradox of Declining Female Happiness."[66] The study boldly claimed that over the past several decades "measures of subjective well-being indicate that women's happiness has declined both absolutely and relative to men. The paradox of women's declining relative well-being is found across various datasets, measures of subjective well-being, and is pervasive across demographic groups and industrialized countries."

The study sent shock waves through the opinion pages of newspapers and magazines and left academia in a tizzy, with everyone scratching their heads about how women could be more liberated than ever before in history, but less happy.

As Ross Douthat of the *New York Times* explained,

> American women are wealthier, healthier and better educated than they were 30 years ago. They're more likely to work outside the home, and more likely to earn salaries comparable to men's when they do. They can leave abusive marriages and sue sexist employers. They enjoy unprecedented control over their own fertility. On some fronts—graduation rates, life expectancy and even job security—men look increasingly like the second sex.
>
> But all the achievements of the feminist era may have delivered women to greater unhappiness. In the 1960s, when Betty Friedan diagnosed her fellow wives and daughters as the victims of "the problem with no name," American women reported themselves happier, on average, than did men. Today, that gender gap has reversed. Male happiness has inched up, and female happiness has dropped. In postfeminist America, men are happier than women.

Postfeminist American women seem to have swapped one "problem with no name" for another. A wave of subsequent studies and research reinforced the notion that when it came to mental and psychological health, women were slipping behind men.

Women are twice as likely to suffer from anxiety as men, according to researchers at Cambridge University, who did a comprehensive review of forty-eight different studies on the subject.[67] Another "overview of research on sex and gender differences in anxiety disorders" confirmed a "well-established female preponderance in prevalence and severity" of mental health problems including agoraphobia, panic disorder, separation anxiety, specific phobia, social anxiety disorder, generalized anxiety disorder, obsessive-compulsive disorder, and acute and posttraumatic stress disorder.[68] Half of the measured sex differences for those categories were classified as "substantial" by the researchers. Scientists and sociologists are puzzled.

Women are also more likely to be depressed. Mayo Clinic has an online entry devoted entirely to "understanding the gender gap" in depression, stating that women are twice as likely as men to be diagnosed with it.[69] It's not surprising, then, that women far outpace men when it comes to using drugs to medicate a mental health issue. "America's State of Mind," a comprehensive study of mental health medication use concluded that women "are far more likely to take a drug to treat a mental health condition than men." One in four women took a drug for mental health reasons in 2010, versus fifteen percent of men.

A full fifth of women over the age of twenty take antidepressants, for example, and their use among women grew by twenty-nine percent between 2001 and 2010. The chart on the following page shows the staggering sex disparity in antidepressant use.[70]

While many psychologists and sociologists are mystified, and others blame everything from the selfie culture to the pressure on women to shoulder both professional work and child care, one psychiatrist offers a different take. In a piece for the *New York Times* based on her book *Moody Bitches*, Julie Holland wrote that many of the symptoms that are medicated in women are part of their female nature. She points out that women are "moody" and more "sensitive to our environments" and

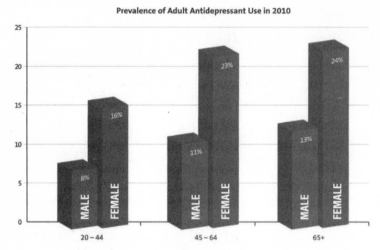

Courtesy of Express Scripts Holding Company

asserts that her "observations [are] rooted in biology, not intended to mesh with any kind of pro- or anti-feminist ideology. But they do have social implications. Women's emotionality is a sign of health, not disease; it is a source of power. But we are under constant pressure to restrain our emotional lives. We have been taught to apologize for our tears, to suppress our anger and to fear being called hysterical."

Rather than understand and accept women as different from men, society is pressuring them into medicating away what makes them different. Women are urged to take drugs that have the effect of artificially regulating female hormones to reduce "emotional sensitivity with its natural fluctuations." They end up "modeling a more masculine, static hormonal balance." The "emotional blunting" produced by the drugs "encourages women to take on behaviors that are typically approved by men: appearing to be invulnerable, for instance, a stance that might help women move up in male-dominated businesses."[71]

In other words, we are medicating being a woman—as if it were a mental illness.

Medicating away women's feelings can lower their sex drive, as can shutting down female fertility with the Pill and other hormonal birth controls. But fear not, there is an antidote: female Viagra. Dubbed "the little pink pill," female Viagra was approved by the FDA in 2015 to "improve" women's sex drive.

Whether it works is one question. Whether it is safe is another. But an even bigger question is this: What is the societal baseline for "healthy" sexual performance? Does something like female Viagra help women to enjoy sex more? Or does it just reinforce the expectation that women should perform sexually just like men?

One woman's account of using female Viagra is illuminating. Amanda Parrish, a participant in the clinical trials for the new drug, wrote: "I read *Fifty Shades of Grey* at least 12 times, and incorporated the fun, frisky stuff from that. I even tried testosterone, but I found that it worked much better in the workout room than the bedroom, and I was concerned about the side effects that I was experiencing." Only female Viagra worked for her.

Parrish points out that whereas male Viagra is intended to fix a functional flaw in a male organ, the female version works entirely differently. It is meant to correct a female lack of desire and alter female performance to be more aggressive. "What I have isn't a functional problem," she writes. "My problem is that my brain doesn't feel desire."[72]

It's no wonder that women are less happy today. *Fifty Shades of Grey*, a glamorized narrative of the most twisted alpha-male fantasy, is presented as a romance manual for women, and Big Pharma markets male hormones to help her get in the mood, or a little pink pill when all else fails.

In the world of blunted sexual difference, it is woman whose unique nature is medicated away, who is caught in a vicious cycle where she is taught to deny what makes her distinct and medicated when her mind and body respond poorly to the attempt to remake her in man's image.

It's a steep price to pay for the mere fact of being a woman.

CHAPTER 9

THE END OF PRIVACY

One of the most pusillanimous things we of the female sex have done throughout the centuries is to have allowed the male sex to assume that mankind is masculine. It is not. It takes both male and female to make the image of God. The proper understanding of mankind is that it is only a poor, broken thing if either male or female is excluded.

—Madeleine L'Engle, *The Irrational Season*

In April of 2016, retail giant Target waded into the raging national debate about whether bathrooms should be maintained as exclusively single-sex. In a post on its blog entitled "Continuing to Stand for Inclusivity," the company announced, "we felt it was important to state our position" that in Target stores, "team members and guests" are permitted "to use the restroom or fitting room facility that corresponds with their gender identity."[1]

No doubt the corporate executives behind the move were prepared for some blowback. But not quite at the decibel level that ensued. Target was in the headlines for weeks, its stock plunged by almost ten percent the following month, and a boycott petition aimed at the retailer garnered over one million signatures.[2] Target insisted it was just stating a longstanding policy, and blamed everything but the boycott and the bad P.R.[3] In one interview about declining sales, Target's CEO actually blamed the weather.[4]

"AN INCLUSIVE PLACE TO SHOP"

Rather than address many customers' apprehensions about its policy—specifically, how a company that boasts eighteen hundred stores[5] would ensure that predators would not take advantage of a policy that permitted anyone to use the restroom of their choice—Target doubled down. Its spokeswoman brushed off such concerns and reiterated that Target strives to be an "inclusive place to shop," and that some Targets offer "single-stall, family restrooms for those who may be more comfortable with that option."[6]

When a *Wall Street Journal* story announcing Target's move popped into my Facebook newsfeed, I had just returned from shopping there with my four-year-old daughter. We were in the middle of the shoe aisle looking for sandals for her when she clutched my hand in panic with a familiar cry: "Mommy, potty! I have to go potty!"

We sprinted to the bathroom, making it without a moment to spare, not even a second to shut the stall door. My daughter relieved herself in plain view of about seven other women, all of whom smiled understandingly. After she went, I had to go, also with the door open, because my very mobile eighteen-month-old son was still in our cart, which would not fit in the stall. And there was no "single-stall, family [restroom] for those who may be more comfortable with that option."

I was grateful for our privacy.

To be specific, I was grateful for a place where my daughter and I could use the bathroom in a rather public way but still with the privacy afforded by being exclusively among members of our own sex.

The members of Target's higher echelons do not seem to understand this everyday reality.

Moms like myself were mocked to kingdom come for registering even the slightest concern about what such a sweeping policy means for our privacy and safety. A wave of articles rushed to point out how silly it is to worry about an assault in the bathroom, forgetting the glaringly obvious reality that since the dawn of civilization, relieving oneself has overwhelmingly been practiced only among members of one's own sex. Until recently, bathrooms were one of the remaining places in society where men were not permitted to be with women and vice versa. Because of that clear barrier, even the sight of a man pushing open the door to a women's restroom would raise eyebrows—and deter any would-be assailant with half a brain.

But all that is changing, as rules designed to protect privacy between the sexes are upended. Shortly after Target made its big announcement, a man recorded himself walking into his local Target and asserting his new right to use the women's restroom. He did not state that he identifies as a woman; he simply said he wanted to make sure he had the right to use the women's restroom. In the video, a manager assures him that he does, and when asked what the store will do if any women are upset, the manager says he will "take care of it."[7]

Apparently it was not long before Target's lawyers got wind of the viral video; it was taken down almost immediately. But the video was not an isolated incident. The following month, the *New York Times* ran the headline "Men Are Posting Videos of Themselves Testing Target's New Bathroom Policy." The piece reported, "Multiple videos have popped up on YouTube showing men confronting store managers about the policy and asking what would stop them from entering the women's bathroom inside the store. In the videos, the managers can be seen (or heard, since some of the video is poorly shot) patiently saying that nothing would stop the men from using the women's room."[8]

Nothing.

THIS REPORT IS REAL

Two weeks after Target announced that its women's bathrooms were open to anyone whose "gender identity" led him there, police in a town in Texas issued a warrant for what was unmistakably a man who was spotted by a girl in a SuperTarget fitting room recording her as she undressed. The warrant charged him with "invasive visual recording."[9] A month later, the same thing happened at a Target in New Hampshire: a man was charged with filming women in the fitting room.[10]

The following month, it happened again. In July, an Idaho paper reported that a "man dressed as a woman" was caught filming a young woman removing her clothes in the dressing room of a local Target.[11] The predator was booked as a male under the name Shaun Smith, and according to a *New York Times* article on the incident, "Both the victim and her mother described the voyeur as a white male wearing a dress and blond wig."[12]

Nevertheless, the Idaho *Post Register* referred to Smith as "she," reporting that "Smith admitted to committing similar crimes in the past, saying she makes the videos for the 'same reason men go online to look at pornography,' court documents show. Smith [said] she finds the videos sexually gratifying."[13]

It was the third such an episode since Target had announced its policy, once for every subsequent month.

The Idaho incident prompted an entry on the rumor-investigating website Snopes, because the story was easily confused with a fake story that had been published on a comedy site just two months before, mocking concern over the possibility that unisex bathrooms might result in…exactly what happened in Idaho.[14] In the fake news story, a man who self-identified as a woman was captured photographing minor females in the bathroom. The only difference between the fake story and the real one was the location: in the real story, the snooping took place in the fitting room. As Snopes was forced to admit in a post about the fake story, "This fake news article was later confused with a somewhat similar real-life incident that subsequently transpired at a Target store."[15] On the post about the real story, Snopes had to clarify, "Unlike a fake news report from April 2016 involving a woman supposedly arrested for taking pictures of underage girls in a Target bathroom, this report is real."

But Target should not have needed these incidents to know that voyeurism is a real problem, because it was an issue even before the retailer broadcasted a policy that makes it easier for male predators to access women's restrooms and fitting rooms. Just one month before Target announced its policy, a fourteen-year-old girl noticed a man photographing her under the door as she changed clothes in a Target fitting room in Florida.[16] She said that when she saw the camera, "I didn't know what to do about it. So my body just locked up and I started shaking.... I don't feel safe in a dressing room anymore." Target knew that even its family restrooms were vulnerable; in 2015, a California man was caught hiding a camera in one.[17]

Just a couple of weeks after Target's announcement, a woman who was being verbally harassed in the swimsuit section of a Target in Florida videotaped herself chasing her harasser out of the store and into the parking lot. The man, it turned out, had a history of bothering women in public places and a previous conviction for photographing women in dressing rooms.[18] Under Target's policy, men exactly like him can now walk right into the women's restroom or fitting room, and any startled woman is the problem to be handled—not the offending man.

VOYEURS UNLEASHED

Stories of male voyeurs are a dime a dozen. Consider a few headlines that emerged in the span of just a few months in 2016.

- "[University of Iowa] Police Locate Suspect Videotaping in Women's Shower"[19] (February 2016)
- "Louisville Man Accused of Voyeurism in Women's Restroom at Sullivan University"[20] (February 2016)
- "Alleged Voyeur Arrested over Cameras in Ladies Restrooms"[21] (March 2016)
- "Quarryville Man Accused of Using Phone to Look at 10-Year-Old Girl in Sheetz Restroom"[22] (April 2016)
- "Man accused of Filming Women in Smyrna Park's Bathroom"[23] (April 2016)

There is no end to headlines like these; and apparently no shortage of predatory men who would love to have access to the private places where women expose themselves. And it's a one-way street. Try doing a

Google search on women peeping on men, and all you get is an article about why it is that only men seem to spy sexually on women.[24] There's a reason it's "peeping Tom," not "Peeping Tina."

In one particularly terrifying case in Chicago, a man attacked an eight-year-old girl who had gone to the bathroom alone. After choking her to the point of unconsciousness, he was caught carrying her into a stall, where he presumably intended to rape her.[25]

Sex-deniers will argue that bad actors can find a way into a ladies' bathroom regardless of the relevant law or policy, and have been doing so for quite some time.

But welcoming men into women's restrooms takes away a valuable protection that women have had up until now. The fact is, the overwhelming majority of sexual predators are men. Even a post on my local listserv for parents in the progressive quarters of northwest D.C. recently asked why do "only men rape women" and not the other way around. And before the spring of 2016, anyone who saw a man going into the ladies' room knew that something was wrong. There was nothing to deter anyone from raising the alarm in that situation. Now someone who sees a burly football player pushing open the door marked "Women" has to weigh the danger to the actual women there against the possibility of being labeled insensitive, bigoted, or a "hater." And Target has put a thumb on the scale; its announced policy essentially warns observant customers who might be able to prevent a sexual assault not to do anything about it.

Finally, in August of 2016, Target announced what CNN called a "$20 million answer" to the boycott that had tanked the chain's stock: "Target has decided to expand its use of a third, single-toilet bathroom at all of its stores, which can be locked by users." According to CNN, these new bathrooms are for "any customer who needs some privacy."[26] (The all-stall nature of the women's restroom wasn't a strong enough indicator of the female preference for privacy?)

But no matter, the regular full-size women's bathrooms will still be open to anyone who claims to "identify" as the sex posted on the door— including, inevitably, some men who will turn out to be voyeurs and predators.

The tide of gender-neutral bathroom laws raises challenges for law enforcement as well. A Giant grocery store security guard in Washington, D.C., was *arrested* for "escorting a man out of the women's restroom after he refused to leave because he identifies as a woman." The security guard, who is female, was taken into custody by Washington, D.C., police, who confirmed "that they are treating the incident as a 'suspected hate crime.'"[27]

Things become slightly more complicated when the predator is a man who is dressed a woman, as happened, for example, in a California Macy's, where a man wearing a wig and women's clothes (according to police) was caught recording women in the bathroom.

Similarly, in November of 2015, NBC Washington reported on a "man dressed as a woman arrested for spying in mall bathroom." The man, as it turned out, had repeatedly dressed as a woman to gain access to women's bathrooms, where he spied on and recorded girls and women ranging from age five to fifty-three.[28]

Just a month before, a college in Canada changed its gender-neutral bathroom policy after two separate reports surfaced of men filming women while they showered. A news article announced the (partial) return to the traditional men's and women's restrooms policy in politically correct, gender-is-a-construct Newspeak, saying that some bathrooms had been re-established "specifically for residents who identify as men or women."

"The purpose of this temporary measure is to provide a safe space for the women who have been directly impacted by the incidents of voyeurism and other students who may feel more comfortable in a single-gender washroom," the school's dean was quoted as saying.[29]

But things entered entirely new territory in February of 2016 when a man walked into a women's locker room at a public pool in Seattle and began to undress.

As a local news outlet reported: "It was a busy time at Evans Pool around 5:30pm Monday February 8. The pool was open for lap swim. According to Seattle Parks and Recreation, a man wearing board shorts entered the women's locker room and took off his shirt." "Women alerted staff," the article went on, "who told the man to leave, but he said 'the law has changed and I have a right to be here.'" According to the article, employees stated that "the man made no verbal or physical attempt to identify as a woman." He did, however, explicitly cite a new ordinance in Seattle that allowed anyone of any sex to use the restroom of their choice.

A hotly contested law passed in December of the previous year required most bathrooms and locker rooms to be open to members of either sex.

The pool incident, which news outlets called a "first-of-a-kind challenge" for implementing the new policy, came just days after the Daily Beast had characterized opposition to the law as "Seattle's Absurd, Discriminatory Trans Bathroom Panic."[30]

And yet according to local news, "As far as policy to protect everyone, Seattle Parks spokesman David Takami says they're still working on the issue. Right now, there's no specific protocol for how someone should demonstrate their gender in order to access a bathroom. Employees just rely on verbal identification or physical appearance, and this man offered neither."

The man was never arrested. Instead, according to the news report, he returned a second time while young girls were changing for swim practice.[31] What an ironic demonstration of Seattle's city government's claim—in its FAQ on "all gender bathrooms"—that making bathrooms unisex makes them more "accessible spaces for everyone." In places like Seattle, and Target stores nationwide, men no longer need to hide cameras to peep on women. They can just walk right in and observe with their own two eyes.

THE "DEAR COLLEAGUE" LETTER

The Obama administration followed Target's example. In May 2016, the same month that Target announced its bathroom policy, the Obama administration stepped into the same storm over gender identity and privacy issues—and short-circuited every state and local government in the country. In what quickly became known as its "Dear Colleague" letter, the Department of Education issued "guidance" (applicable to every school that receives any public funds) which entirely upends the previous legal meaning of Title IX. That's the federal law that, among other things, bars discrimination in educational institutions on the basis of sex.[32]

The Department of Education's letter states that when a student "assert[s] a gender identity that differs from previous representations or records, the school will begin treating the student consistent with the student's gender identity." The document clarifies that that assertion requires no "medical diagnosis or treatment" as a prerequisite; it's enough just to claim that you "identify" as the opposite sex. If a school refuses to act on this bare assertion, it puts all its federal funding in jeopardy and risks legal retribution.

The executive action circumvented Congress, where Title IX originated, essentially replacing the word "sex" in the law with "gender," even though, as we saw in chapter one, the two terms have sharply distinct meanings.

As an editorial in the *Wall Street Journal* put it, "The Administration's letter to its 'colleagues' in the nation's public schools brings to mind Little Red Riding Hood, standing innocently before the large, smiling figure in granny clothes, except for the disconcertingly big, sharp teeth. The Obama teeth emerge on page two of the Education Department's letter: 'As a condition of receiving Federal funds...' Yes, unless the schools 'treat a student's gender identity as the student's sex for the purposes of Title IX,' the school district may lose federal funds."[33]

The letter has monumental implications. It effectively renders unisex every bathroom and locker room at every public school (and every other school where federal aid is granted or used), upends the sex-segregated nature of sports and corresponding scholarships, obliterates the concept of single-sex housing, and flips the table completely on the sex that Title IX was supposed to protect from discrimination: women. Under the new meaning of Title IX, a woman who does not want a man in her locker room is the discriminator. A woman who does not find it fair to have to compete for the same scholarship against a biological male is the sexist. A woman who feels unsafe when a man is present in a private space designated for females, be it a bathroom or a dorm room, is in violation of Title IX. And a school that refuses to comply and insists on preserving safe spaces for girls and women risks civil rights lawsuits, for, of all things, gender discrimination.

UNINTENDED CONSEQUENCES

The outcry that arose in the wake of the Dear Colleague letter made for some strange bedfellows. It wasn't only social conservatives who objected to it. Eyebrows everywhere went up when just two weeks after the letter's release, a director of the Georgia American Civil Liberties Union (ACLU)—raising concerns about the privacy and safety of women—resigned her job over the organization's position on the issue. The African American mother of daughters, citing her girls' personal experience with a fearful encounter in the women's restroom, raised flags about the "implications for women's rights" and said that nothing was being done "to ensure women and girls are safe from those who might have malicious intent."

As she asked in an interview, "What do we do about women who are the survivors of rape, for whom it would be traumatic to share a public restroom where you take down your underwear" while there is the possibility of "men in the bathroom"?[34] Her concerns didn't matter; overnight, in the eyes of liberals, she went from civil rights hero to traitor. ThinkProgress accused her of undergoing an "ugly transformation"[35] into someone hateful and the Huffington Post labeled her "just another 'concern' troll."[36] In an appearance on *The View*, she revealed that she had not quit but rather been pushed out for "asking too many questions." Specifically, she said that despite being a progressive herself, she was "demonized by the progressives for asking too many questions about women's rights" in the debate about bathrooms. "When did women's rights no longer become a progressive value?" she asked pointedly.[37]

Later in the summer, prominent liberal feminist and pro-choice activist Kathleen Sloan penned a piece for the Delaware *News Journal* arguing that the gender identity movement, with its focus on forced sex integration of private spaces, has a mountain of "unintended consequences for women."

The former executive director of the Connecticut chapter of the National Organization for Women, founded by Betty Friedan, argued that abandoning sex and turning gender identity into a purely subjective choice is especially bad for women, "because our biology makes us physically vulnerable to men," she wrote. "The fact that men are generally physically stronger and larger than women, have more upper-body strength and cannot become pregnant, makes women physically vulnerable to men. We are also socially vulnerable due to ubiquitous physical and sexual violence against women based on our biological sex."

The new system of effectively unisex facilities empowers men, because it "allows men to enter women's spaces at any time." The implications of the gender identity movement extend far beyond bathrooms and locker rooms, Sloan argued, to include prisons and even domestic violence shelters, the ultimate safe spaces for women.[38]

In an interview with me, Sloan told the story of her friend and fellow feminist Lee Lakeman's fight to keep a biological man out of a women's rape crisis center. The case of *Kimberly Nixon v. Vancouver Rape Relief Society* went all the way to the British Columbia Court of Appeal, where the women won. In an interview five years later with the *Feminist Current*, Lakeman said, "[I]f you want to fight back as a group of women, you need, at some point, to say 'men can't join the group' and you need to, at some point, say—'even though sex and gender may be on a continuum, where are you marking the line on the continuum for who's in your group?' You still, at some point, have to decide where is the boundary around your group and the group that you're trying to work for or work with."[39]

But the crux of Sloan's argument is about the divorce of gender from biological sex. Severing the connection between the two, she wrote in her provocatively entitled piece "The Gender Identity Movement Erases Women," makes it "impossible to name sex as the source of women's oppression, subjugation and inequality in a patriarchal world." It makes "a material analysis of women's oppression impossible" and would obscure the statistics about sexual violence against women. Her argument calls to mind the judge in Kesha's case, who wrote that "Every rape is not a gender-motivated hate crime." As Sloan explains,

> The threat that the gender identity movement poses to women is that "gender" is detached from the biological differences between males and females (present in all mammalian species) and consequently male supremacy and the oppression of women is obscured and ultimately erased. Instead of challenging dominant and submissive roles and behaviors, the gender identity movement ultimately upholds and perpetuates them. Without being able to name humans as male or female, women have no hope of being able to protect ourselves from the violence men commit against us, much less overturn the patriarchal misogyny that has oppressed and terrorized us for millennia.

Sloan put it a little more simply when speaking with me. The gender identity movement, she said, is just an abstraction of Descartes' (in)famous line, "I think, therefore I am." Today, she argued, it's become, "I think, therefore I demand that society recognize who I say I am based on my subjective interpretation."[40] Even if that demand undermines the Women's Movement.

"EMPOWERED" PROSTITUTES

Perhaps nothing in modern society better embodies the patriarchal misogyny Kathleen Sloan laments than human trafficking and the effort to decriminalize the practice that enables it: prostitution. Amid the rampant confusion over sex, it should come as no surprise that proponents of decriminalizing prostitution cite "gender equity" as their justification.

While most think of slavery as a problem of the past, there are in fact more people living in slavery now than ever before in human history.

Experts put the number of currently enslaved people somewhere between 27 and 30 million.[41] According to the FBI, "Human sex trafficking is the most common form of modern-day slavery."[42] Its victims, the FBI states, are "mostly females and children." The United Nations Office on Drugs and Crime concurs, reporting that "the most common form of human trafficking (79%) is sexual exploitation. The victims of sexual exploitation are predominantly women and girls."[43]

And it's not just festering in brothels in poor countries; it is a serious problem in the U.S., too.

As the FBI explains, "The terms *human trafficking* and *sex slavery* usually conjure up images of young girls beaten and abused in faraway places, like Eastern Europe, Asia, or Africa. Actually, human sex trafficking and sex slavery happen locally in cities and towns, both large and small, throughout the United States, right in citizens' backyards."

ThinkProgress notes that hundreds of thousands of children are being trafficked for sex right here in America, eighty-three percent of them American citizens. Sex slavery is as much a developed world problem as it is a developing world problem. "The majority of these children being sold for sex are girls between the ages of 12 and 14. They are girls abducted or lured by traffickers and then routinely raped, beaten into submission, and sometimes even branded. When the girls try to run away, their traffickers torture and or gang rape them."[44]

In a society that is not yet fully blind to sex differences, sexual trafficking is still recognized as an overwhelmingly sex-selective crime that hurts women the most. Human trafficking is overwhelmingly a female struggle.

But a growing movement is pushing to legalize the "sex trade," as proponents of decriminalization euphemistically call it. While some argue that decriminalizing prostitution will bring the industry out of the dark and help women who are victimized by it, others contend that legalizing prostitution is more equitable to women, empowering them in the trading of sex for money. Some women, they argue, freely choose to sell their bodies, just as men freely choose to buy them.

The human rights world was roiled in 2015 when, despite the mounting evidence that the human sex slave trade disempowers women,

Amnesty International decided to come out in favor of decriminalizing prostitution. In a statement about what it called "state obligations to respect, protect, and fulfill the human rights of sex workers," the International Council of Amnesty cited a list of thirteen different guidelines and principles behind their decision. Number two was, "States must combat discrimination and harmful gender stereotypes, empower women and other marginalized groups, and ensure that no one lacks viable alternatives for making a living."[45] Amnesty's Q&A on why it supports decriminalizing "sex work" cites "Amnesty International's overarching commitment to advancing gender equality and women's rights."[46]

Thanks to "gender equality," the folks at Amnesty can no longer see prostitution as the systematic violation of one sex by another that it is. Suddenly it's a "viable [alternative] for making a living." Instead of being scandalized by the sale of women's bodies for money, they're scandalized by opposition to that transaction—because that opposition arises out of a recognition of women's unique vulnerabilities. Here Amnesty is actually following the lead of the United Nations, branches of which for years had been referring to prostitution as "sex work" and calling for its decriminalization and legalization. In 2013, for example, UN Women, the UN's "Entity for Gender Equality and the Empowerment of Women," issued a report on "Sex Work, Sexual Exploitation, and Trafficking," asserting, "The conflation of consensual sex work and sex trafficking leads to inappropriate responses that fail to assist sex workers and victims of trafficking in realizing their rights. Furthermore, failing to distinguish between these groups infringes on sex workers' right to health and self-determination and can impede efforts to prevent and prosecute trafficking."[47] UN Women joined other UN entities such as the UN Development Program and the UN Program on HIV/AIDS in calling for the removal of legal obstacles to prostitution. The latter actually blamed the spread of AIDS on the "stigma" associated with illegal prostitution.[48]

Amnesty's move triggered a wave of articles in elite liberal publications suggesting that legalizing "sex work" constitutes a step forward for gender equity. The *New York Times* published two back-to-back pieces about the push to decriminalize prostitution.[49] Author Emily

Bazelon wrote that the belief that "sex work" "can be authentically feminist" is one that "poses a deep challenge to Western feminism, which treats the commercial sex industry as an ugly source of sexual inequality."[50]

A lengthy piece in *New York* magazine asked "Is Prostitution Another Job?" It answered with one story after another of women who make great money selling themselves.[51] The first woman profiled tells of returning to her car for the first time after selling sex for cash. "I counted and was like, 'Holy shit, that's 300!' At this point, I'm 18 and working at Sears. I was excited." She shrugs off the downsides of the job: "There have been two clients throughout my entire time that made me feel dirty," she says, "[b]ut that was two out of hundreds."

The *New York* magazine piece quotes sociology professor Barb Brents, who argues that critics of prostitution approach the subject with "gendered norms of sex: Men are active and have a tireless sexual drive. Women are passive and don't." To advocates of "sex workers," banning prostitution is paternalistic and sexist, and deprives women of the chance to be "free economic agents, capable of making choices in their own self-interest, empowered to own their sexuality and use their bodies however they choose."

Of course it's easy for the "gender equity" lobby to make its opponents look silly and create a straw man by exaggerating the case for gender difference. But nobody really believes that men's sex drive is literally "tireless," or that women are simply "passive." Still the—average, by and large—difference between men's and women's sex drives is a basic fact of reality. Indeed, it would be difficult to explain the very existence of prostitution without that difference. Otherwise, why is it that men pay women for sex, rather than the other way around?

The "gender equity" line of argument for legalizing prostitution stems directly from the sex-blind equality push of the Sexual Revolution. If women could be as sexually free as men, detached from the "consequences" rooted in their biological differences, they would obtain ultimate freedom. And yet the feminist leaders of that period seem marginally less out of touch with reality than the leadership of the current "gender equity" movement. Second wave feminists have long opposed legalizing prostitution and still do so today. Gloria Steinem rejects the modern push for legalization and even the label "sex work," giving prostitution her own name: "commercial rape." Along with scores of prominent activists and celebrities like Lena Dunham and Emily Blunt, Steinem signed a letter protesting Amnesty's move. They went so far as to call a regime of legal prostitution "gender apartheid," a new system of sexual discrimination in which "one category of women may gain protection from sexual violence and sexual harassment, and [be] offered economic and educational opportunities; while another category of women, whose lives are shaped by absence of choice, are instead set apart for consumption by men and for the profit of their pimps, traffickers and brothel owners."[52]

In an interview with the *Guardian*, Steinem said, "We need to eroticize equality. Prostitution is about buying a body, not mutual pleasure and free choice.... Make no mistake: as long as women are for sale, no woman will be viewed as equal in corporate boardrooms, in the halls of legislature, or in the home."[53]

Despite opposing Amnesty's proposal, Steinem and friends champion their own version of legalized prostitution in which the prostitute's "work" is decriminalized but the john's purchase of sex remains illegal. Known as the Nordic model, because it is based on the systems of countries like Sweden, many of today's liberal feminists view it as the happy middle ground on the question that Liesl Gerntholtz, the executive director of Human Rights Watch's women's rights division, called "the most contentious and divisive issue in today's women's movement."[54]

But plenty of women still understand that laws against prostitution protect women.

As Naomi Riley wrote about the pieces questioning the criminalization of prostitution in *New York* magazine and the *New York Times*, "Both of these articles are ostensibly written because human-rights organizations across the world are debating whether decriminalization of prostitution would result in less sex-trafficking and greater safety for women who choose to do what we are now quaintly supposed to refer to as 'sex work.' But really these articles are part of a cultural push to makes us think that women selling their bodies is no different from women who bartend or become management consultants.[55]

"Surely feminists of another era would smell a conspiracy," she concluded. "Someone has managed to persuade young women that their ultimate fulfillment lies in trading their bodies for better coffee drinks."

THE NEW NORMAL

The most iconic feminist of the previous era was rather flip when she talked about the trendiest new form of prostitution: the so-called sugar babies—college students who have sex with wealthy men for tuition money. In her *Guardian* interview, Steinem sighed and said, "I mean, somewhere, I'm sure, there's a happy call girl who's financing her PhD. But it's not the norm."[56]

Or is it?

As we saw in chapter three, there are plenty of well-educated women who are perfectly happy to sell themselves—whether it's appearing in violent porn, auctioning off their virginity as an extension of a senior thesis, or opening up a profile on SeekingArrangement.com—and call it empowering. You can hardly open a women's magazine or a gossipy website without reading about the experiences of these women.

"I Was a Real-Life 'Sugar Baby' for Wealthy Men," reads one *Marie Claire* headline. The piece begins:

> "I'm the tall brunette in the romper," I texted from the lobby of the Ritz-Carlton.
>
> I felt a tap on my shoulder. "Nice outfit. I'm Rich."
>
> The 65-year-old business executive looked old but well preserved. After martinis and a cheese plate, we got a room—Rich undressed, I de-rompered. We popped champagne, toasted in the Jacuzzi, and dried off.
>
> On my way out, Rich slipped an envelope in my purse. "Your allowance, babe."

"Thanks, daddy," I replied, counting five crisp hundreds.

The anonymous writer mentions *The Girlfriend Experience*, a new show on Starz about a "savvy yet detached student turned high-end call girl," a story that she says "is, essentially, my own." "From age 22 to 26," she writes, "I juggled 30 different men between the ages of 42 and 75, and made close to $300,000 in total." Imagine my (lack of) surprise when I read that the author, who maintains anonymity, went to my alma mater, land of the Sex Fair and the Naked Quad Run, Tufts University.

Hooking up with guys she found via computer dating sites seemed to lead naturally to prostitution: "I was astounded to realize I could get paid to wear a slinky dress, sip cocktails, and chat, just as I'd done for free with guys my age. I thought back to one particularly cute guy I'd met through OkCupid: tan, toned, and 27. We'd dined at the local Pizzeria Uno's. Afterwards, I went back to his place for sex—a fair trade, I thought. For two vodka cranberries and a flatbread, it seemed natural to return the favor. That's the thing though: Seeking Arrangement was just like OkCupid—but for money."[57]

Contrary to Ms. Steinem's supposition, there is a mountain of articles about sugar babies, including a Villanova law grad who used sugar daddies to finance her $50,000-a-year law degree.[58] "Candice Kashani," one article informs us, "graduated from law school debt-free this spring, thanks to a modern twist on an age-old arrangement."[59] A subhead in a *Vanity Fair* article entitled, "Desperately Seeking Sugar Daddies" reads, "Looking to give up her day job but maintain a steady income, the author joined a Website where rich older men shop for girlfriends. Is that so wrong?" Just about every major magazine and website offers at least one story on the subject.

Perhaps the most unusual sugar baby story, however, appeared in *Vogue*. A profile on Grace Jones, a singer the article describes as having an "unconventional gender identity, describing herself as possessing two completely distinct selves," explains, "Jones's ability to inhabit both genders makes her self-sufficient. 'I never ask for anything in a relationship,' she proclaims, 'because I have this sugar daddy I have created for myself: me. I am my own sugar daddy. I have a very strong male side, which I developed to protect my female side. If I want a diamond necklace I can go and buy myself a diamond necklace.'"

The rest of the sugar babies, however, are stuck trading sex for cash, in that "age-old arrangement"—with a thin coat of feminism slapped on it.

So here we are. Women today are stuck fighting over whether the sale of the female body for profit should be given legal sanction and declared "empowering." One side calls full legalization "gender apartheid" because it separates women into two categories, those who freely choose prostitution and the trafficked—all while calling for a different kind of gender apartheid, in which men are punished for buying what women can legally sell. Advocates of "sex work" see opposition to legalization as a throwback to the "darkest periods of left-wing paternalism," in the words of one professor in the Huffington Post.[60]

Somehow the fight for sexual equality made it sexist to point out that paying a woman for sex is sexist. Feminist advocates for gender equity—essentially gender neutrality—are hoisted on their own ideological petard. They are tasting the fruits of their labors in the campaign for women's legal right to sell their bodies to please the corporate men who embody the patriarchy they were supposed to be fighting all along. And when human trafficking, one of the biggest modern threats to true equality between the sexes, is brought to light, the solution proposed by the proponents of gender equity is for women to do as men do and become their own pimps.

Denying the reality of sexual difference ensures that women will continue to be at a disadvantage. It makes it impossible even to talk about—let alone resolve—the very real injustices, vulnerabilities, and discrimination that women suffer on account of our sex.

It obliterates our right to privacy, flipping the tables to make *women* the abusers when we don't want a man in our private spaces.

Indeed, when gender is a vast spectrum to which biological sex is irrelevant, gender equality comes crashing into the right to privacy. As one woman wrote in a letter to the editor of the *Wall Street Journal* in the wake of the Obama administration's Dear Colleague letter, "I am a woman in my 60s with two granddaughters who are minors. I agree with Justice Ruth Bader Ginsburg, who in 1975 opposed unisex restrooms. A transgender male's right to equality does not trump our right to privacy—particularly when performing one of the most intimate of bodily functions. I am shocked the Justice Department doesn't get that."[61]

As her words imply, the question of men in women's facilities is several decades old; in the U.S., it first popped up in the debate about the Equal Rights Amendment. Justice Ginsberg, no social conservative, was one of the leading voices against the idea of unisex bathrooms. As prominent legal scholar Eugene Volokh recently wrote, "it's worth noting that, when sex equality rules were championed in the 1970s, now-Justice Ginsburg—one of the most prominent feminist lawyers of her era—rejected as 'emphatically' unsound the argument that those rules might lead to males being allowed to use women's restrooms."[62] He cites Ginsburg's own words from the *Washington Post* in 1975: "Separate places to disrobe, sleep, perform personal bodily functions are permitted," she wrote, "in some situations required, by regard for individual privacy. Individual privacy, a right of constitutional dimension, is appropriately harmonized with the equality principle."

Yet we are barreling forward in the gender revolution without pausing for a moment to ask ourselves about the implications of making every last space sex-integrated in the name of equality. What will become of prisons, summer camps, domestic violence shelters?

The gender identity movement parades under the mantle of equality, but it only makes the world a less equal place. By denying the sexual binary inherent to human bodies, the gender revolutionaries just tip the scales toward men, making it easier for them to buy women for sex and easier for them to violate women's safe spaces. And they make it impossible for women even to complain about the abuse on the basis of sex—a category they are intent on eliminating.

CHAPTER 10

GENDER REVEAL

The world doesn't need what women have, it needs what women are.

—Edith Stein

"This Couple Had an Insanely Unique Baby Gender Reveal," read the Buzzfeed headline.[1] "Prepare for a Cuteness Overload," read the subheader. The Florida couple, massage therapist Jamie Indiveri and her fiancé, U.S. Army Special Forces soldier Keith Batchelder, had opted for an unusual way to tell their friends and family the sex of their unborn baby. They hired a professional photographer to document the couple sitting on a blanket in the woods together as Batchelder fired his rifle at a distant box, which immediately exploded into a blue plume of colored chalk powder.

On the box were the decorative words, "It's a..." The blue cloud finished the sentence.

The couple's "reveal" went viral, getting picked up everywhere from the *Daily Mail* to gun aficionado website, BearingArms.com. The *Daily Mail* got the vocab right, claiming that the couple used the dramatic method "to discover the sex of their unborn baby."[2]

Indiveri and Batchelder may have gone a bit overboard, but they are just one of countless couples swept up in the "gender-reveal" craze, in which an expecting couple has the sonogram technician write down on a piece of paper the sex of their baby, which they keep as a surprise and announce either at a party or on social media. One common method of announcing the sex is to slice open a cake that is either pink or blue on the inside to indicate boy or girl. It's less common—though certainly dramatic—to shoot a gun at a box filled with pink or blue explosives.

As the *New York Times* put it: "Until recently a little-known practice, the concept is quickly becoming a pre-parenting custom, a dress rehearsal of sorts—or sometimes a replacement—for the baby shower. In a culture where many expectant parents feel obligated to tweet their pregnancy announcement, live-post their ride to the hospital via Instagram, and Skype the baby's first smile, it's the latest example of one of parenthood's formerly private moments becoming a matter of public consumption."[3]

The article cites one of the Internet's most visited parenting websites, BabyCenter, which experienced a nine hundred percent increase in threads on gender-reveal parties in just one year. In one six-month stretch, YouTube saw an even larger increase in gender-reveal videos uploaded to the site.

Pinterest has endless pages dedicated to creative ideas for announcing a baby's sex, with one cheeky pin suggesting a cake decorated with the words, "We're here for the sex."[4]

Despite all the scaremongering about the dangers of assigning a child's sex at birth, plenty of couples are more than happy to do it *before* birth—in gender-stereotyped colors to boot.

SEX STILL MATTERS

Sex, it would appear, still matters. And for many couples, its significance begins in the womb.

The gender-reveal phenomenon is a fun and healthy manifestation of how modern society still recognizes sex. But there are other, darker ways that show how much sex differences still matter to some—including sex-selective in vitro fertilization. In a 2012 article entitled "How to Buy a Daughter," *Slate* reported that new technologies had turned choosing a baby's sex into "a multimillion-dollar industry."

More like a $100 million industry. With the average cost to choose a baby's sex in the range of $20,000 and thousands of couples requesting the procedure annually, sex-selection is booming.[5]

And, as we have already seen, thanks to celebrity couples like John Legend and Chrissy Teigen, the practice has moved beyond the realm of creepy science fiction into the mainstream. More and more couples are openly discussing their desire for a child of one sex or the other, and the enormous sums they'll spend to get their preference.

"We Spent $100k to Guarantee a Baby Girl," read one headline in the *New York Post*. The article quotes the mother as saying, "You feel incomplete as a mother until you have a girl."[6]

In the 2016 season premiere of the HBO nightly news series *Vice*, correspondent Isobel Yeung highlighted the growing trend of using reproductive technologies for sex-selection. One couple that she interviewed for the program called their decision to spend $16,500 to select their baby's sex a "no brainer."

In an interview with the *Daily Mail*, Yeung said, "It is actually crazy considering the amount of time the whole abortion debate gets, and at the same time, we're actually able to choose the sex and eye color of our children. Insane that that doesn't get more airtime."

Sex-selection, illegal in many countries, but not in the United States, has spawned something called "fertility tourism" for couples around the world looking to pick their baby's sex. Meanwhile, according to *Slate*, the P.C. powers that be have renamed sex-selection "family balancing." Yes, that's the very same publication that called the mere labeling of a baby as a "boy" or "girl" a human rights abuse.[7]

Even as we insist that sex is an arbitrary label assigned at birth, in America it's legal to design, choose, or even kill an embryo based on his or her sex. While the British parliament voted 181–1 in 2014 to outlaw abortion based on a baby's sex,[8] a similar measure in the United States failed along party lines.[9]

In America, we insist that parents have a right to choose the sex of their baby, to build a family that is "balanced" by the presence of both sexes. The ironic implication, of course, is that the sexes are different and that those differences are significant.

The burgeoning industries launched by these trends, to which Americans have devoted hundreds of millions of dollars, prove that sex still matters. A lot.

SEX GETS SCHOOLED

Over the past couple of years, reporters and writers began to notice that something curious was happening. Single-sex education was making a comeback. News about this trend tended to be lost in the shuffle as more outlandish stories about sex and education, like boys being banned from playing with Legos or the forced sex-integration of locker rooms, grabbed the public's attention. But even as schools around the country were rewriting their sex-ed curricula to teach kindergarteners that gender is a fluid spectrum, plenty of schools were returning to the old-fashioned model of sorting schoolchildren by their sex.

"Old Tactic Gets New Use: Public Schools Separate Girls and Boys," announced one 2014 *New York Times* article.[10] "The Resurgence of Single-Sex Education" read an *Atlantic* headline in late 2015. A *Christian Science Monitor* piece explained "Why single-sex education is spreading across the US." "Public Schools Increasing Single Sex Education," said *Parenting* magazine's blog. "Single Sex Education Belongs in the 21st Century," proclaimed a writer in *Forbes*.

The headlines were not exaggerating the resurgence of single-sex schooling. In the past ten to fifteen years, as sex-denial was steaming ahead full-throttle, single-sex education has made a robust return. In 2004, there were only thirty-four single-sex public schools in America. In the following decade, that number exploded twenty-five-fold to 850 such schools by 2014.[11] The same-sex education revival was largely due to the passage of the No Child Left Behind Act in 2001, which constituted a major upheaval in public education, and to what the *Atlantic* called a "historic rewriting of Title IX" five years later, which "gave local districts the option of offering single-gender public schools and programs for the first time in more than 30 years."

Researchers aren't in agreement about the benefits of sex-segregated education. Some experts argue that teaching boys and girls separately, especially during puberty, eliminates some distractions and enables teachers and administrators to tailor education to boys' and girls' strengths and needs. One of the leading advocates for single-sex public education, Leonard Sax, argues that ignoring sex differences in education is harmful. According to Sax, founder of the National Association for Choice in Education and author of multiple books on sex differences, "What we're doing right now—pretending that gender doesn't matter—is not working. We are losing ground."[12] His group argues that single-sex education may not work for everyone, but can bring clear benefits to many children.[13] In his research, for example, Sax has found that boys and girls learn differently given different room temperatures,[14] seating styles,[15] and volume of instruction,[16] among other more profound cognitive differences in how they process subjects like art and math.

Some scholars argue that positive educational outcomes in single-sex schools can't be attributed to that factor alone. And others outright oppose single-sex education, suggesting that it reinforces stereotypes and leads to inadequate preparation for real life. "School is preparation for adult life," says one former president of the American Psychological Association. "How can boys and girls learn how to interact as equals in the workplace if they have no experience interacting as equals in school?"[17] Yet when the Supreme Court considered the constitutionality of single-sex schools, all of the justices agreed that they have their merits, even while striking down the Virginia Military Institute's male-only admissions policy. Even Justice Ruth Bader Ginsburg, known for her lifelong advocacy for "gender equality," pointed out in her opinion that "single-sex education affords pedagogical benefits to at least some students. That reality is uncontested in this litigation."

What's also uncontested is the fact that single-sex schooling is on the rise again. When given the freedom, it has become clear, parents and educators have found a lot to like about educating children in a same-sex environment.

FROM THE SLOPES TO THE GYM TO THE OFFICE

And it's not just schools where segregating by sex has seen a revival in popularity. From the boardroom to the gym to the slopes, women are driving a demand for single-sex environments.

Take skiing. As the *New York Times* reports, women's-only ski clinics were "dismissed as irrelevant" up until recently. In the past five years or so, they've made a comeback. The *Times* explains, "'It used to be, "I'm a really good skier, so I don't need to ski just with women,"' said Kim Reichhelm, an extreme skiing champion and a former United States Ski Team member who is teaching clinics in Vail, Aspen and Steamboat, Colo., this season. In high-level clinics now, she said, 'Rather than skiing with a pack of guys who might have a tendency to get in over their heads, you're with a bunch of women whom you trust. Women look at one another and think, "If she's doing it, I can do it."'"[18]

And it's not happening with advanced female skiers only. More recreational female skiers are demanding an all-female learning environment, too. A travel writer detailed one such experience for the UK *Independent*:

> "Based in the quiet Les Bosons area of the sprawling Chamonix valley," writes Sally Newall, "the five-day trip with luxury specialist Amazon Creek is aimed at girls who want to up their ski game in a supportive environment" without what she calls "the pressures that can come with large, testosterone-fuelled groups." Newall describes the female instructor, Rachel Kerr, as "a passionate advocate of what women can achieve in a specialised group. 'We want to unite like-minded women to explore the mountains,' [Kerr] told me, explaining that, in her experience, women feel pressure

to keep up with the pace of the boys and take a back seat in a mixed group. 'I'd like women not to be afraid to voice their opinions and share their experiences so we can target exactly the skills to improve,' she said."[19]

Women looking to break a sweat without dealing with men ogling them or outright harassing them have also spurred the spread of female-only gyms, the most famous among them being the Curves chain. The women's-only gym, ironically founded by a man, became one of the fastest-growing franchises in history and now boasts thousands of outlets around the world. Founder Gary Heavin revealed to a franchising blog that he learned quickly that the best market for single-sex gyms was women, not men. "[M]en [already] have places to exercise. Men don't care if women look at their butts while they're working out," he said in an interview. "It was women that didn't have a place to go, women who were intimidated by the men, women who didn't have two hours to spend at the gym."[20]

One fitness writer elaborates on the appeal of all-female gyms, noting that "women may feel more comfortable exercising in a gym where there are no men around. In a women-only gym, they would be more likely to give and receive open advice on their health condition and their workout plan. With women-centric trainers females could likely get better advice as well as have options for activities that may not be available in co-ed gyms."[21]

Other fitness chains are adding female-only options. Women's fitness magazine *Self* reported in 2014 that CrossFit classes for women only are "popping up all over the country." "That's right—no boys allowed," read an online post on the all-female classes that allow women to do the course "in peace" and without "bros."[22]

A major factor motivating women to opt for female-only gyms is the sexual harassment they frequently encounter in coed gyms. One woman explained in the *Guardian* why female fitness clubs should be allowed even if men can't ban women from their golf courses: "You want to know why we have women-only gym and swimming sessions? It's not some shiny, special privilege bestowed on us lucky women because we just deserve nice things. It is a direct result of the male harassment, sexism and sexual violence that has driven a quarter of women to give up exercising outside altogether and countless others to abandon the gym in frustration."

She recounts her own experience of sexual harassment in a coed pool and points out that "In three years the Everyday Sexism Project has received a whopping 984 testimonies from women writing about their experiences of sexism, harassment and assault at the gym; 541 related to swimming pools." She concludes, "Many women-only spaces exist for one reason: to avoid male harassment."[23]

Despite their popularity as safe spaces from harassment and discrimination, women-only gyms have faced their share of lawsuits over, naturally, discrimination. These gyms, frequented by millions of women, have been sued up and down and across the country, with mixed results. Some states have exempted women's gyms from sex discrimination lawsuits on the grounds that they help to *prevent* sex discrimination, but others have required the gyms to begin admitting men.[24] In one of the more high-profile lawsuits, a Boston trial lawyer sued when a women's club opened across the street from his home in Boston's luxe Back Bay neighborhood and refused to admit him. As the *New York Times* said of his lawsuit: "It may sound frivolous. But his argument has touched such deep nerves that it has divided women's advocates here, incited talk show hosts around the country and, when the Massachusetts Legislature examined it this month, is said to have prompted more calls from irate voters than capital punishment."

(Giving new meaning to sex-based frivolity in law, the same trial lawyer also sued over happy hour specials benefiting only women.)[25]

LEAN IN

But perhaps the mother of all women's-only spaces are the Lean In Circles founded by Facebook COO Sheryl Sandberg. The "circles," which sprang from her wildly popular book about professional empowerment for women, are described on her website as "small groups that meet monthly to encourage and support each other in an atmosphere of confidentiality and trust." Nearly thirty thousand circles exist in more than a hundred countries.[26]

The circles, and indeed Sandberg's entire initiative, make no secret of the fact that they are designed for women. Men are not barred, but their popularity is with the female sex. The *Washington Post* describes Lean In circles as "clusters of women who meet regularly and keep one another focused on their goals."[27] One woman, writing about her personal experience with the circles, described them for *Slate* as gatherings of "like-minded professional women who were interested in talking about career advancement."[28] Another woman described her particular circle for *New York* magazine's blog *The Cut* as a collection of "women [who] could have been pulled from the pages of a Benetton ad."[29]

Nobody is calling Lean In Circles a "gender-neutral" enterprise. And on the heels of Lean In comes SheWorks, a women-only coworking space. Coworking spaces, which allow freelancers and entrepreneurs to pay a monthly fee to rent a desk or small space in a hip office space, have become very popular in recent years. They allow for a quiet place to make phone calls, a more formal environment for the occasional meeting, and a buzzing professional atmosphere filled with other self-employed people. SheWorks caters to professional women in New York City who want to get their work done in a women-only environment, which as its founder put it, ditches the "beer-pong" found in some mixed-sex coworking spaces for female-oriented perks like "a lactation room or the green room, where you can go to relax."[30] Other similar women-only set-ups have popped up elsewhere, including Bizzy Mamas in Philadelphia, described as "a group made up of mostly young, working moms that own their own businesses,"[31] and the "spa-inspired" Hera Hub in Washington, D.C., and San Diego.[32]

The circles and women-centric workspaces come at a time when the professional world is gaining insight into the unique contribution that women make in the workplace.

SEX AND THE BOTTOM LINE

For decades, female employees were typically viewed as a financial liability for a business, but a mound of recent studies have shown that companies that strive to cultivate women in the workplace, and in particular, get them to the top and keep them there, see rewards by multiple measures. In early 2016, the nonprofit Peterson Institute for International Economics released the most significant study to date on how "gender makeup" affects a company's bottom line. The researchers found a clear connection between greater profitability and having more women in executive roles and on corporate boards. The authors attributed this result to the fact that, among other things, "women increase a firm's skill diversity."[33]

That study confirmed what another had demonstrated in 2015, namely that companies with what the researchers described as "strong female leadership" saw three times the rate of return on equity over five years as companies lacking a robust female presence at high levels did.[34] In 2014, a major Credit Suisse study on the gender balance of executives at three thousand companies found the same thing.[35] In their words, "Enhanced female participation in management positions should not be seen as 'nice-to-have' or a necessary box ticking exercise imposed to satisfy quotas. More women in senior management positions," they said, "improves companies' financial performance and makes a difference for investors in terms of equity market returns."[36]

In other words: more women, more money.

But why? As it turns out, despite the fiction that "gender difference" is a meaningless construct, the benefits that flow from having women at the top stem from fundamental *differences* between men and women. The difference, not the lack of contrast, between the sexes is the source of strength and growth for businesses.

New studies are revealing that, on the whole, men and women work differently and bring very different things to the table. And those differences enhance their employers' profitability. One study conducted by economics professors at the University of California at Santa Barbara and the National Center for Scientific Research concluded that women are far more likely to gravitate to "team-based" workplace structures, whereas men tend to prefer to work alone. This held true when compensation was added to the mix; women even preferred "team-based compensation," while the men preferred payment based on individual performance.[37]

In the financial crash of 2008, female-owned hedge funds lost less money than those owned by men, something many attributed to women's more cautious and connected approach to handling risk.[38] "I think it's because we're considering more connections so the decision is like how many people will it really affect.... It's not that we're slower decision makers, we just take more into consideration, and in senior positions, that's really important," behavioral scientist Dr. Marcia Reynolds explained. In fact, the most vocal financial analyst to warn of what would eventually become the financial crash of 2008 was a woman, Meredith Whitney.[39]

It may be politically incorrect, but countless executives today openly tout the benefits that sex difference brings to the workplace. According to a comprehensive piece on sex difference in the workplace in the *Fiscal Times*:

> [M]en and women can be just as different in the professional world as they are in their personal lives. What executives are just beginning to understand is that these differences can be great for business. Typically, "men are linear in thought process and more narrow in their focus, so they are able to break down problems into their component parts and solve it," says Keith Merron a senior associate [at] Barbara Annis & Associates, a consulting firm specializing in gender diversity. "Women more often see a problem holistically and are able to coming up [sic] with an understanding of that situation without needing to know what all the parts are. When it comes to problem solving—particularly in business—you need a balance of both perspectives."[40]

Democratic Senator Kristen Gillibrand of New York expressed the same insight when she explained why she works to get more women elected to Congress. "Women," she says, "are very good at being able to find what they have in common and building from there. In my own experience, anytime I've been successful in moving legislation, I've had the help of a Republican woman."[41] (Senator Gillibrand also happens to be a product of an all-girls' education at the elite Emma Willard prep school in New York.)

Gillibrand's sentiments are backed by neuroscience. One study found that when stressed about giving a major speech, women were more likely to draw on empathy for the perspectives of others in a room for calmness and confidence, whereas men found motivation by gravitating toward narcissism. The same study also discovered that women make better decisions under stress by seeking out smaller but more certain successful outcomes. When men are placed under pressure, by contrast, their decision-making became riskier and more questionable.[42]

WE'RE BETTER TOGETHER

The female propensity for communicative and inter-connected empathy extends beyond the workplace and into communities and families. One landmark study, for example, conducted in 1999 asked the question, "Social Ties and Crime: Is the Relationship Gendered?" The sociologists who conducted the study found that "not all social ties are equally effective in producing informal social control and decreasing crime rates." If you want to see real results, call in the women. "Female social ties," their abstract states, "are more effective in controlling crime."[43]

If you also want to see who cares for humanity, look for the women. It's no secret that women are more likely to spend more time caring for their children than men, but they are also more likely to care for their elderly parents. According to the Family Caregiver Alliance, the percentage of family caregivers that are female ranges from half to two-thirds, depending on the study. In addition, women are more likely to handle the most intimate aspects of care, such as toileting and bathing, whereas men are more likely to handle things like finances.[44] In the headline of a press release documenting that daughters spend an average of twelve hours a month caring for an elderly parent compared with sons' five and a half, the American Psychological Association summed up the research bluntly: "Daughters provide as much elderly parent care as they can, sons do as little as possible."[45] Women's dedication does not come without a cost; almost half of all caregivers for the elderly spend more than $5,000 a year on care. And that's not counting the costs incurred from missing work and neglecting other activities.[46]

Women don't just care more for others; their very presence makes others care more. *New York Times* columnist Ross Douthat called this principle "the daughter theory," after recent research found a slew of ways that having daughters changes fathers for the better. For starters, it tends to make them more socially conservative, something Douthat attributes to a father's realization, on seeing the world in the context of his daughter, that we need a "romantic culture in which more is required of young men before the women in their lives will sleep with them."[47] Writing about a study that showed a "statistically significant" and "substantively large"[48] connection between having daughters and warming up to the GOP, Douthat argues that, "To the extent that parents tend to see the next generation's world through their children's eyes, that's an insight that's more immediately available through daughters than through sons."[49]

Numerous studies have found that having daughters doesn't just make men more conservative, it makes them more helpful around the home and more magnanimous in other parts of their lives. One study found that men who have daughters, or even simply work with women, are more likely to agree that men should help more with chores at home.[50]

Another study found that men who grow up with sisters go on to spend more time with their own families, as well as to be more generous with charitable giving. In a piece for the *New York Times*, Adam Grant reports that, "Social scientists believe that the empathetic, nurturing behaviors of sisters rub off on their brothers."[51] He also cites Bill Gates, who attributes his decision to launch one of the largest charities in the world and give the vast majority of his fortune to it to the women in his life—his mother, his wife, and his daughter.

The piece cites a different study reporting that while women generally opt for a more even distribution of resources, "men are more likely to be either perfectly selfish or perfectly selfless."[52] "It may be," Grant notes, "that meaningful contact with women is one of the forces that tilt men toward greater selflessness."[53]

Unsurprisingly, the research has also found that the influence of women in the home is good for business. In one widely cited study, researchers discovered that male CEOs paid their employees less money after having sons, but the effect was reduced if the child was a daughter, and CEOs paid employees *more* if the daughter was the CEO's first.[54]

"Daughters apparently soften fathers and evoke more caretaking tendencies," writes Grant. "The speculation is that as we brush our daughters' hair and take them to dance classes, we become gentler, more empathetic and more other-oriented."[55]

Whether it's profit, charity, or chores that motivate your interest in sex difference, it's clear that women impact it all. Not all men are stingy egomaniacs, and not all women are selflessly bathing their elderly parents. But the social science makes clear that women bring out the best in men, that the inherent differences between the sexes help make the world a more just place. Call it yin and yang, Venus and Mars, Harry and Sally, we need each other, and we better each other.

EQUAL BUT NOT THE SAME

Since the dawn of the Sexual Revolution, the ship of society has slowly been steered in one direction: gender neutrality. But nature and biology are pesky realities that are impossible to wipe out, so when we strive for gender neutrality, we are left with a frustrating mess. If anything, the effort to stamp out sex difference has only enhanced sex stereotypes such as aggressive masculinity and hyper-sexualized femininity. And the members of the sex whose characteristics are often more subtle, more mysterious, and more complex are being swept up and pressed into a masculine mold. Women are set up to fail.

The one-size-fits-all model simply does not work when it comes to male and female, even when the aims are noble. Take, for example, maternity and paternity leave. Women have been rightly pressuring society for policies that enable them to take time off to care for newborns without forfeiting their job or their paycheck. Plenty of employers, especially those who see the financial benefits of retaining and promoting female talent, are responding to that pressure. Others have recognized the benefits of offering leave to new fathers as well.

But when men and women are offered *equal* workplace benefits after children are born, the effort to create gender neutrality backfires on women. A recent study of gender-neutral policies at universities aimed at making it easier for new parents to gain tenure as professors found that the "gender-neutral policies" led to "substantially reduced female tenure rates while substantially increasing male tenure rates."[56] The study was titled "Equal but Inequitable," and noted that this phenomenon spans numerous fields such as law and medicine, where women and men are afforded the same or similar parental benefits even though women bear far more of the burdens of childbearing. "[F]athers usually receive the same benefits without bearing anything close to the same burden," wrote one economist for the University of Michigan. "Given this asymmetry, it's little wonder some recently instituted benefits have given men an advantage."[57]

A gender-neutral society effectively stacks the deck in favor of men by blinding itself, in the name of political correctness and equality, to everything that makes women more vulnerable. Women are then forced to compete on male terms, and the male model of accomplishment is the default, the paradigm against which women are judged. Playing with Legos is better than playing with dolls, because building is better than nurturing. Women can't be good soldiers unless they are delivering hand-to-hand blows like the strongest man. Women can't be sexually free unless they can sell their own bodies like a pimp. These are the assumptions that would be written into a gender-blind society, and we can already see them taking hold.

The entire list of assumptions about sex needs to be re-written, starting with the notion that women must overcome what makes us different in order to be equal with men. Rather, the starting point for authentic equality between the sexes must be recognition of what makes us different and the acceptance that some of those differences cannot be altered. Only then can society accept what we call vulnerabilities in women and begin to view them as strengths.

There are signs that all is not yet lost. They are little, quirky signs, like the viral popularity of gender-reveal parties, despite the chorus of naysayers. Or the celebrities who rush to defend a fellow starlet who was taken advantage of because of her sex. Or the booming line of Legos for girls. Or the lone university returning its dorms to single-sex status.

Notwithstanding such hopeful signs, these are chaotic times. Because sex is such an essential part of who we are, we can hardly expect anything but the overthrow of reason when we try to deny that it matters—even that it exists as a category. When we deny sex, we cast ourselves into the most brute state of nature: a battle of strengths that pits men and women against each other as rivals and enemies.

But sex doesn't need to be a fault line in a battle, or a source of national scandal. The difference between the two sexes should be the starting point for a more authentic equality. This does not mean a return to the times when women were denied basic goods like an education or the vote. Those times suffered under an equally problematic misunderstanding of the difference between the sexes, one that denied where the sexes truly are the same, namely in their intellectual capacity and their contributions to civic life. But it is also an affront to equality to say men and women are identical, and to deny that a civilized society requires certain corrections to accommodate the unique needs of the female sex.

Only when we can all say *vive la différence* can men and women truly begin to live as equals.

EPILOGUE

I wrote most of this book while recovering from major surgery. While I have always chafed at the labeling of women as "nurturing," I was made acutely aware of the reality that women, in general, simply are nurturing in a way men are not. For weeks on end, not only did my mother and sister care for my two children night and day while I was helpless to do so myself, but they also took care of me, while the men in my life faded into the background. I was the most physically vulnerable that I had ever been in my adult life, apart from brief periods after childbirth.

Some men are warriors and some men are poets. Some women are trial lawyers and some women are nurses. Some men are nurses, some women are warriors. Individuals vary widely in how they live out their masculinity and femininity. But our current culture insists on denying the value of the more nurturing and domestic roles that have typically been ascribed to women. We laud the female CEO and scorn the stay-at-home mom. Perhaps nothing better sums up our culture's unspoken take on "gender" than Democratic strategist Hilary Rosen's quip during the 2012 presidential campaign about Ann Romney, mother to five sons—that she had "never worked a day in her life."[1] In other words, a woman's work is entirely invalid unless it looks identical to her husband's.

I grew up subscribing to the Hilary Rosen school of feminism, determined to be a cutthroat lawyer with a husband who cooked, split the chores 50–50, kept separate bank accounts, and so on. God as my witness, I would have my "gender equity!"

But my feminist worldview imploded at Tufts University, land of the empowered and educated female, when I saw the existence of modern woman under attack. While I certainly found strong and intelligent women there, women I still call friends today, I could see plainly the way that denying certain truths about our sexual identities had the effect of reducing women to sex objects for male pleasure.

Urging women to deny the experienced reality of their sexuality and prostrate themselves to liberal feminist narratives about sex and gender persists into adulthood. We are told to delay marriage for our careers, to move in with men instead of demanding that they marry us, and to delay children as long as is physically possible, and then we are lied to about the basic biological realities about our bodies. And now I see women of the "separate bank account" school of feminism stuck in their own patriarchy Catch-22s, doing everything from paying rent to their husbands to shouldering the costs of child care entirely out of their own pocketbooks. Women stuck bearing the physical burden of hormonal contraception for two decades of their lives because reproduction is her "problem." Women torn up by guilt for wanting a different work-life arrangement from men.

It has become anathema to suggest that a woman might want something different out of life, even a life where women have all the opportunities in the world and increasingly outpace men in the educational and professional worlds. It has become anathema even to point out that biological sex is a real scientific phenomenon. Increasingly, I see scare quotes used around the phrase biological sex, a phrase you will find in any medical textbook. We've actually become scared of sex. Scared of our own selves.

I emphasize the effect this has on women, because I am a woman and can speak from my experience as one. I am well aware that sex denial has created a crisis for masculinity as well. I focus on women in particular in this book, because it is we who have the most to lose in a world where sex is in scare quotes. Trigger warning: we are the reproductively more vulnerable and physically weaker sex, and when we give society a pass to deny that reality, we give society a frightening amount of cover when it comes to endangering women. It is here that social conservatives and radical feminists increasingly line up together. And so in a strange way, I have come full circle to the feminism of my youth.

Pope Francis recently ruffled feathers when he said that "gender theory" amounts to a "global war on the family."[2] It's true, because if sex is meaningless, and the sexes don't need each other or have different contributions to make, then why band together? Why should a man stick around to help the mother of his children when the media celebrates the record number of households headed by single moms as some sort of feminist triumph?[3]

But gender theory is also a war on women because it delegitimizes claims of abuse that originate from our sex. Ultimately, though, gender theory is a war on ourselves. It creates an anarchy of identity, a sort of sexual Hobbesian state of nature, a Leviathan of a world where, trust me, women don't want to be. In that world, our world, gender stereotypes are actually reinforced as the gender barometer defaults not just to the masculine, but to the macho masculine. Even men get held to a more alpha male standard in a world where we are sent flailing and grasping for any kind of standards when it comes to biological sex.

That being said, it's important we not lose empathy for those who genuinely do experience confusion about their sex. Our culture is no help here, but I can only imagine how feeling trapped in the wrong body would be the ultimate form of psychological claustrophobia.

But the reality is that we are not disembodied. We are body and soul. And from the moment of our conception, we are male and female. Rather than trying to quash that reality, which can only lead to more suffering, not less, we should step back and marvel at it. Only then does the extraordinary and equal contribution of woman dazzle.

I sincerely hope this book sheds some light on the important quest to understand what makes us different and how we can help to better each other for the good of all.

ACKNOWLEDGMENTS

Writing this book while pregnant, recovering from major surgery, and with two children under the age of four was a feat made possible only by the help and support of others.

Eternal gratitude is owed to my mother Linda, who logged countless hours helping me through it all and who raised me in such a way that I always remained tethered to my femininity. I am equally indebted to my father Randy, who always pushed me to strive harder, to never give up in the pursuit of my passions, and to never let me think that a man's world was not mine to conquer.

Every girl must be in want of a sister, and I was blessed with two. Thank you to Chelsea, my writing doppelgänger, for never tiring of assuring me that I could in fact pull this off, and to Lindsey for being the kind of barrier-breaking woman I hope this book inspires.

I am a better woman and mother because of the strong and spirited women in my life, in particular my grandmother Ruth Penner, my mother-in-law Roni McGuire, my cousin Joy Schwarting, and my professional mentors Ann Corkery and Kristina Arriaga. Special thanks are also due to Mary Eberstadt, Susan Arellano, Dan Casey, and Mollie Ziegler Hemingway for giving me essential advice, both in my writing career and regarding this book.

This book would never have happened were it not for the generous confidence of Tom Spence, the vision of Harry Crocker, and the patient wisdom of Elizabeth Kantor. Nor would it have been possible without the indispensable help of Anna Sutherland.

My optimism about the future for women in society would not exist without the inspiring friendships I find in Montse Alvarado, Sarah Smith, Stephanie DiNapoli, Ashley Wickham, Amy Helms, Megan Donley, Liza Bowen, Stephanie Acosta Inks, Kim Hicks, Mary Rose Somarriba, Angela Wu Howard, Rachel Currie, Melissa Langsam Braunstein, Liz Tenety, Asma Uddin, and Leigh Snead. To quote Queen Bey, "Girls! Who runs the world?"

My trajectory toward truth in a world that roundly rejects it would not have been possible without the enduring friendship and guidance of Father Thomas Joseph White, O.P.

Finally, to Max and Stella, who bring me endless joy, my hope is that this book in some tiny way contributes toward a world where you can grow into the man and woman you are meant to be.

Above all, thank you to Brian. You both inspire and complete my thoughts. Nothing I do would be possible without you.

NOTES

INTRODUCTION

1. Jesse Greenspan, "Billie Jean King Wins the 'Battle of the Sexes,' 10 Years Ago," History Channel, September 20, 2013, http://www.history.com/news/billie-jean-king-wins-the-battle-of-the-sexes-40-years-ago.
2. Ibid.
3. "Billie Jean King Wins in Straight Sets against Bobby Riggs in 1973's 'Battle of the Sexes.'" *New York Daily News*, September 19, 2015, http://www.nydailynews.com/sports/billie-jean-wins-straight-sets-riggs-1973-article-1.2355262.
4. Greenspan, "Billie Jean King Wins."
5. Cyd Zeigler, "Fallon Fox Comes Out as Trans Pro MMA Fighter," Outsports, March 5, 2013, http://www.outsports.com/2013/3/5/4068840/fallon-fox-trans-pro-mma-fighter.

6. Alan Murphy, "Transgender Fighter Fallon Fox Sends Opponent to Hospital," WHOA TV, September 15, 2014, http://whoatv.com/transgender-fighter-fallon-fox-sends-opponent-to-hospital/.

7. Adam Campbell, "Transgender 'Female' MMA Fighter Brutally Injures Female Opponent," Liberty News Now, June 8, 2015, http://www.libertynewsnow.com/transgender-female-mma-fighter-brutally-injures-female-opponent/article1545.

8. Scott Gleeson and Erik Brady, "Will Transgender Olympian Come Out for Rio Games?," *USA Today*, July 20, 2016, http://www.usatoday.com/story/sports/olympics/rio-2016/2016/07/19/out-transgender-olympics-rio-caitlyn-jenner-chris-mosier/87188798/.

9. Rich Lowry, "If You Don't Want to Study White Writers, Don't Major in English," *New York Post*, June 6, 2016, http://nypost.com/2016/06/06/if-you-dont-want-to-study-white-writers-dont-major-in-english/.

10. Debra Heine, "Army Cadets on Campus Forced to Wear Red High Heels and Raise Awareness of Debunked 'Rape Culture,'" PJ Media, April 21, 2015, https://pjmedia.com/blog/army-cadets-on-campus-forced-to-wear-red-high-heels-and-raise-awareness-of-debunked-rape-culture/.

11. Ian Duncan, "Female Midshipmen to Wear Trousers, Not Skirts, at Graduation: Naval Academy Ditches Skirts at Graduation, Orders Female Mids to Don Trousers," *Baltimore Sun*, February 23, 2016, http://www.baltimoresun.com/news/maryland/bs-md-naval-academy-pants-20160223-story.html.

12. Trevor MacDonald, "Transphobia in the Midwifery Community," Huffington Post, September 15, 2015, http://www.huffingtonpost.com/trevor-macdonald/transphobia-in-the-midwif_b_8131520.html.

CHAPTER 1: THE KIDS ARE NOT ALRIGHT

Epigraph Jean-Jacques Rousseau, *Emile* (Basic Books 1979), 90.

1. Christin Scarlett Milloy, "Don't Let the Doctor Do This to Your Newborn," *Slate*, June 26, 2014, http://www.slate.com/blogs/outward/2014/06/26/infant_gender_assignment_unnecessary_and_potentially_harmful.html.
2. "What's in Store: Moving Away from Gender-Based Signs," Target, August 7, 2015, https://corporate.target.com/article/2015/08/gender-based-signs-corporate.
3. Caroline Bologna, "13 Empowering Photos Show There's No 'Right' Way to Be a Boy," Huffington Post, July 7, 2016, http://www.huffingtonpost.com/entry/13-empowering-photos-show-theres-no-right-way-to-be-a-boy_us_576ab3b5e4b09926ce5d46a4?ir=Good+News&.
4. Ruth Margolis, "Target Is Abolishing Boy/Girl Toy Labels: Here's Why Kids' Clothes Should Be Next," *Week*, August 13, 2015, http://theweek.com/articles/571312/target-abolishing-boygirl-toy-labels-heres-why-kids-clothes-should-next.
5. Amy Joyce, "Beyond the Girl and Boy Aisles: How Funneling Kids into a Category Can Hurt," *Washington Post*, September 9, 2015, https://www.washingtonpost.com/lifestyle/beyond-the-girl-and-boy-aisles-how-funneling-kids-into-a-category-can-hurt/2015/09/08/dfd00af2-50de-11e5-8c19-0b6825aaa4a3a_story.html.
6. Princess Awesome, https://princess-awesome.com.
7. "Clothes Without Limits," http://www.clotheswithoutlimits.com/participating-companies/.
8. Rebecca Hains, "Target Will Stop Labeling Toys for Boys or for Girls. Good.," *Washington Post*, August 13, 2015, https://www.washingtonpost.com/posteverything/wp/2015/08/13/target-will-stop-selling-toys-for-boys-or-for-girls-good/.
9. "A dot Bech," @abianne, Twitter, https://twitter.com/abianne; "Abi Bechtel, Writer," https://abibechtel.com/.
10. Peggy Orenstein, "What's Wrong with Cinderella?," *New York Times*, December 24, 2006, http://www.nytimes.com/2006/12/24/magazine/24princess.t.html?pagewanted=all&_r=0.

11. Claire Suddath, "The $500 Million Battle over Disney's Princesses: How Hasbro Grabbed the Lucrative Disney Doll Business from Mattel," Bloomberg, December 17, 2015. http://www.bloomberg.com/features/2015-disney-princess-hasbro/.

12. Peggy Orenstein, "Tips for Raising Well-Rounded Girls in a Princess Dominated World, PBS, May 6, 2014, http://www.pbs.org/newshour/updates/navigating-princess-culture/.

13. Adam McCabe, "VIDEO: Disney's 'Dream Big, Princess' Campaign Brings Inspiring Girl Power to the Masses," Inside the Magic, February 12, 2016, http://www.insidethemagic.net/2016/02/video-disneys-dream-big-princess-campaign-brings-inspiring-girl-power-to-the-masses/.

14. "Potty-Mouthed Princesses Drop F-Bomb for Feminism," FCKH8, October 21, 2014, https://www.youtube.com/watch?v=XqHYzYn3WZw.

15. "'Potty-Mouthed Princesses' and the Feminist Rabbit Hole, *Federalist*, October 23, 2014, http://thefederalist.com/2014/10/23/potty-mouthed-princesses-and-the-feminist-rabbit-hole/.

16. Isha Aran, "The Potty Mouthed Princesses Are Back and Now They Have Black Eyes," *Jezebel*, November 25, 2014, http://jezebel.com/the-potty-mouth-princesses-are-back-and-now-they-have-b-1663329964.

17. "Kindergarten Teacher Bans Legos for Boys Citing 'Gender Equity,'" CBS Seattle, November 19, 2015, http://seattle.cbslocal.com/2015/11/19/kindergarten-teacher-bans-legos-for-boys-citing-gender-equity/>.

18. Elyse Wanshel, "Teacher's Comments about Legos Cause Controversy in School District: The School Has Denied What She Told a Local Paper," Huffington Post, November 20, 2015, http://www.huffingtonpost.com/entry/karen-keller-bans-boys-legos_us_564f5009e4b0879a5b0abc9e.

19. Emanuella Grinberg, "6 Ways to Embrace Gender Differences at School," CNN, January 3, 2015, http://www.cnn.com/2014/10/03/living/children-gender-inclusive-schools/.

20. Cavan Sieczkowski, "'Gender Bender' Day at School Stirs Controversy; Parent Suggests It Promotes Homosexuality," Huffington Post, May 28, 2013, http://www.huffingtonpost.com/2013/05/28/gender-bender-day-homosexuality_n_3346285.html.

21. Julia Glum, "Wisconsin Gender-Neutral Homecoming Court: Madison High School to Crown 'Regent Royalty' in LGBT-Friendly Tradition," International Business Times, October 16, 2015, http://www.ibtimes.com/wisconsin-gender-neutral-homecoming-court-madison-high-school-crown-regent-royalty-2144130.

22. "School's Father-Daughter Dance Cancelled After Some Complaints It Wasn't Inclusive," Fox News, May 6, 2016, http://www.foxnews.com/us/2016/05/06/schools-father-daughter-dance-canceled-after-some-complaints-it-wasn-t-inclusive.html.

23. Todd Starnes, "Parents Furious over School's Plan to Teach Gender Spectrum, Fluidity," Fox News, May 15, 2015, http://www.foxnews.com/opinion/2015/05/15/call-it-gender-fluidity-schools-to-teach-kids-there-s-no-such-thing-as-boys-or-girls.html.

24. T. Rees Shapiro, "Fairfax School Board Approves Adding Transgender Topic to Teens' Class," *Washington Post*, June 26, 2015, https://www.washingtonpost.com/local/education/school-board-approves-adding-transgender-issues-to-the-classroom/2015/06/26/d484c7c2-1c14-11e5-93b7-5eddc056ad8a_story.html.

25. "Kindergarten-12th Grade: Health &Physical Education," Washington State Learning Standards, 2016, http://www.k12.wa.us/HealthFitness/Standards/HPE-Standards.pdf.

26. "Bernice Sandler," http://www.bernicesandler.com.

27. Steve Wulf, "Title IX: 37 Words That Changed Everything," ESPN, April 29, 2012, http://espn.go.com/espnw/title-ix/article/7722632/37-words-changed-everything.

28. Diane Pucin, "FloJo's Name Isn't Only Reminder of Her at Meet," *Lost Angeles Times*, April 7, 2000, http://articles.latimes.com/2000/apr/07/sports/sp-17012.

29. Emily Sweeney, "MIAA to Study Boy-Girl Swim Team Records," *Boston Globe*, January 1, 2012, http://archive.boston.com/sports/schools/articles/2012/01/01/miaa_to_discuss_issue_of_boys_breaking_girls_swim_records_1325369322/?page=1.

30. Stephanie Kogut, "Boys Playing Girls' Sports: Does Equality Trump Fairness?," Jurist, November 27, 2013, http://www.jurist.org/sidebar/2013/11/alan-boynton-piaa-gender-equality.php.

31. Sweeney, "MIAA to Study Boy-Girl Swim Team Records."

32. J. Brady McCoullough, "Issue of Boys Playing on Girls Sports Teams to Be Debated in Pa.," *Pittsburgh Post-Gazette*, May 3, 2013, http://www.post-gazette.com/sports/hsother/2013/05/03/Issue-of-boys-playing-on-girls-sports-teams-to-be-debated-in-Pa/stories/201305030285.

33. "Title IX Myths and Facts," Women's Sports Foundation, https://www.womenssportsfoundation.org/home/advocate/title-ix-and-issues/what-is-title-ix/title-ix-myths-and-facts.

34. Ibid.

35. *Commonwealth of Pennsylvania v. Pennsylvania Interscholastic Athletic Association*, http://www.jurist.org/sidebar/83%20-%20PIAA%20-%20Packel%20-%202013%20Court%20Opinion%20%28A3528337%29.pdf.

36. Ibid; Ben Rohrbach, "Transgender Track Athlete Makes History As Controversy Swirls around Her," *USA Today*, June 2, 2016, http://usatodayhss.com/2016/transgender-track-athlete-makes-history-as-controversy-stirs-around-her.

37. "'It's Not Fair': Transgender Student's Success in Girls Track Causes Backlash," Fox News, June 7, 2016, http://insider.foxnews.com/2016/06/07/nattaphon-wangyot-transgender-athlete-wins-all-state-honors-girls-track-and-field.

38. Beth Bragg, "At Alaska State Track Meet, a Transgender Athlete Makes Her Mark," *Alaska Dispatch News*, May 31, 2016, http://www.adn.com/sports/2016/05/27/at-alaska-state-track-meet-a-transgender-athlete-makes-her-mark/.

39. Interview of Neena Chaudhry by the author on June 21, 2016.
40. McCollough, "Issue of Boys Playing on Girls Sports."
41. "Successful Lego Strategy Delivers Continued Strong Growth," Lego, February 21, 2013, http://www.lego.com/en-gb/aboutus/news-room/2013/february/annual-result-2012.
42. Kate Stanton, "Lego Gets Sales Boost from Girl-Friendly Toy Series," UPI, February 8, 2013, http://www.upi.com/blog/2013/02/28/Lego-gets-sales-boost-from-girl-friendly-toy-series/9651362066350/.
43. "Friends," Lego, http://www.lego.com/en-us/friends/products.
44. Jonathan V. Last, "The Lego Disney Castle: Finally a Death Star for Girls," *Weekly Standard*, July 12, 2016, http://www.weeklystandard.com/the-lego-disney-castle-finally-a-death-star-for-girls/article/2003261.
45. "FACT SHEET: Breaking Down Gender Stereotypes in Media and Toys So That Our Children Can Explore, Learn, and Dream without Limits," White House, April 6, 2016, https://www.whitehouse.gov/the-press-office/2016/04/06/factsheet-breaking-down-gender-stereotypes-media-and-toys-so-our.
46. Naomi Schaefer Riley, "The Tuth about Boys and Girls, Toys and TV," *New York Post*, July 28, 2016, http://nypost.com/2016/07/28/the-truth-about-girls-and-boys-toys-and-tv/.
47. "Tell LEGO to Stop Selling Out Girls! #LiberateLEGO," Change.org, https://www.change.org/p/tell-lego-to-stop-selling-out-girls-liberatelego.
48. Susanna Kim, "Lego Friends Triples Sales despite Feminist Critique," ABC News, September 3, 2012, http://abcnews.go.com/blogs/business/2012/09/lego-friends-triples-sales-to-girls-despite-feminist-critique/.

CHAPTER 2: DENYING THE DIFFERENCE

1. "Sex/Gender," *AMA Manual of Style: A Guide for Authors and Editors*, 10th ed. (Oxford: Oxford University Press, 2007), http://www.amamanualofstyle.com/view/10.1093/jama/9780195176339.001.0001/med-9780195176339-div2-350.

2. "Definition of Terms: Sex, Gender, Gender Identity, Sexual Orientation," *The Guidelines for Psychological Practice with Gay, Lesbian, and Bisexual Clients*, February 18–20, 2011, https://www.apa.org/pi/lgbt/resources/sexuality-definitions.pdf.

3. "Sex Redefined: The Idea of Two Sexes Is Simplistic: Biologists Now Think There Is a Wider Spectrum than That," *Nature*, February 18, 2015, http://www.nature.com/news/sex-redefined-1.16943.

4. "What Do We Mean by 'Sex' and 'Gender'?," World Health Organization, http://apps.who.int/gender/whatisgender/en/.

5. "Sex and Gender-Based Medical Education Summit: A Roadmap for Curricular Innovation," Mayo Clinic, October 18–19, 2015, https://ce.mayo.edu/special-topics-in-health-care/content/sex-and-gender-based-medical-education-summit-roadmap-curricular-innovation.

6. Ethan Grove, "Mayo Co-Sponsors Landmark Summit on Sex and Gender Based Medical Education," Mayo Clinic, October 16, 2015, http://newsnetwork.mayoclinic.org/discussion/mayo-clinic-co-sponsors-landmark-summit-on-sex-and-gender-based-medical-education/.

7. Virginia M. Miller et al., "Embedding Concepts of Sex and Gender Health Differences into Medical Curricula," *Journal of Women's Health*, 22:3 (March 2013): 194–202, https://www.ncbi.nlm.nih.gov/pmc/articles/PMC3601631/.

8. "Exploring the Biological Contributions to Human Health: Does Sex Matter?," Institute of Medicine, 2001, https://www.nationalacademies.org/hmd/~/media/Files/Report%20Files/2003/Exploring-the-Biological-Contributions-to-Human-Health-Does-Sex-Matter/DoesSexMatter8pager.pdf.

9. Miller et al., "Embedding Concepts of Sex and Gender."

10. Ibid.

11. "Sex," *Oxford Dictionaries*, http://www.oxforddictionaries.com/us/definition/american_english/sex.

12. "Gender," *Oxford Dictionaries*, http://www.oxforddictionaries.com/us/definition/american_english/gender.
13. "Sex," *American Heritage Dictionary*, https://www.ahdictionary.com/word/search.html?q=sex.
14. "Sex," Online Etymology Dictionary, http://www.etymonline.com/index.php?term=sex&allowed_in_frame=0.
15. "Gender," Online Etymology Dictionary, http://www.etymonline.com/index.php?allowed_in_frame=0&search=gender.
16. Ibid.
17. "Featured Politics and Social Science Categories," Amazon, https://www.amazon.com/s/ref=lp_283155_nr_n_21?fst=as%3Aoff&rh=n%3A283155%2Cn%3A%211000%2Cn%3A3377866011&bbn=1000&ie=UTF8&qid=1477063574&rnid=1000.
18. Judith Butler, "Sex and Gender in Simone de Beauvoir's *Second Sex*," *Yale French Studies* 72 (1986), https://www.jstor.org/stable/2930225?seq=1#page_scan_tab_contents.
19. The entry on "Feminist Perspectives on Sex and Gender" in the *Stanford Encyclopedia of Philosophy* explains, "One way to interpret Beauvoir's claim that one is not born but rather becomes a woman is to take it as a claim about gender socialisation: females become women through a process whereby they acquire feminine traits and learn feminine behaviour. Masculinity and femininity are thought to be products of nurture or how individuals are brought up. They are *causally constructed* (Haslanger 1995, 98): social forces either have a causal role in bringing gendered individuals into existence or (to some substantial sense) shape the way we are *qua* women and men. And the mechanism of construction is social learning." The *Encyclopedia* also cites another prominent second wave feminist, Kate Millett, who "takes gender differences to have 'essentially cultural, rather than biological bases' that result from differential treatment (1971, 28–9). For her, gender is 'the sum total of the parents', the peers', and the culture's notions of what is appropriate to each

gender by way of temperament, character, interests, status, worth, gesture, and expression' (Millett 1971, 31). Feminine and masculine gender-norms, however, are problematic in that gendered behaviour conveniently fits with and reinforces women's subordination so that women are socialised into subordinate social roles: they learn to be passive, ignorant, docile, emotional helpmeets for men (Millett 1971, 26). However, since these roles are simply learned, we can create more equal societies by 'unlearning' social roles. That is, feminists should aim to diminish the influence of socialisation." "Feminist Perspectives on Sex and Gender," *Stanford Encyclopedia of Philosophy*, January 29, 2016, http://plato.stanford.edu/entries/feminism-gender/.

20. Rebecca Reilly-Cooper, "Gender Is Not a Spectrum," *Aeon*, June 28, 2016, https://aeon.co/essays/the-idea-that-gender-is-a-spectrum-is-a-new-gender-prison.

21. Riki Wilchins, "We'll Win the Bathroom Battle When the Binary Burns," *Advocate*, April 29, 2016, http://www.advocate.com/commentary/2016/4/29/well-win-bathroom-battle-when-binary-burns.

22. Jen Yamato, "Inside Kesha's Battle against Dr. Luke: Allegations of Rape, Sketchy Deleted Photos, and More," Daily Beast, February 23, 2016, http://www.thedailybeast.com/articles/2016/02/23/inside-kesha-s-battle-against-dr-luke-allegations-of-rape-sketchy-deleted-photos-and-more.html.

23. Joe Coscarelli, "New York State Judge Rejects Kesha's Claims in Dr. Luke's Case," *New York Times*, April 7, 2016, http://www.nytimes.com/2016/04/07/arts/new-york-state-judge-rejects-keshas-claims-in-dr-luke-case.html?_r=0.

24. Reilly-Cooper, "Gender Is Not a Spectrum."

25. Charles Pope, "Our Bodies Reveal Things about God and His Creation," *National Catholic Register*, May 10, 2016, http://www.ncregister.com/site/article/our-bodies-reveal-things-about-god-and-his-creation/.

26. Jocelyn McClurg, "John Gray Looks Back at 'Men Are from Mars,'" *USA Today*, October 30, 2013, http://www.usatoday.com/story/life/books/2013/10/30/men-are-from-mars-women-are-from-venus/3297375/.

27. "The Top 100 Bestselling Books of All Time: How Does Fifty Shades of Grey Compare?," Data Blog, http://www. theguardian.com/news/datablog/2012/aug/09/best-selling-books-all-time-fifty-shades-grey-compare.

28. Markus MacGill, "Oxytocin: What Is It and What Does It Do?," Medicla News Today, September 21, 2015, http://www. medicalnewstoday.com/articles/275795.php.

29. Navneet Magon and Sanjay Kalra, "The Orgasmic History of Oxytocin: Love, Lust, and Labor," *Indian Journal of Endocrinology and Metabolism* 15: Suppl3 (September 2011), S156-61, http://www.ncbi.nlm.nih.gov/pmc/articles/ PMC3183515/.

30. Tori DeAngelis, "The Two Faces of Oxytocin: Why Does the 'Tend and Befriend' Hormone Come into Play at the Best and Worst of Times?," *American Psychological Association Science Watch* 39:2 (February 2008), 30, http://www.apa.org/ monitor/feb08/oxytocin.aspx.

31. Barbara F. Meltz, "Hooking Up Is the Rage, but Is It Healthy?," *Boston Globe*, February 13, 2007, http://archive. boston.com/yourlife/relationships/articles/2007/02/13/ hooking_up_is_the_rage_but_is_it_healthy/.

32. Katie Haller, "The Truth Behind Why Women Find It Harder to Have Casual Sex than Men Do," Elite Daily, April 18, 2014, http://elitedaily.com/women/oxytocin-science-makes-harder-women-casual-sex/.

33. Maya Szalavitz, "How Ocytocin Makes Men (Almost) Monogamous," *Time*, November 27, 2013, http://healthland. time.com/2013/11/27/how-oxytocin-makes-men-almost-monogamous/.

34. Lindsay Abrams, "Study: Oxytocin ('the Love Hormone') Makes Men in Relationships Want to Stay Away from Other Women," *Atlantic*, November 16, 2012, http://www. theatlantic.com/health/archive/2012/11/study-oxytocin-the-love-hormone-makes-men-in-relationships-want-to-stay-away-from-other-women/265314/.

35. "Biological Evidence May Support Idea That Women Talk More than Men," Huffington Post, February 22, 2013, http://www.huffingtonpost.com/2013/02/21/women-talk-more-than-men-study_n_2734215.html.

36. "Language Protein Differs in Males, Females," Society for Science, February 20, 2013, http://www.sfn.org/Press-Room/News-Release-Archives/2013/Language-Protein.

37. Kate Wheeling, "The Brains of Men and Women Aren't Really That Different, Study Finds," *Science*, November 30, 2015, http://www.sciencemag.org/news/2015/11/brains-men-and-women-aren-t-really-different-study-finds.

38. Karen Kaplan, "There's No Such Thing as a 'Male Brain' or 'Female Brain,' and Scientists Have the Scans to Prove It," *Los Angeles Times*, November 30, 2015, http://www.latimes.com/science/sciencenow/la-sci-sn-no-male-female-brain-20151130-story.html.

39. Louann Brizendine, "Love, Sex, and the Male Brain," CNN March 25, 2010, http://www.cnn.com/2010/OPINION/03/23/brizendine.male.brain/.

40. Jesse L. Hawke et al., "Gender Ratios for Reading Difficulties," *Dyslexia* 15:3 (August 2009), 239–42, http://www.ncbi.nlm.nih.gov/pmc/articles/PMC2739722/.

41. Georgetown University Medical Center, "Brain Anatomy of Dyslexia Is Not the Same in Men and Women, Boys and Girls," Science Daily, May 8, 2013, https://www.sciencedaily.com/releases/2013/05/130508131831.htm.

42. Ehud Yairi, "On the Gender Factor in Stuttering," The Stuttering Foundation, Fall 2005, http://www.stutteringhelp.org/gender-factor-stuttering.

43. "Women and Sleep," National Sleep Foundation, https://sleepfoundation.org/sleep-topics/women-and-sleep.

44. Susan Stamberg, "Girls Are Taught to 'Think Pink,' but That Wasn't Always So," NPR, April 1, 2014, http://www.npr.org/2014/04/01/297159948/girls-are-taught-to-think-pink-but-that-wasnt-always-so.

45. Russell Goldman, "Here' a List of 58 Gender Options for Facebook Users," ABC News, February 13, 2014, http://

abcnews.go.com/blogs/headlines/2014/02/heres-a-list-of-58-gender-options-for-facebook-users/.

46. Facebook Diversity, https://www.facebook.com/facebookdiversity/posts/774221582674346.
47. Dannielle Owens-Reid and Kristin Russo, "Facebook's New Gender Terms, Explained," *Cosmopolitan*, February 17, 2014, http://www.cosmopolitan.com/lifestyle/news/a5630/facebook-gender-terms/.
48. Fiona Macdonald, "The Ultimate 21st-Century Word?," BBC, June 23, 2016, http://www.bbc.com/culture/story/20160623-the-ultimate-21st-century-word.
49. "German MP Speaks Out on Diversity Bill, Addressing 60 Genders (VIDEO)," RT, June 22, 2016, https://www.rt.com/viral/347812-germany-gender-bill-afd/.

CHAPTER 3: PASSED-OUT GIRLS IN SHOPPING CARTS

1. James Gordon, "Vox Changes Its Tone," *Tufts Observer*, October 15, 2014, http://tuftsobserver.org/vox-changes-its-tone/.
2. Belle Knox, "In Defense of Kink: My First Role as the Duke Porn Star Was on a Rough Sex Website, and No, That Doesn't Make Me a Bad Feminist," *xoJane*, March 18, 2014, http://www.xojane.com/sex/belle-knox-duke-porn-star-rough-sex-feminism-kink.
3. Alex Morris, "The Blue Devil in Miss Belle Knox: Meet Duke Porn Star Miriam Weeks, *Rolling Stone*, April 23, 2014, http://www.rollingstone.com/culture/news/the-blue-devil-in-miss-belle-knox-meet-duke-porn-star-miriam-weeks-20140423.
4. Natalie Dylan, "Why I'm Selling My Virginity," Daily Beast, January 23, 2009, http://www.thedailybeast.com/articles/2009/01/23/why-im-selling-my-virginity.html.
5. Nancy Jo Sales, "Daddies, 'Dates,' and the Girlfriend Experience: Welcome to the New Prostitution Economy," *Vanity Fair*, August 2016, http://www.vanityfair.com/style/2016/07/welcome-to-the-new-prostitution-economy.

6. Caroline Kitchener, "How Sugar Daddies Are Financing College Education," *Atlantic*, September 19, 2014, http://www.theatlantic.com/education/archive/2014/09/how-sugar-daddies-are-financing-college-education/379533/.

7. Sales, "Daddies, 'Dates,' and the Girlfriend Experience."

8. Dylan, "Why I'm Selling My Virginity."

9. Ibid.

10. "'Why Should I Wait Any Longer?': Student Auctions Her VIRGINITY Online to Pay Her Tuition Fees—and Bids Start at £130K," *Daily Mail*, September 28, 2016, http://www.dailymail.co.uk/femail/article-3811309/Student-auctions-virginity-online-130-000.html.

11. Angelica Bonus, "Fraternity Pledges' Chant Raises Concerns at Yale," CNN, October 18, 2010, http://www.cnn.com/2010/US/10/18/connecticut.yale.frat.chant/.

12. Lisa W. Foderaro, "At Yale, Sharper Look at Treatment of Women," *New York Times*, April 7, 2011, http://www.nytimes.com/2011/04/08/nyregion/08yale.html?mtrref=undefined&gwh=0DC9A6DD70E6C47BB1DA6DB6D8919D12&gwt=pay.

13. Nicole Allan, "Title IX Investigation into Climate for Women at Yale," *Yale Alumni Magazine*, May/June 2011, https://yalealumnimagazine.com/articles/3147/span-title-ix-investigation-into-climate-for-women-at-yale-span.

14. Sandra Y. L. Korn, "When No Means Yes," *Harvard Crimson*, November 12, 2010, http://www.thecrimson.com/article/2010/11/12/yale-dke-harvard-womens/.

15. "Queer: Common Questions," Wesleyan University, http://www.wesleyan.edu/queer/commonquestions.html.

16. "Pronouns—a How to Guide," University of Wisconsin Milwaukee, 2011, http://dc.uwm.edu/cgi/viewcontent.cgi?article=1000&context=lgbt_instruct.

17. Julie Scelfo, "A University Recognizes a Third Gender: Neutral," *New York Times*, February 3, 2015, http://www.nytimes.com/2015/02/08/education/edlife/a-university-recognizes-a-third-gender-neutral.html?_

r=0&module=ArrowsNav&contentCollection=Education%20
Life&action=keypress&region=FixedLeft&pgtype=article.

18. Katherine Timpf, "Wesleyan Now Offering
LGBTTQQFAGPBDSM Housing (Not a Typo)," *National
Review*, February 25, 2015, http://www.nationalreview.com/
article/414398/weslyan-offering-lgbttqqfagpbdsm-housing-
not-typo-katherine-timpf.

19. Scelfo, "A University Recognizes a Third Gender."

20. Steven Petrow, "Gender-Neutral Pronouns: When 'They'
Doesn't Identify as Either Male or Female, *Washington Post*,
October 27, 2014, https://www.washingtonpost.com/lifestyle/
style/gender-neutral-pronouns-when-they-doesnt-identify-as-
either-male-or-female/2014/10/27/41965f5e-5ac0-11e4-b812-
38518ae74c67_story.html.

21. The Writing Center, "Gender-Sensitive Language," UNC
College of Arts & Sciences, http://writingcenter.unc.edu/
files/2012/09/Gender-Sensitive-Language-The-Writing-Center.
pdf.

22. The Writing Center, "Gender-Sensitive Language," University
of North Carolina, http://writingcenter.unc.edu/files/2012/09/
Gender-Sensitive-Language-The-Writing-Center.pdf.

23. Scott Jaschik, "What Larry Summers Said," *Inside Higher
Ed*, February 18, 2005, https://www.insidehighered.com/
news/2005/02/18/summers2_18; Wendy Wang, "Mothers and
Work: What's 'Ideal'?," Pew Research Center, August 19,
2013, http://www.pewresearch.org/fact-tank/2013/08/19/
mothers-and-work-whats-ideal/.

24. Sara Rimer, "A 'Rebellious Daughter' to Lead Harvard," *New
York Times*, February 12, 2007, http://www.nytimes.
com/2007/02/12/education/12harvard.html?_r=0.

25. Jodi Kantor, "Harvard Business School Case Study: Gender
Equity," *New York Times*, September 7, 2013, http://www.
nytimes.com/2013/09/08/education/harvard-case-study-
gender-equity.html?pagewanted=all&_r=0.

26. C. Ramsey Fahs, "In Historic Move, Harvard to Penalize
Final Clubs, Greek Organizations," *Harvard Crimson*, May

8, 2016, http://www.thecrimson.com/article/2016/5/6/college-sanctions-clubs-greeklife/.

27. Nick Anderson and Justin Wm. Moyer, "Harvard Intensifies Battle against Single-Gender Clubs," *Washington Post*, May 6, 2016, https://www.washingtonpost.com/news/grade-point/wp/2016/05/06/harvard-intensifies-battle-against-single-gender-clubs/.

28. The Costume King, "CEOs & Office Hoes," College Party Guru, http://collegepartyguru.com/themes/pages.php?link=CEOs_Office_Hoes.

29. Martha Sorren, "10 Sorority Rush Hazing Horror Stories That Will make You Think Twice about Pledging," *Bustle*, March 25, 2004, http://www.bustle.com/articles/16574-10-sorority-rush-hazing-horror-stories-that-will-make-you-think-twice-about-pledging.

30. Anderson and Moyer, "Harvard Intensifies Battle."

31. Juliet Lapidos, "Sororities Should Throw Parties," *New York Times*, January 20, 2015, http://www.nytimes.com/2015/01/21/opinion/sororities-should-throw-parties.html?_r=0.

32. Naomi Schafer Riley, "Harvard Tells Its Women: Go Where the Rapes Are," *New York Post*, March 14, 2016, http://nypost.com/2016/03/14/harvard-tells-its-women-go-where-the-rapes-are/.

33. Caitlin Flannagan, "The Dark Power of Fraternities," *Atlantic*, March 2014, http://www.theatlantic.com/magazine/archive/2014/03/the-dark-power-of-fraternities/357580/.

34. Riley, "Harvard Tells Its Women."

35. Kim Bellware, "Gender-Neutral Bathrooms Are Quietly Becoming the New Thing at Colleges," Huffington Post, July 18, 2014, http://www.huffingtonpost.com/2014/07/18/gender-neutral-bathrooms-colleges_n_5597362.html; Scott Jaschick, "A Bathroom of Her Own," *Inside Higher Ed*, December 21, 2009, https://www.insidehighered.com/news/2009/12/21/bathrooms.

36. "List of Colleges with Gender Neutral Housing," College Equality Index, http://www.collegeequalityindex.org/list-colleges-gender-neutral-housing?page=1.

37. Barbara Booth, "One of the Most Dangerous Places for Women in America," CNBC, September 22, 2015, http://www.cnbc.com/2015/09/22/college-rape-crisis-in-america-under-fire.html.

38. Maureen Downey, "What Colleges Don't Tell You: Most Campus Sexual Assaults Happen in Dorms; Freshmen Particularly Vulnerable," *Atlanta Journal-Constitution*, April 11, 2016, http://getschooled.blog.myajc.com/2016/04/11/what-colleges-dont-tell-you-most-campus-sexual-assaults-happen-in-dorms-freshmen-particularly-vulnerable/.

39. "Analysis of College Campus Rape and Sexual Assault Reports, 2000–2011," Massachusetts Executive Office of Public Safety and Security, Office of Grants and Research, Research and Policy Analysis Division, September 2012, http://www.mass.gov/eopss/docs/ogr/lawenforce/analysis-of-college-campus-rape-and-sexual-assault-reports-2000-2011-finalcombined.pdf.

40. John Garvey, "Why We're Going Back to Single-Sex Dorms," *Wall Street Journal*, June 13, 2011, http://www.wsj.com/articles/SB10001424052702304432304576369843592242356.

41. Brit Peterson, "The Unintended Consequences of Catholic University's Sex Experiment," *Washingtonian*, November 4, 2014, https://www.washingtonian.com/2014/11/04/the-unintended-consequences-of-catholic-universitys-sex-experiment/.

42. Interview of John Garvey by the author on July 22, 2016.

43. "Harvard's Final Insult: The University Will Ban Students from Governing Their Own Social Lives," *Wall Street Journal*, April 17, 2016, http://www.wsj.com/articles/harvards-final-insult-1460759189.

44. Justin Wm. Moyer, "Harvard Women Protest Sanctions on Single-Gender Clubs," *Washington Post*, May 9, 2016, https://

www.washingtonpost.com/news/grade-point/wp/2016/05/09/
harvard-women-protest-sanctions-on-single-gender-clubs/.
45. Ibid.

CHAPTER 4: FEMMES FATALES

1. Associated Press, "Women Allowed on Submarines," *New York Times*, April 30, 2010, http://www.nytimes.com/2010/04/30/us/30brfs-WOMENALLOWED_BRF.html?_r=0.
2. Luis Martinez, "Smooth Sailing for 1st Women to Serve on Navy Submarines," ABC News, May 24, 2012, http://abcnews.go.com/blogs/politics/2012/05/smooth-sailing-for-first-women-to-serve-on-navy-submarines/.
3. Meghann Myers, "Navy: Sophisticated Sub Ring Repeatedly Filmed Women," *USA Today*, December 9, 2015, http://www.usatoday.com/story/news/nation-now/2015/12/09/navy-sophisticated-sub-ring-repeatedly-filmed-women/77068836/.
4. Meghann Myers, "Navy: Women Secretly Filmed in Shower aboard Sub," *Navy Times*, December 3, 2014, http://www.navytimes.com/story/military/crime/2014/12/03/submarine-wyoming-women-camera-shower/19827247/.
5. Steven Beardsley, "Navy: USS Wyoming Shower Videos Hard to Prevent," *Stars and Stripes*, November 12, 2015, http://www.stripes.com/news/navy-uss-wyoming-shower-videos-hard-to-prevent-1.378504.
6. Commander, Submarine Forces Public Affairs, "Navy Policy Will Allow Women to Serve aboard Submarines," America's Navy, April 29, 2010, http://www.navy.mil/submit/display.asp?story_id=52954.
7. Matthew Roseberg and Dave Philipps, "All Combat Roles Now Open to Women, Defense Secretary Says," *New York Times*, December 3, 2015, http://www.nytimes.com/2015/12/04/us/politics/combat-military-women-ash-carter.html?_r=0.
8. Elisabeth Bumiller and Thom Shanker, "Pentagon Is Set to Lift Combat Ban for Women," *New York Times*, January 23,

2013, http://www.nytimes.com/2013/01/24/us/pentagon-says-it-is-lifting-ban-on-women-in-combat.html.

9. "Marine Corps Force Integration Plan—Summary," https://www.documentcloud.org/documents/2394531-marine-corps-force-integration-plan-summary.html.

10. "Presidential Commission on the Assignment of Women in the Armed Forces: Report to the President," November 15, 1992, http://babel.hathitrust.org/cgi/pt?id=umn.31951d00277676f;view=1up;seq=68.

11. Luke Sharrett, "Women in the Infantry? Forget about It, Says Female Marine Officer," NBC News, July 12, 2012, http://usnews.nbcnews.com/_news/2012/07/12/12684555-women-in-the-infantry-forget-about-it-says-female-marine-officer?lite.

12. Thomas Neven, "Putting Women in Combat Endangers More Lives," *Federalist*, December 7, 2015, http://thefederalist.com/2015/12/07/putting-women-in-combat-endangers-more-lives/.

13. See, for example, Tom Bowman, "Controversial Marine Corps Study on Gender Integration Published in Full," NPR, November 4, 2015, http://www.npr.org/sections/thetwo-way/2015/11/04/454672813/controversial-marine-corps-study-on-gender-integration-published-in-full and Stassa Edwards, "Marine Corps Study on Women in Combat 'Flawed' and Incomplete," *Jezebel*, October 17, 2015, http://jezebel.com/marine-corps-study-on-women-in-combat-flawed-and-incomp-1737108138.

14. Aaron McLean, "Ray Mabus Can't Handle the Truth," *Weekly Standard*, September 28, 2015, http://www.weeklystandard.com/ray-mabus-cant-handle-the-truth/article/1032570.

15. "Navy Secretary Believes Combat Positions Should Be Open to Qualified Women," NPR, September 11, 2015, http://www.npr.org/2015/09/11/439381272/navy-secretary-ray-mabus-takes-issue-with-marine-combat-study.

16. "Marine Force Integration Plan—Summary," https://www. documentcloud.org/documents/2394531-marine-corps-force-integration-plan-summary.html.

17. Thomas Gibbons-Neff, "Navy Secretary 'Threw Us under the Bus' Say Marines in Gender-Integrated Infantry Unit," Stars and Stripes, September 14, 2015, http://www.stripes.com/news/us/navy-secretary-threw-us-under-the-bus-say-marines-in-gender-integrated-infantry-unit-1.368066/.

18. Hope Hodge Seck, "Marine War Hero: SecNav 'Off Base' on Women in Combat," *Marine Corps Times*, September 14, 2015, https://www.marinecorpstimes.com/story/military/2015/09/14/marine-war-hero-secnav-off-base-women-combat/72251362/.

19. Thomas Gibbons-Neff, "Secretary of the Navy 'Threw Us under the Bus,' Say Marines in Gender-Integrated Infantry Unit," *Washington Post*, September 14, 2015, https://www.washingtonpost.com/news/checkpoint/wp/2015/09/14/navy-secretary-threw-us-under-the-bus-say-marines-in-gender-integrated-infantry-unit/.

20. The Scrapbook, "Mabus Strikes Again (Marines Hardest Hit)," *Weekly*, January 18, 2016, http://www.weeklystandard.com/mabus-strikes-again/article/2000481.

21. Bill Chappell, "Pentagon Says Women Can Now Serve in Front-Line Ground Combat Positions," NPR, December 3, 2015, http://www.npr.org/sections/thetwo-way/2015/12/03/458319524/pentagon-will-allow-women-in-frontline-ground-combat-positions.

22. The Scrapbook, "Mabus Strikes Again."

23. Jude Eden, "The Many Problems with Coed Marine Boot Camp: Goodbye High Standards, Hello Misconduct," Polizette, January 13, 2016, http://lifezette.com/polizette/the-perils-of-coed-marine-boot-camp/.

24. Aaron MacLean, "Coed Boot Camp: Who Will Defend the Marines?," *Weekly Standard*, January 25, 2016, http://www.weeklystandard.com/co-ed-boot-camp/article/2000598.

25. Richard Leiby, "The Marines Pull-Up Controversy: An Unexpected Battle in the Gender Wars," *Washington Post*, January 1, 2014, https://www.washingtonpost.com/lifestyle/style/the-marines-pull-up-controversy-an-unexpected-battle-in-the-gender-wars/2014/01/01/8d5e7f7a-726d-11e3-8b3f-b1666705ca3b_story.html.
26. "Marine Corps Force Integration Plan."
27. Stew Smith, "USMC PFT Score Charts," Military.com, http://www.military.com/military-fitness/marine-corps-fitness-requirements/usmc-pft-charts.
28. Jude Eden, "The Many Problems with Coed Marine Bootcamp: Goodbye High Standards, Hello Misconduct," Lifezette, January 13, 2016, http://www.lifezette.com/polizette/the-perils-of-coed-marine-boot-camp/.
29. Hope Hodge Seck, "Marine Corps Rolls Out Biggest Fitness Standard Overhaul in 40 Years," Military.com, July 1, 2016, http://www.military.com/daily-news/2016/07/01/marine-corps-rolls-biggest-fitness-standard-overhaul-40-years.html.
30. Lance M. Bacon and Gina Harkins, "11 Things Marines Need to Know about the New PFT, CFT, and Body Composition Rules," *Marine Times*, July 1, 2016, http://www.marinecorpstimes.com/story/military/2016/07/01/11-things-marines-need-know-corps-new-fitness-rules/86582012/.
31. Seck, "Marine Corps Rolls Out Biggest Fitness Standard Overhaul."
32. "General Warns: Military Will Face 'Great Pressure' to Lower Standards for Women in Combat to Please 'Agenda-Driven' in D.C.," CNS News, January 9, 2016, http://www.cnsnews.com/news/article/cnsnewscom-staff/general-warns-military-will-lower-standards-women-combat-please-agenda.
33. Seck, ""Marine Corps Rolls Out Biggest Fitness Standard Overhaul."
34. Eden, "The Many Problems."
35. Derrick Perkins, "Mabus: 1 in 4 Marine Recruits Should Be Women," *Marine Times*, May 26, 2015, http://www.

marinecorpstimes.com/story/military/2015/05/26/diversifying-the-marine-corps/27606749/.

36. Thomas Gibbons-Neff, "How Marine Corps Boot Camp Became the New Battlefield for Gender Integration in the Military," *Washington Post,* January 8, 2016, https://www.washingtonpost.com/news/checkpoint/wp/2016/01/08/how-marine-corps-boot-camp-became-the-new-battlefield-for-gender-integration-in-the-military/.

37. Chappell, "Pentagon Says Women Can Now Serve."

38. Neven, "Putting Women in Combat."

39. "Democratic Primary Debate at the Citadel, Sponsored by Youtube and CNN: On Homeland Security," ontheissues.org, July 23, 2007, http://www.ontheissues.org/Archive/2007_YouTube_Dems_Homeland_Security.htm.

40. Theodore Schleifer, "Ted Cruz: Making U.S. Women Eligible to Be Drafted Is 'Nuts,'" CNN, February 8, 2016, http://www.cnn.com/2016/02/07/politics/ted-cruz-drafting-women-nuts/.

41. Richard Sisk, "Women Will Likely Have to Register for the Draft, Army Secretary Says," Military.com, October 12, 2015, http://www.military.com/daily-news/2015/10/12/women-likely-have-register-draft-army-secretary-says.html.

42. "Selective Service System: Official Site of the United States Government," https://www.sss.gov/.

43. Jennifer Steinhauer, "Senate Votes to Require Women to Register for the Draft," *New York Times,* June 14, 2016, http://www.nytimes.com/2016/06/15/us/politics/congress-women-military-draft.html?_r=0.

44. Mary Eberstadt, "Mothers in Combat Boots," *Policy Review,* February 1, 2010, http://www.hoover.org/research/mothers-combat-boots.

45. Interview of Aaron MacLean by the author on March 4, 2016.

46. Michael S. Schmidt, "Pentagon to Offer Plan to Store Eggs and Sperm to Retain Young Troops," *New York Times,* February 3, 2016, http://www.nytimes.com/2016/02/04/us/

politics/pentagon-to-offer-plan-to-store-eggs-and-sperm-to-retain-young-troops.html?_r=0.

47. Ian Duncan, "Female Midshipmen to Wear Trousers, Not Skirts, at Graduation," *Baltimore Sun*, February 23, 2016, http://www.baltimoresun.com/news/maryland/bs-md-naval-academy-pants-20160223-story.html.

CHAPTER 5: FIGHTING FIRE WITH FEMALES

1. Scott Stump, "Meet the Hero Dad Who Saved His Son from Being Hit by a Flying Baseball Bat, *Today*, March 8, 2016, http://www.today.com/parents/meet-hero-dad-who-saved-his-son-being-hit-flying-t78556.

2. "Injuries, Illnesses, and Fatalities: Firefighter Factsheet," Bureau of Labor Statistics, July 2013, http://www.bls.gov/iif/oshwc/cfoi/osar0017.htm.

3. Anna Merlan, "The FDNY Is a Force of More than 10,000. Can You Guess How Many Are Women?," *Village Voice*, February 12, 2014, http://www.villagevoice.com/news/the-fdny-is-a-force-of-more-than-10-000-can-you-guess-how-many-are-women-6440901.

4. Joseph P. Fried, "Women Win Ruling on Fire Dept. Test," *New York Times*, March 6, 1982, http://www.nytimes.com/1982/03/06/nyregion/women-win-ruling-on-fire-dept-test.html.

5. Norman D. Henderson et al., "Field Measures of Strength and Fitness Predict Firefighter Performance on Physically Demanding Tasks," *Personnel Psychology* 60 (2007): 431–73, https://home.ubalt.edu/tmitch/645/Predictors/FIELD%20MEASURES%20OF%20STRENGTH%20AND%20FITNESS.pdf.

6. "Fire Service Joint Labor Management Wellness-Fitness Task Force Candidate Physical Ability Test Summary," IAFF Firefighters, http://www.iaff.org/hs/cpat/cpat_index.html.

7.   Denise M. Hulett et al., "A National Report Card on Women in Firefighting," April 2008, https://i-women.org/wp-content/uploads/2014/07/35827WSP.pdf.

8.   The changes are detailed on the IAFF website:

> All candidates will attend at least two mandatory orientation sessions commencing within eight weeks before the actual official CPAT test date, during which they will receive "hands on" familiarity with the actual CPAT apparatus. Candidates may voluntarily attend up to one additional orientation session.

> Within 30 days prior to the actual CPAT test date, all candidates will perform at least 2 timed practice runs, using actual CPAT apparatus, and in which the candidate is allowed to take as much time as necessary to complete the entire course.

> A candidate may waive all of the fore-mentioned program components and be eligible to participate in a CPAT test. Such a waiver shall only be acceptable if it is in writing, and is made on a wholly knowing and voluntary basis.

> During the orientations and practice runs certified Peer Fitness Trainers, fitness professionals and/or CPAT trained fire fighters (proctors) will be present to help all candidates understand the test elements and how they can improve their physical performance and conditioning prior to taking the test.

> "Fire Service Summary."

9.   "IAFF Signs CPAT Conciliation Agreement with EEOC," *Indiana Professional Firefighters Newsletter*, summer 2006, p. 8, http://www.pffui.com/news/Fall_06.pdf.

10. "The Fire Service Joint Labor Management Wellness-Fitness Task Force Candidate Physical Ability Test," 2nd ed., International Association of Firefighters, 2007, p. 6, http://www.iaff.org/et/becomeff/documents/cpatmanual-lorez.pdf.

11. Barbara Russo, who directs the Fire and Emergency Services Administration program at North Carolina's Fayetteville State

University and has studied gender issues in firefighting, told the *Dallas Morning News* in 2015 that the CPAT "tends to weed women out." Todd Davis, "Female Firefighters Are Few, Far Between in D-FW Station Houses," *Dallas News*, November 29, 2016, http://www.dallasnews.com/news/headlines/20151129-female-firefighters-are-few-far-between-in-local-station-houses.ece. A recent report in the *Kansas City Star* echoes Russo's assessment. Jill Sederstrom, "Just Part of the Team: Female Firefighters," *Kansas City Star*, January 26, 2016, http://www.kansascity.com/news/local/community/joco-913/article56575658.html#1.

12. Christine Pelisek, "Women Firefighters: The Gender Boondoggle," *LA Weekly*, January 23, 2008, http://www.laweekly.com/news/women-firefighters-the-gender-boondoggle-2151639.

13. Susan Edelman, "FDNY Recruit Failed Her Way into $81,000 Desk Job," *New York Post*, July 26, 2015, http://nypost.com/2015/07/26/fdny-recruit-failed-her-way-into-81000-desk-job/; "FDNY Rookie Who Failed Physical Tests Injured 10 Days into Job," FireRescue1, November 23, 2015, http://www.firerescue1.com/health/articles/31267018-FDNY-rookie-who-failed-physical-tests-injured-10-days-into-job/.

14. Pelisek, "Women Firefighters."

15. Susan Edelman, "Woman to Become NY Firefighter Despite Failing Crucial Fitness Test," *New York Post*, May 3, 2015, http://nypost.com/2015/05/03/woman-to-become-ny-firefighter-despite-failing-crucial-fitness-test/.

16. Susan Edelman, "Woman Who Failed FDNY Physical Test 6 Times Gets Another Chance," *New York Post*, December 27, 2015, http://nypost.com/2015/12/27/unfireable-female-firefighter-returns-to-the-fdny/.

17. Betsy McCaughey, "Perils of the Push for Female Firefighters," *New York Post*, May 5, 2015, http://nypost.com/2015/05/05/fdnys-unfit-the-perils-of-pushing-women-into-firefighting/.

18. Jay Newton-Small, "There Is a Simple Solution to America's Policing Problem: More Female Cops," *Time*, July 14, 2016,

http://time.com/4406327/police-shootings-women-female-cops/.

19. Peter Horne, "Policewomen: Their First Century and the New Era," *Police Chief*, September 2016, http://www. policechiefmagazine.org/magazine/index.cfm?article_ id=1000&fuseaction=display.

20. Dean Scoville, "The First Female Patrol Officers," *Police*, September 21, 2012, http://www.policemag.com/channel/ women-in-law-enforcement/articles/2012/09/the-first-female-patrol-officers.aspx.

21. Susan Ehrlich Martin and Nancy J. Jurik, *Doing Justice, Doing Gender: Women in Legal and Criminal Justice Occupations*, second edition (Sage Publications, 2006). Quotations are from page 55.

22. Val Van Brocklin, "Physical Fitness Double Standards for Male and Female Cops?," PoliceOne.com, December 8, 2013, https://www.policeone.com/patrol-issues/articles/6681168-Physical-fitness-double-standards-for-male-and-female-cops/.

23. Some departments ask applicants to complete a timed obstacle course meant to mimic chasing a suspect, drag a human dummy a certain number of feet, and/or scale a five- or six-foot wall. "Tearing Down the Wall: Problems with Consistency, Validity, and Adverse Impact of Physical Agility Testing in Police Selection," National Center for Women & Policing, spring 2003, pp. 4–5, http://womenandpolicing.com/ pdf/PhysicalAgilityStudy.pdf; Stew Smith, "The 'Common PFT,'" Military.com, http://www.military.com/military-fitness/fitness-test-prep/common-pft.

24. "Tearing Down the Wall," p. 5, http://womenandpolicing. com/pdf/PhysicalAgilityStudy.pdf. As of 2003, according to a limited survey of departments, "less than one-third of the [55 surveyed] agencies [that use physical agility testing of some kind] use gender norming (27.3%) and/or age norming (25.5%) as part of their scoring procedure."

25. "General Information on How to Become a Law Enforcement Officer," Michigan Commission on Law Enforcement

Standards, http://www.michigan.gov/mco
les/0,4607,7-229-41624_43155—-,00.html.

26. "Physical Fitness Test," Michigan Commission on Law
Enforcement Standards, http://www.michigan.gov/
mcoles/0,1607,7-229—147713—,00.html; "Police Academy
Application Instructions 2015–2016," Kellogg Community
College, p. 31, http://www.kellogg.edu/wp-content/
uploads/2013/10/2015-Academy-Application.pdf.

27. When the FBI reinstated physical fitness testing in 2015, its
standards varied by age and gender. Claire Zillman, "So You
Want to Be an FBI Agent? Here's What It Takes," *Fortune*,
April 6, 2015, http://fortune.com/2015/04/06/fbi-agent-
fitness-test/.

28. Marc Levy, "U.S. Sues Pa. State Police, Saying Physical Fitness
Test Discriminates against Women," Associated Press, July 30,
2014, http://www.pennlive.com/midstate/index.ssf/2014/07/
us_sues_pa_state_police_saying.html.

29. Ibid.

30. Michael Muskal, "Pennsylvania State Police Fights Suit
Alleging Discrimination," *Los Angeles Times*, July 30, 2014,
http://www.latimes.com/nation/nationnow/la-na-nn-
pennsylvania-state-police-doj-20140730-story.html.

31. Pam Zubeck, "Female Cops Sue over Fitness Test," *Colorado
Springs Independent*, May 1, 2015, http://www.csindy.com/
IndyBlog/archives/2015/05/01/female-cops-sue-over-fitness-
test.

32. Ibid.; "Springs Officers Will No Longer Take Fitness Tests
after Discrimination Lawsuit," CBS Denver, November 10,
2015, http://denver.cbslocal.com/2015/11/10/female-springs-
officers-win-lawsuit-no-longer-have-to-take-physical-fitness-
tests/.

33. Ama Sarfo, "DOJ Settles Police Discrimination Suit with
Corpus Christi," Law 360, May 16, 2013, http://www.
law360.com/articles/442086/doj-settles-police-discrimination-
suit-with-corpus-christi.

34. Tessa Berenson, "FBI Head Calls Lack of Data on Police Shootings 'Embarrassing,'" *Time*, October 8, 2015, http://time.com/4406327/police-shootings-women-female-cops/ and https://www.washingtonpost.com/graphics/national/police-shootings/.

35. "Men, Women, and Police Excessive Force: A Tale of Two Genders," The National Center for Women & Policing, April 2002, http://womenandpolicing.com/PDF/2002_Excessive_Force.pdf.

36. Interview of Lieutenant Colonel Matthew Bucholz by the author on November 6, 2016.

37. Newton-Small, "There Is a Simple Solution."

38. Interview of Bucholz.

39. "Tale of Two Genders."

40. Drake Baer, "If You Want Less Police Violence, Hire More Female Cops," *New York* magazine, July 15, 2016, http://nymag.com/scienceofus/2016/07/more-female-cops-less-police-violence.html.

41. Jay Newton-Small, "There Is a Simple Solution to America's Policing Proglem: More Female Cops," *Time*, July 14, 2016, http://time.com/4406327/police-shootings-women-female-cops/.

42. Baer, "If You Want Less Police Violence."

43. Interview of Bucholz.

CHAPTER 6: VALLEY OF THE DOLLS

1. "Chrissy Teigen Shares Why She Chose to Have a Daughter: John 'Deserves That Bond,'" *People*, February 24, 2016, http://celebritybabies.people.com/2016/02/24/chrissy-teigen-john-legend-picked-girl-embryo/?utm_source=popsugar.com&utm_medium=referral&utm_campaign=pubexchange_article.

2. "Sex Selection and Discrimination" in *Gender and Genetics*, World Health Organization Genomic Resource Center, http://www.who.int/genomics/gender/en/index4.html.

3. Ross Douthat, "160 Million and Counting," *New York Times*, June 26, 2011, http://www.nytimes.com/2011/06/27/opinion/27douthat.html?_r=0.

4. Byron Kaye and Khettiya Jittapong, "In Thailand, Baby Gender Selection Loophole Draws China, HK Women to IVF Clinics," Reuters, July 15, 2014, http://www.reuters.com/article/us-thailand-ivf-gender-selection-idUSKBN0FK2H020140715; Jasmeet Sidhu, "How to Buy a Daughter: Choosing the Sex of Your Baby Has Become a Multimillion-Dollar Industry," *Slate*, September 14, 2012, http://www.slate.com/articles/health_and_science/medical_examiner/2012/09/sex_selection_in_babies_through_pgd_americans_are_paying_to_have_daughters_rather_than_sons_.html.

5. Monica Kim, "Should You Select Your Child's Gender? The Debate Surrounding Chrissy Teigen's IVF Reveal," *Vogue*, February 26, 2016, http://www.vogue.com/13406421/chrissy-teigen-ivf-gender-selection-controversy-explained/.

6. Kensington Palace, birth announcement, Twitter, https://twitter.com/kensingtonroyal/status/594443545118924800.

7. "BREAKING NEWS: They Royal Baby Doesn't Have Gender Apparently," imgur, May 15, 2015, http://imgur.com/2xeUTz2.

8. Ashley McGuire, "Gender Confusion: How to Ruin a Royal Birth," *New York Post*, May 8, 2015, http://nypost.com/2015/05/08/gender-confusion-how-to-ruin-a-royal-birth/.

9. Emily Fox, "Royal Wedding One of the Most Watched Events in TV History," *Daily Express*, May 2, 2011, http://www.express.co.uk/news/uk/244200/Royal-Wedding-one-of-most-watched-events-in-TV-history.

10. "You Old Romantics You…72 Million Live Streams in 188 Countries for the Royal Wedding on YouTube," YouTube Official Blog, May 6, 2011, https://youtube.googleblog.com/2011/05/you-old-romantics-you72-million-live.html.

11. Olivia Goldhill, "Kate Middleton: Highs and Lows of Her Popularity," *Telegraph*, September 26, 2014, http://www.

telegraph.co.uk/news/uknews/kate-middleton/11122883/Kate-Middleton-highs-and-lows-of-her-popularity.html.

12. Aida Edemariam, "I Accumulated an Anger That Would Rip a Roof Off," *Guardian*, September 11, 2009, http://www.theguardian.com/theguardian/2009/sep/12/hilary-mantel-booker-prize-interview.

13. Mark Brown and Jane Martinson, "Hilary Mantel Reveals She Fantasised about Killing Margaret Thatcher," *Guardian*, September 19, 2014, https://www.theguardian.com/books/2014/sep/19/hilary-mantel-fantasised-killing-margaret-thatcher.

14. Hilary Mantel, "Royal Bodies," *London Review of Books* 35:4 (February 20, 2013), 3–7, http://www.lrb.co.uk/v35/n04/hilary-mantel/royal-bodies.

15. Charlotte Alter, "Feminists Hang on Prince Dad's Every Word," *Time*, September 15, 2013, http://time.com/2051/prince-william-is-on-dad-parade-but-women-want-kate/.

16. April Daniels Hussar, "Survey: Most College Women Want to Be Married by 30," *Self*, August 30, 2012, http://www.self.com/flash/sex-and-relationships/2012/08/survey-most-college-women-want/.

17. Frank Newport and Joy Wilke, "Desire for Children Still Norm in U.S.," Gallup, September 25, 2013, http://www.gallup.com/poll/164618/desire-children-norm.aspx.

18. Ed Docx, "The Duchess of Cambridge: How Britain Stopped Believing in the Royal Fairytale," *Newsweek*, September 25, 2014, http://www.newsweek.com/2014/10/03/duchess-cambridge-how-britain-stopped-believing-royal-fairytale-273100.html.

19. Alter, "Feminists Hang on Prince Dad's Every Word."

20. Alessandra Stanley, "There's Sex, There's the City, but No Manolos: Lena Dunham's 'Girls' Begins on HBO," *New York Times*, April 12, 2012, http://www.nytimes.com/2012/04/13/arts/television/lena-dunhams-girls-begins-on-hbo.html.

21. Heather Wilhelm, "Commentary: Lena Dunham's Brand of Feminism Is Scarier than Halloween," *Chicago Tribune*,

October 30, 2015, http://www.chicagotribune.com/news/
opinion/commentary/ct-lena-dunham-abortion-steinem-
feminism-wilhelm-perspec-1030-20151029-column.html.

22. Katey Rich, "Lena Dunham Explains Feminism with Nipple
Tape and Armpit Hair," *Vanity Fair*, October 22, 2015, http://
www.vanityfair.com/hollywood/2015/10/lena-dunham-
explains-feminism.

23. "Kate Middleton is pregnant! Will she keep it?" Lena
Duhnam tweet, Twitter, https://twitter.com/lenadunham/
status/509491066702028800.

24. "The Girl Can't Help It: The Unstoppable Lena Dunham,"
Planned Parenthood of the Pacific Southwest, https://www.
plannedparenthood.org/planned-parenthood-pacific-
southwest/who-we-are/carematters/the-girl-cant-help-it-the-
unstoppable-lena-dunham.

25. Rose Walano, "Lena Duham Wears a Fallopian Tube Sweater
to a Planned Parenthood Conference and It's Everything," *US
Weekly*, October 2, 2015, http://www.usmagazine.com/
celebrity-style/news/lena-dunham-womb-sweater-planned-
parenthood-event-photos-2015210.

26. Jane Mulkerrins, "*Girls'* Lena Dunham: Women Saying, 'I'm
Not a Feminist' Is My Greatest Pet Peeve," Metro, January 14,
2013, http://metro.co.uk/2013/01/14/lena-dunham-the-fact-
my-girls-character-is-not-a-size-4-is-meaningful-3348636/.

27. Sarah Kliff, "Only 18 Percent of Americans Consider
Themselves Feminists," Vox, April 8, 2015, http://www.vox.
com/2015/4/8/8372417/feminist-gender-equality-poll.

28. Radhika Sanghani, "Only 7 Percent of Britons Consider
Themselves Feminists," *Telegraph*, January 15, 2016, http://
www.telegraph.co.uk/women/life/only-7-per-cent-of-britons-
consider-themselves-feminists/.

29. Emily Swanson, "Poll: Few Identify as Feminists, but Most
Believe in Equality of Sexes," Huffington Post, April 16, 2013,
http://www.huffingtonpost.com/2013/04/16/
feminism-poll_n_3094917.html.

30. Steve Watson, "Poll: Less than One Third of Women Identify
as 'Feminist,'" Infowars, February 24, 2016, http://www.

infowars.com/poll-less-than-one-third-of-women-identify-as-feminist/.

31. Hermione Hoby, "Taylor Swift: 'Sexy? Not on My Radar,'" *Guardian*, August 23, 2014, https://www.theguardian.com/music/2014/aug/23/taylor-swift-shake-it-off.

32. Russ Weakland, "Beyonce Hints That Jay-Z Took Her Virginity: No Wonder He Put a Ring on It!," Hollywood Life, January 20, 2011, http://hollywoodlife.com/2011/01/20/beyonce-jay-z-virginity-sex/.

33. Ashley E. McGuire, "Beyoncé's Soulful Feminism," *Acculturated*, February 4, 2016, http://acculturated.com/beyonces-soulful-feminism/.

34. Kia Makarechi, "Obama Says 'Beyonce Could Not Be a Better Role Model for My Girls' As Event with Jay-Z Nets $4 Million," Huffington Post, September 19, 2012, http://www.huffingtonpost.com/2012/09/19/obama-beyonce-role-model-jay-z-4-million_n_1896368.html.

35. Naomi Schaefer Riley, "Jay-Z a Poor Excuse for a Husband," *New York Post*, January 28, 2014, http://nypost.com/2014/01/28/beyonce-jay-z-this-is-marriage/.

36. Beyoncé Knowles-Carter, "Gender Equality Is a Myth," Shriver Report, January 12, 2014, http://shriverreport.org/gender-equality-is-a-myth-beyonce/.

37. "Sheryl Sandburg, "Beyoncé : She's the Boss," *Time*, April 23, 2014, http://time.com/70716/beyonce-2014-time-100/.

38. Mollie Hemingway, "Feminism or Sexism? Depends. Is It Beyonce's VMAs or Vergara's Emmys?," *Federalist*, August 24, 2014, http://thefederalist.com/2014/08/26/feminism-or-sexism-depends-is-it-beyonces-vmas-or-vergaras-emmys/.

39. Ibid.

40. Perez Hilton, "Sofia Vergara Covers *Harper's Bazaar* Arabia & Opens Up about Having Babies with Joe Manganiello!," perezhilton.com, February 29, 2016, http://perezhilton.com/cocoperez/2016-02-29-sofia-vergara-harpers-bazaar-arabia-march-2016-cover-spread-interview#.WEhKrxSgJ5g.

41. Tricia Romano, "'Blurred Lines,' Robin Thicke's Summer Anthem, Is Kind of Rapey," Daily Beast, June 17, 2013, http://www.thedailybeast.com/articles/2013/06/17/blurred-lines-robin-thicke-s-summer-anthem-is-kind-of-rapey.html.

42. Elly Brinkley, "Is 'Blurred Lines' a 'Rapey' Song?," *Wall Street Journal*, August 8, 2013, http://blogs.wsj.com/speakeasy/2013/08/08/is-blurred-lines-a-rapey-song/.

43. Rauly Ramirez, "Robin Thicke's 'Blurred Lines' Breaks Record Atop Hot R&B/Hip-Hop Songs," Billboard, September 25, 2013, http://www.billboard.com/articles/columns/the-juice/5733206/robin-thickes-blurred-lines-breaks-record-atop-hot-rbhip-hop.

44. Jennifer Lai, "'Blurred Lines Is Cocky, Yes. But Rapey? No.," *Slate*, June 27, 2013, http://www.slate.com/blogs/xx_factor/2013/06/27/robin_thicke_s_blurred_lines_is_cocky_yes_but_rapey_and_misogynistic_no.html; Alyson Penn, "In Defense of Robin Thicke's Song 'Blurred Lines,'" The Frisky, June 21, 2013, http://www.thefrisky.com/2013-06-21/in-defense-of-robin-thickes-song-blurred-lines/.

45. Laura Barcella, "How Do the 'Blurred Lines' Lyrics Stack Up with the Words of Rapists?," *xoJane*, September 18, 2013, http://www.xojane.com/issues/how-do-the-blurred-lines-lyrics-stack-up-to-the-words-of-actual-rapists.

46. "35 Huge Songs Written by Kesha's Former Mentor Dr. Luke," CBS News, http://www.cbsnews.com/pictures/35-huge-pop-songs-written-produced-by-keshas-former-mentor-dr-luke/.

47. Jaime Lutz, "Katy Perry Supports Hillary Clinton on Her Nails," *Glamour*, October 25, 2015, http://www.glamour.com/story/katy-perry-wears-her-clinton-s.

48. Chris Spargo, "Sony's Biggest Star Adele Donates Her Brit Award Win to Kesha After Judge Ruled Singer Must Stay with the Label Despite Her Claims Producer Raped and Drugged Her," *Daily Mail*, February 24, 2016, http://www.dailymail.co.uk/tvshowbiz/article-3462690/Adele-dedicates-BRIT-Awards-win-Kesha-scoops-four-possible-gongs.html.

49. Todd Leopold, "Taylor Swift Donates $250K to Kesha, Offers Support During 'Trying Time,'" CNN, February 23, 2016, http://www.cnn.com/2016/02/22/entertainment/taylor-swift-kesha-feat/.

50. Lady Gaga, Twitter, https://twitter.com/ladygaga/status/700813758067830786.

51. Kaya, Payseno, "Rape Culture Puts Kesha in a Horrifying, Impossible Situation," *Bust*, April 7, 2016, http://bust.com/feminism/15011-kesha-stuck-between-a-rock-and-a-rapey-place-dr-luke-sony.html.

52. Joe Coscarelli, "New York State Judge Rejects Kesha's Claims in Dr. Luke Case," *New York Times*, April 7, 2016, http://www.nytimes.com/2016/04/07/arts/new-york-state-judge-rejects-keshas-claims-in-dr-luke-case.html?_r=0.

53. Andrea Mandell, "Thandie Newton Reveals Sexual Abuse by Director," *USA Today*, July 1, 2016, http://www.usatoday.com/story/life/people/2016/07/01/thandie-newton-reveals-sexual-abuse-director/86619408/.

54. Andrea Park, "Rose McGowan Tweets That She Was Raped by Hollywood Exec," CBS News, October 17, 2016, http://www.cbsnews.com/news/rose-mcgowan-tweets-that-she-was-raped-by-hollywood-exec/.

55. Mark Seal, "The One Accuser Who May Finally Bring Bill Cosby Down for Good," *Vanity Fair*, August 2016, http://www.vanityfair.com/news/2016/07/bill-cosby-andrea-constand-sexual-assault-trial.

56. Andi Zeisler, "Music Business 'Feminism' Is Little More than Branding. Just Ask Kesha," *Guardian*, April 26, 2016, https://www.theguardian.com/music/2016/apr/26/feminism-music-business-branding-beyonce-kesha.

57. Lara Baker, "Women in the Music Business: Mind the Gender Gap," Huffington Post, June 21, 2013, http://www.huffingtonpost.co.uk/lara-baker/women-in-the-music-business_b_3472612.html.

58. "Billboard's 2015 Power 100 List Revealed, *Billboard*, February 5, 2015, http://www.billboard.com/biz/6458403/billboards-2015-power-100-list-revealed.

59. Margaret Magnarelli, "The 25 Careers with the Smallest Wage Gaps for Women," *Time*, April 14, 2015, http://time.com/money/3819230/careers-wage-gap-equal-pay/.

60. Katie McDonough, "'Hollywood Is a Cesspool of Misogyny and Racism. Bring on the Lawsuits': Why the ACLU's Bold Action Is So Necessary," *Salon*, May 12, 2015, http://www.salon.com/2015/05/12/hollywood_is_a_cesspool_of_misogyny_and_racism_bring_on_the_lawsuits_why_the_aclus_bold_action_is_so_necessary/.

61. Cara Buckley, "A.C.L.U., Citing Bias against Women, Wants Inquiry into Hollywood's Hiring Practices," *New York Times*, May 12, 2015, http://www.nytimes.com/2015/05/13/movies/aclu-citing-bias-against-women-wants-inquiry-into-hollywoods-hiring-practices.html?smid=tw-share.

62. Jacob Stolworthy, "Quentin Tarantino–Produced Project Casting Call Asks for 'Whores,'" *Independent*, June 6, 2016, http://www.independent.co.uk/arts-entertainment/films/news/new-quentin-tarantino-project-casting-call-asks-for-whores-a7067246.html.

63. Kate Erbland, "10 Things You Might Not Know about 'Pretty Woman,'" Mental Floss, January 6, 2016, http://mentalfloss.com/article/62303/20-things-you-might-not-know-about-pretty-woman.

64. Colette Dowling, "The Cinderella Syndrome," *New York Times*, March 22, 1981, http://www.nytimes.com/1981/03/22/magazine/the-cinderella-syndrome.html?pagewanted=all.

65. Chase Olsen, "Daddies or Dummies: Is the Media Teaching Our Youth to Disregard Dad?," FHSS Blog, June 7, 2016, https://fhssbyu.com/2016/06/07/daddies-or-dummies-is-the-media-teaching-our-youth-to-disregard-dad./

66. Naomi Schaefer Riley, "How Disney Teaches Contempt for Dads," *New York Post,* June 14, 2016, http://nypost.com/2016/06/14/how-disney-teaches-contempt-for-dads/.

67. Rich, "Lena Dunham Explains."

68. Joanna Robinson, "Is This the One Flaw in the Otherwise Great *Captain America: Civil War*?," *Vanity Fair,* May 8, 2016, http://www.vanityfair.com/hollywood/2016/05/captain-america-civil-war-steve-rogers-sharon-carter-bucky-barnes.

69. "Franchise Index," Box Office Mojo, http://www.boxofficemojo.com/franchises/?view=Franchise&sort=sumgross&order=DESC&p=.htm.

70. Russell Scott Smith, "Killer Sex—Hot Tales of Brad and Angelina from the Set of 'Mr. and Mrs. Smith,'" *New York Post,* June 5, 2005, http://nypost.com/2005/06/05/killer-sex-hot-tales-of-brad-and-angelina-from-the-set-of-mr-and-mrs-smith/.

71. Radhika Sanghani, "Marvel Editor: I Won't Say No to Sexy Female Superheroes. Comics Still Need to Be Naughty and Fun," *Telegraph,* September 10, 2014, http://www.telegraph.co.uk/women/womens-life/11071016/Marvel-comic-book-editor-I-wont-say-no-to-sexy-female-superheroes.-Comics-still-need-to-be-naughty-and-fun.html.

72. Patrick Ryan, "Lena Dunham Tailors HBO Film on Gender Identity," *USA Today,* June 19, 2016, http://www.usatoday.com/story/life/music/2016/06/19/lena-dunham-hbo-suited/86026398/.

73. Mary Emily O'Hara, "Miley Cyrus Just Dropped a Bomb about Her Sexuality," The Daily Dot, December 11, 2015, http://www.dailydot.com/entertainment/miley-cyrus-genderqueer-foundation/.

74. Jackie Wattles, "Meet CoverGirl's First Cover Boy," CNN, October 11, 2016, http://money.cnn.com/2016/10/11/news/companies/covergirl-cover-boy-james-charles/.

CHAPTER 7: THE SEXUAL DEVOLUTION

Epigraph Midge Dector, "The New Chastity and Other Arguments Against Women's Liberation," 1972, in *A Speaker's Treasury of Quotations: Maxims, Witticisms, and Quips for Speeches and Presentations*, ed. Michael C. Thomsett and Linda Rose Thomsett (McFarland & Company, 2009), 44.

1. Peter Yang, "Hugh Hefner: What I've Learned: Philosopher King, 76, Los Angeles," *Esquire*, January 29, 2007, http://www.esquire.com/entertainment/interviews/a1229/esq0602-jun-wil/.

2. Harvey Mansfield, *Manliness* (Yale University Press, 2007), 12.

3. Hannah Smothers, "Reversible, Condomless Male Birth Control Will Be Here in 2018," *Cosmopolitan*, March 29, 2016, http://www.cosmopolitan.com/sex-love/news/a55978/vasalgel-male-birth-control-2018/.

4. Aaron Hamlin, "The Male Pill Is Coming—and It's Going to Change Everything," *Telegraph*, June 18, 2015, http://www.telegraph.co.uk/women/womens-health/11646385/Contraception-Male-Pill-is-coming-and-its-going-to-change-everything.html.

5. Arikia Millikin, "The Perfect Birth Control for Men Is Here. Why Can't We Use It?," *Vice*, April 1, 2015, http://motherboard.vice.com/read/the-perfect-birth-control-for-men-is-here-why-cant-we-use-it.

6. Martha Kempner, "Male Birth Control Pill Is Still 'Right around the Corner,' Like It Has Been for Years," Rewire, October 20, 2015, https://rewire.news/article/2015/10/20/male-birth-control-pill-still-right-around-corner-like-years/.

7. Kathleen Doheny, "Male Birth Control: More Options Soon?," WebMD, March 25, 2016, http://www.webmd.com/men/news/20160325/male-birth-control.

8. Katherine Ellen Foley, "There's a Birth Control Shot for Men, but They Can't Seem to Handle the Side Effects," Quartz, October 28, 2016, http://qz.com/822177/a-birth-control-shot-for-men-was-successful-

in-stopping-pregnancy-but-many-study-participants-quit-because-of-the-side-effects/.

9. L. Maren Wood, "The Women's Movement" in *Protest, Change, and Backlash: The 1960s,* Learn NC, http://www.learnnc.org/lp/editions/nchist-postwar/6055.

10. Margaret Sanger, "A Parents' Problem or Woman's?," *Birth Control Review,* March 1919, 6–7, https://www.nyu.edu/projects/sanger/webedition/app/documents/show.php?sangerDoc=226268.xml.

11. Marjorie Dannenfelser, "The Sufragettes Would Not Agree with Feminists Today on Abortion," *Time,* November 4, 2015, http://time.com/4093214/suffragettes-abortion/.

12. Emma Brockes, "Gloria Steinem: 'If Men Could Get Pregnant, Abortion Would Be a Sacrament,'" *Guardian,* October 17, 2015, https://www.theguardian.com/books/2015/oct/17/gloria-steinem-activist-interview-memoir-my-life-on-the-road.

13. Gloria Steinem, *My Life on the Road* (Random House, 2015), vii.

14. Douglas Marti, "Lawrence Lader, Champion of Abortion Rights, Is Dead at 86," *New York Times,* May 10, 2006, http://www.nytimes.com/2006/05/10/nyregion/10lader.html?_r=0.

15. Bernard Nathanson, *Aborting America* (Toronto: Life Cycle), 1979, 32, qtd. in Sue Ellen Browder, *Subverted: How I Helped the Sexual Revolution Hijack the Women's Movement* (Ignatius, 2015), 52.

16. Alan Wolfe, "The Mystique of Betty Friedan," *Atlantic,* September 1999, http://www.theatlantic.com/past/docs/issues/99sep/9909friedan.htm.

17. Betty Friedan, *It Changed My Life: Writings on the Women's Movement* (Cambridge, Massachusetts: Harvard University Press, 1975), 158.

18. Wolfe, "The Mystique."

19. Friedan, *It Changed My Life,* 397.

20. Christina Hoff Somers, "This House Believes That a Woman's Place Is at Work—Concluding Remarks," aei.org, December 14, 2011, https://www.aei.org/publication/this-house-believes-that-a-womans-place-is-at-work-concluding-remarks/.
21. Miral Fahmy, "Is a Woman's Place in the Home? 1 in 4 Say Yes—Poll," Reuters, March 8, 2010, http://uk.reuters.com/article/women-poll-idUKLNE62704620100308.
22. "John F. Kennedy: XXXV President of the United States: 1961–1963," The American Presidency Project at the University of California at Santa Barbara, http://www.presidency.ucsb.edu/ws/?pid=9267.
23. "The Equal Pay Act of 1963," U.S. Equal Employment Opportunity Commission, https://www.eeoc.gov/laws/statutes/epa.cfm.
24. Clay Risen, "The Accidental Feminist: Fifty Years Ago a Southern Segregationist Made Sure the Civil Rights Act Would Protect Women. No Joke," *Slate*, February 7, 2014, http://www.slate.com/articles/news_and_politics/jurisprudence/2014/02/the_50th_anniversary_of_title_vii_of_the_civil_rights_act_and_the_southern.html.
25. "By 1977, three court cases confirmed that a woman could sue her employer for harassment under Title VII of the 1964 Civil Rights Act, using the EEOC as the vehicle for redress. The Supreme Court upheld these early cases in 1986 with *Meritor Savings Bank v. Vinson*." Sascha Cohen, "A Brief History of Sexual Harassment in America before Anita Hill," *Time*, April 11, 2016, http://time.com/4286575/sexual-harassment-before-anita-hill/.
26. See sections 1 and 5 of the law, Title IX, Education Amendments of 1972, United States Department of Labor, https://www.dol.gov/oasam/regs/statutes/titleix.htm and Jon Birger, "Why Getting into Elite Colleges Is Harder for Women," *Washington Post*, July 30, 2015, https://www.washingtonpost.com/posteverything/wp/2015/07/30/achieving-perfect-gender-balance-on-campus-isnt-that-important-ending-private-colleges-affirmative-action-for-

men-is/. There were also exceptions for some schools run by religious institutions and for fraternities, sororities, Girl Scouts, Boy Scouts, etc.

27. Melanie A. Farmer, "College Marks 25 Years of Coeducation," *Record*, http://www.columbia.edu/cu/news/record/coeducation.html.

28. Caryn McTighe Musil, "Scaling Ivory Towers," *Ms.*, fall 2007, p. 44, http://www.feminist.org/education/TriumphsOfTitleIX.pdf.

29. "Degrees Conferred by Degree-Granting Institutions, by Level of Degree and Sex of Student: Selected Years, 1869–70 through 2021–22," in *Digest of Education Statistics*, National Center for Education Statistics, 2012, Table 310, https://nces.ed.gov/programs/digest/d12/tables/dt12_310.asp.

30. Betty Friedan, *The Feminine Mystique* (first published in 1963; New York: Norton, 2001), 425.

31. Amanda Chatel, "10 Gloria Steinem Facts That Will Make You Love Her Even More," *Bustle*, March 25, 2015, https://www.bustle.com/articles/71389-10-gloria-steinem-facts-that-will-make-you-love-her-even-more; Jane Kramer, "Road Warrior: After Fifty Years, Gloria Steinem Is Still at the Forefront of the Feminist Cause, *New Yorker*, October 19, 2015, http://www.newyorker.com/magazine/2015/10/19/road-warrior-profiles-jane-kramer. On feminists and divorce more generally, see Nancy Levit and Robert R. M. Verchick, *Feminist Legal Theory: A Primer* (New York: NYU Press, 2006), 171.

32. Rates rose from 10.6 divorces per 1,000 married women in 1965 to 22.6 divorces per 1,000 married women in 1980. "Number of Divorces per 1,000 Married Women Age 15 and Older, by Year, United States," in *The State of Our Unions: Social Indicators of Marital Health & Well-Being: Trends of the Last Five Decades*, 2011, figure 5, http://www.stateofourunions.org/2011/social_indicators.php#divorce. Legal changes were not the sole cause of this increase, of course. Sociologist W. Bradford Wilcox names not just

no-fault divorce as a factor but also the sexual revolution, changing expectations of marital relationships, increases in women's employment, feminist consciousness-raising, and an increasing "focus on individual fulfillment and personal growth" in relationships as factors. In "The Evolution of Divorce," *National Affairs*, fall 2009, http://nationalaffairs. com/publications/detail/the-evolution-of-divorce.

33. Robert Schoen and Vladimir Canudas-Romo, "The Timing Effects of Divorce: 20th Century Experience in the United States," *Journal of Marriage and Family* 68:3 (August 2006): 749–58, https://www.jstor.org/stable/3838889?seq=1#page_ scan_tab_contents.

34. "Divorce Costs Thousands of Women Health Insurance Coverage Every Year," University of Michigan Institute for Social Research, http://home.isr.umich.edu/sampler/divorce-costs-thousands-of-women-health-insurance-coverage-every-year/.

35. Sandra Yin, "Older Women, Divorce, and Poverty," Population Reference Bureau, http://www.prb.org/ Multimedia/Audio/2008/olderwomen.aspx.

36. Marcia Pappas, "Divorce New York Style," *New York Times*, February 19, 2006, http://www.nytimes.com/2006/02/19/ opinion/nyregionopinions/divorce-new-york-style.html.

37. Ashley McGuire, "The Feminist, Pro-Father, and Pro-Child Case against No-Fault Divorce, *Public Discourse*, May 7, 2013, http://www.thepublicdiscourse.com/2013/05/10031/.

38. Evan Gahr, "All the Fault of No-Fault," *Insight on the News* 28 (October 1996): 41, https://www.questia.com/ magazine/1G1-18791713/all-the-fault-of-no-fault.

39. Pappas, "Divorce New York Style."

40. Chicago-Kent College of Law at Illinois Tech, "*Griswold v. Connecticut*," in *Body Politic: The Supreme Court and Abortion Law*, Oyez, https://www.oyez.org/cases/1964/496.

41. "Title X Funding History," Office of Population Affairs, http://www.hhs.gov/opa/title-x-family-planning/title-x-policies/title-x-funding-history/.

42. Paul VI, *Humanae Vitae*, 1968, http://w2.vatican.va/content/paul-vi/en/encyclicals/documents/hf_p-vi_enc_25071968_humanae-vitae.html.
43. Michael Brendan Dougherty and Pascal-Emmanuel Gobry, "Time to Admit It: The Church Has Always Been Right on Birth Control," Business Insider, February 8, 2012, http://www.businessinsider.com/time-to-admit-it-the-church-has-always-been-right-on-birth-control-2012-2.
44. George A. Akerlof and Janet L. Yellen, "Why Kids Have Kids: Don't Blame Welfare, Blame 'Technology Shock,'" *Slate*, November 16, 1996, http://www.slate.com/articles/briefing/articles/1996/11/why_kids_have_kids.html.
45. Sally Kohn, "The Sex Freak-Out of the 1970s," CNN, July 21, 2015, http://www.cnn.com/2015/07/21/opinions/kohn-seventies-sexual-revolution/.

CHAPTER 8: DISPARATE IMPACT

1. Brent Lang, "Box Office: 'Fifty Shades of Grey' Explodes with Record-Breaking $81.7 Million," *Variety*, February 15, 2015, http://variety.com/2015/film/news/box-office-fifty-shades-of-grey-explodes-with-record-breaking-81-7-million-1201434486/.
2. Ashley E. McGuire, "Feminist Failure Leaves Women to Self-Objectify as Pornographic Playthings," USA *Today*, February 15, 2015, http://www.usatoday.com/story/opinion/2015/02/13/fifty-shades-of-grey-movie-glamorizes-sexual-violence-column/23366077/.
3. Emily Esfahani Smith, "Let's Give Chivalry Another Chance," *Atlantic*, December 10, 2012, http://www.theatlantic.com/sexes/archive/2012/12/lets-give-chivalry-another-chance/266085/.
4. John Picciuto, "Why Chivalry Is Dead, from a Man's Perspective," Elite Daily, August 21, 2013, http://elitedaily.com/dating/sex/why-chivalry-is-dead-from-a-mans-perspective/.

5. Evan Marc Katz, "Is Online Dating Different for Men and Women?," Evan Marc Katz: Understand Men, Find Love, http://www.evanmarckatz.com/blog/online-dating-tips-advice/is-online-dating-different-for-men-and-women/.

6. J. Money, "Girls Care about Money, Guys Care about Looks. Here's Why Girls Get Screwed on Dating Sites," Budgets Are Sexy, October 11, 2012, http://www.budgetsaresexy.com/2012/10/girls-care-about-money-guys-care-about-looks-heres-why-girls-get-screwed-on-dating-sites/.

7. Louisa Peacock, "Pregnant Woman Forced to Sit on Train Floor: What Is It about Us Brits on Public Transport?," *Telegraph*, February 19, 2014, http://www.telegraph.co.uk/women/womens-life/10648256/Pregnant-Victoria-Poskitt-forced-to-sit-on-train-floor-What-is-it-about-Brits-on-public-transport.html.

8. Tom Namako, "Pregnant Woman Slapped with Ticket during Subway Seat Search," *New York Post*, April 9, 2010, http://nypost.com/2010/04/09/pregnant-woman-slapped-with-ticket-during-subway-seat-search/.

9. Dana Hedgpeth, "Pregnant and Hunting for a Seat on Metro," *Washington Post*, June 8, 2012, https://www.washingtonpost.com/blogs/dr-gridlock/post/pregnant-and-hunting-for-a-seat-on-metro/2012/06/08/gJQAWsf1NV_blog.html.

10. Dana Hedgpeth, "Riding Metro while Pregnant," *Washington Post*, April 11, 2012, https://www.washingtonpost.com/news/dr-gridlock/wp/2014/04/11/riding-metro-while-pregnant/#comments.

11. Roberto A. Ferdman, "There Are Only Three Ways to Meet Anyone Anymore," *Washington Post*, March 8, 2016, https://www.washingtonpost.com/news/wonk/wp/2016/03/08/how-much-life-has-changed-in-one-incredible-chart-about-dating/.

12. David M. Buss et al., "A Half Century of Mate Preferences: The Cultural Evolution of Values," *Journal of Marriage and Family* 63 (May 2001): 491–503, http://labs.la.utexas.edu/buss/files/2015/09/half-century-of-mate-prefs-2001-jmf.pdf.

13. Diana B. Elliott et al., "Historical Marriage Trends from 1890–2010: A Focus on Race Differences: SEHSD Working Paper Number 2012–12," United States Census Bureau, 2012, https://www.census.gov/content/dam/Census/library/working-papers/2012/demo/SEHSD-WP2012-12.pdf.

14. "Married Women's Property Laws," Law Library of Congress, https://memory.loc.gov/ammem/awhhtml/awlaw3/property_law.html.

15. W. Bradford Wilcox argues convincingly that Brookings Institution scholar Richard V. Reeves (in "How to Save Marriage in America," *Atlantic*, February 13, 2014, http://www.theatlantic.com/business/archive/2014/02/how-to-save-marriage-in-america/283732/) "obscures the extent to which the cast of modern American family life remains gendered." "Surprisingly, Most Married Families Today Tilt Neo-Traditional," Family Studies, February 26, 2014, http://family-studies.org/the-real-modern-family-surprisingly-most-married-families-today-tilt-neo-traditional/.

16. Kim Parker and Wendy Wang, "Modern Parenthood: Roles of Moms and Dads Converge as They Balance Work and Family," Pew Research Center, March 14, 2013, http://www.pewsocialtrends.org/2013/03/14/modern-parenthood-roles-of-moms-and-dads-converge-as-they-balance-work-and-family/.

17. The most notable change since the mid-1990s is an increase in the hours per week that both mothers and fathers spend on child care. Mothers' hours in paid employment have actually declined. "Parental Time Use," Pew Research Center, http://www.pewresearch.org/data-trend/society-and-demographics/parental-time-use/.

18. "Changing Views about Work" in Parker and Wang, "Modern Parenthood," http://www.pewsocialtrends.org/2013/03/14/chapter-1-changing-views-about-work/.

19. The 2000 Survey of Marriage and Family Life. The work categories were staying at home, working part time, and working full time. See W. Bradford Wilcox and Jeffrey Dew,

"No One Best Way: Work-Family Strategies, the Gendered Division of Parenting, and the Contemporary Marriages of Mothers and Fathers," in *Gender and Parenthood: Biological and Social Scientific Perspectives*, ed. W. Bradford Wilcox and Kathleen Kovner Kline (New York: Columbia University Press, 2013), p. 283, table 10.2.

20. Eleanor Maccoby, *The Two Sexes: Growing Up Apart, Coming Together* (Cambridge, MA: Harvard University Press, 1998), 314.

21. Jane Riblett Wilkie et al., "Gender and Fairness: Marital Satisfaction in Two-Earner Couples," *Journal of Marriage and Family* 60:3 (August 1998): 579, http://www.jstor.org/stable/353530.

22. Robert Schoen et al., "Wives' Employment and Spouses' Marital Happiness: Assessing the Direction of Influence Using Longitudinal Couple Data," *Journal of Family Issues* 27:4 (April 2006), 506–28, http://jfi.sagepub.com/content/27/4/506.abstract.

23. Liana C. Sayer et al., "She Left, He Left: How Employment and Satisfaction Affect Men's and Women's Decisions to Leave Marriages," *American Journal of Sociology* 116:6 (May 2011): 1982–2018, https://www.ncbi.nlm.nih.gov/pmc/articles/PMC3347912/; Robert Schoen, "Women's Employment, Marital Happiness, and Divorce," *Social Forces* 81:2 (2002): 643–62, http://sf.oxfordjournals.org/content/81/2/643.short.

24. Laurie DeRose, "Essay: No One Best Way: Work, Family, and Happiness the World Over," World Family Map, 2015, http://worldfamilymap.ifstudies.org/2015/articles/essay-2.

25. But the top determinant of women's marital happiness was their self-reported satisfaction with the love, affection, and understanding their husbands gave them. "University of Virginia Study Finds Commitment to Marriage, Emotional Engagement Key to Wives' Happiness," University of Virginia News, March 1, 2006, http://www.virginia.edu/topnews/releases2006/20060301Wilcox_Nock_Study.html; W. Brad

Wilcox and Steven L. Nock, "What's Love Got to Do with It? Equality, Equity, Commitment, and Women's Marital Quality," *Social Forces* 84:3 (2006), 1321–45, http://sf. oxfordjournals.org/content/84/3/1321.abstract.

26. The researchers controlled for race/ethnicity as well as for "number of marriages, marital duration, education, family income (logged), and age of youngest child." W. B. Wilcox and Jeffrey Dew, "No One Best Way: Work-Family Strategies, the Gendered Division of Parenting, and the Contemporary Marriages of Mothers and Fathers," conference at the University of Virginia, 2008.

27. Wilkie et al., "Gender and Fairness," 589.

28. "Wives Who Earn More than Their Husbands, 1987–2014," U.S. Census Bureau, April 6, 2016, http://www.bls.gov/cps/ wives-earn-more.htm.

29. Wilcox and Dew, "No One Best Way," 287.

30. Ibid., 289.

31. Marianne Bertrand et al., "Gender Identity and Relative Income within Households, *Quarterly Journal of Economics* (2015): 571–614, http://qje.oxfordjournals.org/ content/130/2/571.full.pdf.

32. Cristin L. Munscha, "Her Support, His Support: Money, Masculinity, and Marital Infidelity," *American Sociological Review* 80:3 (June 2015), 469–95, http://asr.sagepub.com/ content/80/3/469.abstract.

33. Lamar Pierce et al., "In Sickness and in Wealth: Psychological and Sexual Costs of Income Comparison in Marriage," *Personality and Social Psychology Bulletin* 39:3 (March 2013), 359–74, http://psp.sagepub.com/content/39/3/359.

34. Liana C. Sayer et al., "He Left, She Left: How Employment and Satisfaction Affect Men's and Women's Decisions to Leave Marriages," *American Journal of Sociology* 116:6 (May 2011), 1982–2018, ahttps://www.ncbi.nlm.nih.gov/pmc/ articles/PMC3347912/.

35. Melissa Ruby Banzhaf, "When It Rains, It Pours: Under What Circumstances Does Job Loss Lead to Divorce," The Society

of Labor Economists, p. 2, http://www.sole-jole.org/14357. pdf.

36. Kathleen Kovner Kline and W. Bradford Wilcox, *Mother Bodies, Father Bodies: How Parenthood Changes Us from the Inside Out* (New York: Institute for American Values, 2014), 33.

37. Michael W. Yogman et al., "Father Involvement and Cognitive/Behavioral Outcomes of Preterm Infants," *Journal of the American Academy of Child & Adolescent Psychiatry* 34:1 (Jan. 1995): 58–66; Daniel Paquette and Caroline Dumont, "The Father-Child Activation Relationship, Sex Differences, and Attachment Disorganization in Toddlerhood," *Child Development Research* 2013, http://www.hindawi.com/journals/cdr/2013/102860/.

38. Maccoby, *The Two Sexes*, 266–67; Kyle Pruett and Marsha Kline Pruett, *Partnership Parenting: How Men and Women Parent Differently—Why It Helps Your Kids and Can Strengthen Your Marriage* (New York: Da Capo Lifelong Books, 2009), 18–19.

39. Maccoby, *The Two Sexes*, 267.

40. Ibid; Pruett and Pruett, *Partnership Parenting*, 19.

41. Sue Shellenbarger, "Roughhousing Lessons From Dad," *Wall Street Journal*, June 11, 2014, http://www.wsj.com/articles/roughhousing-lessons-from-dad-1402444262.

42. Sara McLanahan et al., "The Causal Effects of Father Absence," *Annual Review of Sociology* 39 (July 2013): 399–427, http://www.annualreviews.org/doi/abs/10.1146/annurev-soc-071312-145704.

43. W. Bradford Wilcox, "The Distinct, Positive Impact of a Good Dad: How Fathers Contribute to Their Kids' Lives," *Atlantic*, June 14, 2013, http://www.theatlantic.com/sexes/archive/2013/06/the-distinct-positive-impact-of-a-good-dad/276874/; "Atlantic Dads," The National Marriage Project, http://nationalmarriageproject.org/wordpress/atlanticdads/; Marcia J. Carlson, "Family Structure, Father Involvement, and Adolescent Behavioral Outcomes," *Journal*

of Marriage and Family 68:1 (February 2006): 137–54, http://eric.ed.gov/?id=EJ732973.

44. C. A. Bush et al., "Differences in Empathy between Offender and Nonoffender Youth," *Journal of Youth and Adolescence* 29 (2000): 467, https://link.springer.com/article/10.1023/A:1005162526769.

45. Bruce J. Ellis et al., "Does Father Absence Place Daughters at Special Risk for Early Sexual Activity and Teenage Pregnancy?," *Child Development* 74:3 (May 2003), 801–21, http://onlinelibrary.wiley.com/doi/10.1111/1467-8624.00569/abstract.

46. Wilcox, "The Distinct, Positive Impact of a Good Dad."

47. Marc H. Bornstein and Catherine S. Tamis-Lamonda, "Maternal Responsiveness and Cognitive Development in Children," *New Directions for Child and Adolescent Development* 43 (spring 1989): 49–61, http://onlinelibrary.wiley.com/doi/10.1002/cd.23219894306/abstract.

48. Diane Benoit, "Infant-Parent Attachment: Definition, Types, Antecedents, Measurement and Outcome," *Pediatric Child Health* 8:9 (October 2004), 541–45, https://www.ncbi.nlm.nih.gov/pmc/articles/PMC2724160/#b5-pch09541.

49. Kline and Wilcox, *Mother Bodies, Father Bodies*, 39.

50. Paul Raeburn, *Do Fathers Matter? What Science Is Telling Us About the Parent We've Overlooked* (New York: Scientific American/Farrar, Straus and Giroux, 2014).

51. Eve Gerber, "Kyle Pruett on Fatherhood," Salon, July 23, 2012, https://www.salon.com/2012/07/23/kyle_pruett_on_fatherhood_salpart/.

52. Judith Shulevitz, "Mom: The Designated Worrier," *New York Times*, May 8, 2015, http://www.nytimes.com/2015/05/10/opinion/sunday/judith-shulevitz-mom-the-designated-worrier.html?_r=0.

53. "'Ongoing, Severe Epidemic' of STDs in US, Report Finds," NBC News, February 13, 2013, http://vitals.nbcnews.com/_news/2013/02/13/16951432-ongoing-severe-epidemic-of-stds-in-us-report-finds.

54. "HPV and Men—Fact Sheet," Centers for Disease Control and Prevention, http://www.cdc.gov/std/hpv/stdfact-hpv-and-men.htm.

55. Daniel J. DeNoon, "HPV Cancer Hits 8,000 Men, 18,000 Women a Year," WebMD, April 19, 2012, http://www.webmd.com/cancer/news/20120419/hpv-cancer-hits-8000-men-18000-women-a-year.

56. Eileen F. Dunne et al., "Prevalence of HPV Infection among Men: A Systematic Review of the Literature," *Journal of Infectious Disease* 194:8: 1044–57, http://jid.oxfordjournals.org/content/194/8/1044.long.

57. "What Women Should Know about Cervical Cancer and the Human Papilloma Virus," American Cancer Society, http://www.cancer.org/acs/groups/content/@editorial/documents/document/acspc-043803.pdf.

58. "10 Ways STDs Impact Women Differently from Men," Centers for Disease Control, April 2011, https://www.cdc.gov/std/health-disparities/stds-women-042011.pdf.

59. Faran Krentcil, "Chloë Grace Moretz: "I Found a Lot of Power Within My Insecurities," *Elle*, June 23, 2016, http://www.elle.com/culture/celebrities/interviews/a37312/chloe-grace-moretz-hillary-clinton-brooklyn-beckham-interview/.

60. Erik Sass, "Social Media Fueling Women's Body Image Issues," MediaPost, October 27, 2014, http://www.mediapost.com/publications/article/236998/social-media-fueling-womens-body-image-issues.html.

61. "New Statistics Reflect the Changing Face of Plastic Surgery" (press release), American Society of Plastic Surgeons, http://www.plasticsurgery.org/news/2016/new-statistics-reflect-the-changing-face-of-plastic-surgery.html.

62. Roni Caryn Rabin, "More Teenage Girls Seeking Genital Cosmetic Surgery," *New York Times*, April 25, 2016, http://well.blogs.nytimes.com/2016/04/25/increase-in-teenage-genital-surgery-prompts-guidelines-for-doctors/?_r=0.

63. Christina Cauterucci, "Why Are More and More Teen Girls Getting Cosmetic Genital Surgery?," *Slate*, April 26, 2016,

http://www.slate.com/blogs/xx_factor/2016/04/26/why_is_
cosmetic_genital_surgery_on_the_rise_among_teen_girls.
html.

64. "See All the New Barbies from Curvy to Tall and Petitie," *Time*, January 28, 2016, http://time.com/4197499/barbies-new-body-photos-of-curvy-tall-and-petite/.

65. Conor Clarke, "Why Are Women Better Off, but Less Happy?," *Atlantic*, May 26, 2009, http://www.theatlantic. com/politics/archive/2009/05/why-are-women-better-off-but-less-happy/18293/.

66. Betsey Stevenson and Justin Wolfers, "The Paradox of Declining Female Happiness: NBR Working Paper No. 14969," National Bureau of Economic Research, May 2009, http://www.nber.org/papers/w14969.

67. Olivia Remes et al., "A Systematic Review of Reviews on the Prevalence of Anxiety Disorders in Adult Populations," *Brain and Behavior* 6:7 (July 2016), http://onlinelibrary.wiley.com/doi/10.1002/brb3.497/abstract.

68. Dorte Mølgaard Christiansen, "Examining Sex and Gender Differences in Anxiety Disorders," in F. Durbano, *A Fresh Look at Anxiety Disorders* (Tech Open Access Publishers, 2015), http://findresearcher.sdu.dk/portal/files/116134994/examining_sex_and_gender.pdf.

69. "Depression in Women: Understanding the Gender Gap," Mayo Clinic, January 16, 2016, http://www.mayoclinic.org/diseases-conditions/depression/in-depth/depression/art-20047725.

70. "America's State of Mind," Medco, http://apps.who.int/medicinedocs/documents/s19032en/s19032en.pdf.

71. Julie Holland, "Medicating Women's Feelings," *New York Times*, February 28, 2015, http://www.nytimes. com/2015/03/01/opinion/sunday/medicating-womens-feelings. html.

72. Amanda Parrish, "Here's What It's Like to Take 'Female Viagra,'" *Time*, June 17, 2015, http://time.com/3924245/flibanserin-female-viagra/.

CHAPTER 9: THE END OF PRIVACY

Epigraph Madeleine L'Engle, *The Irrational Season (The Crosswicks Journal, Book 3)* (HarperOne, 1984), p. 7.

1. "Continuing to Stand for Inclusivity," A Bullseye View (Target corporate website), April 19, 2016, https://corporate.target.com/article/2016/04/target-stands-inclusivity.
2. Hayley Peterson, "The Target Boycott Has Reached a Boiling Point—and Sales May Suffer as a Result," Business Insider, May 14, 2016, http://www.businessinsider.com/target-boycott-impact-on-sales-2016-5.
3. Hadley Malcolm, "Target Shares Plunge as Sales Fall, Outlook Spooks Street," *USA Today*, May 18, 2016, http://www.usatoday.com/story/money/2016/05/18/target-first-quarter-earnings/84530886/.
4. Khadeeja Safdar and Lisa Beilfuss, "Target Gives Weak Forecast as Sales Decline," *Wall Street Journal*, May 18, 2016, http://www.wsj.com/articles/target-sales-decline-profit-edges-lower-1463572937.
5. "Corporate Fact Sheet," Target, https://corporate.target.com/press/corporate.
6. Hadley Malcolm, "More than 700,000 Pledge to Boycott Target over Transgender Bathroom Policy," *USA Today*, April 28, 2016, http://www.usatoday.com/story/money/2016/04/25/conservative-christian-group-boycotting-target-transgender-bathroom-policy/83491396/.
7. David French, "A Viral Video Illustrates Why Target Is Making Me Rethink My Opposition to Boycotts," *National Review*, April 26, 2016, http://www.nationalreview.com/corner/434613/viral-video-illustrates-why-target-making-me-rethink-my-opposition-boycotts.
8. "Men Are Posting Videos on YouTube of Themselves Testing Target's New Bathroom Policy," *New York Times*, May 3, 2016, http://nytlive.nytimes.com/womenintheworld/2016/05/03/men-are-posting-videos-on-youtube-of-themselves-testing-targets-new-bathroom-policy/.

9. Tom Steele, "Frisco Police Identify Man They Say Recorded Girl in Target Changing Room," *Dallas Morning News*, May 24, 2016, http://crimeblog.dallasnews.com/2016/05/frisco-police-identify-man-they-say-recorded-girl-at-target-changing-room.html/.

10. "Man Charged with Recording Girls in Bedford, NH Target Fitting Room," CBS Boston, June 24, 2016, http://boston.cbslocal.com/2016/06/24/bedford-target-fitting-room-recording-zachery-bishop/.

11. Stefan Rockefeller, "Transgender Woman Arrested for Voyeurism at Ammon Target," *East Idaho News*, July 12, 2016, http://www.eastidahonews.com/2016/07/man-dressed-woman-caught-taking-photos-dressing-room/. The *East Idaho News* later changed the wording of the article to "transgender" without issuing a correction.

12. Niraj Chokshi, "Transgender Woman Is Charged with Voyeurism Target in Idaho," *New York Times*, July 15, 2016, http://www.nytimes.com/2016/07/15/us/target-transgender-idaho-voyeurism.html?_r=0.

13. "Court Docs: Transgender Voyeur Admits to Pattern," *Post Register*, July 13, 2016, http://www.postregister.com/articles/news-daily-email-todays-headlines-west/2016/07/13/court-docs-transgender-voyeur-admits.

14. Jeff Zarronandia, "Transgender Woman Arrested for Taking Pictures in Target Changing Room," Snopes, July 15, 2016, http://www.snopes.com/2016/07/13/transgender-woman-arrested-for-taking-pictures-in-target-changing-room/.

15. Dan Evon, "Transunder Arrest," Snopes, July 14, 2016, http://www.snopes.com/transgender-arrested-target-photos/.

16. "'I Don't Feel Safe': Victim of Target Voyeur in Davie Speaks Out," NBC Miami, March 25, 2016, http://www.nbcmiami.com/news/local/Man-Wanted-for-Placing-Camera-Under-Fitting-Room-Door-at-Target-Davie-Police-373572501.html.

17. "Hanford Man Confesses to Hiding Camera in Target Store Restroom, Police Say," ABC Fresno, July 18, 2015, http://

abc30.com/news/hanford-man-confesses-to-hiding-camera-in-target-restroom-police-say/862164/.

18. "See It: A Convicted Voyeur Picked the Wrong Woman to Harass at Target," Fox News Insider, May 3, 2016, http://insider.foxnews.com/2016/05/03/florida-woman-chases-convicted-voyeur-out-target-store-viral-video.

19. Max Walker, "Update: UI Police Locate Suspect Videotaping in Women's Shower," KCRG-TV-9, February 16, 2016, http://www.kcrg.com/content/news/University-of-Iowa-Police-Investigate-Report-of-Man-Videotaping-in-Womens-Shower-368990061.html.

20. "Louisville Man Accused of Voyeurism in Women's Restroom at Sullivan University," WDRB, February 29, 2016, http://www.wdrb.com/story/31343333/louisville-man-accused-of-voyeurism-in-womens-restroom-at-sullivan-university.

21. Wes Wade, "Alleged Voyeur Arrested over Cameras in Ladies Restrooms," *Daily Times*, March 26, 2016, http://www.thedailytimes.com/news/alleged-voyeur-arrested-over-cameras-in-ladies-restrooms/article_8b7c865a-5f12-5680-89fa-8d72adf04340.html.

22. Paul Smith, "Quarryville Man Accused of Using Phone to Look at 10-Year-Old Girl in Sheetz Restroom," Fox 43, April 18, 2016, http://fox43.com/2016/04/18/quarryville-man-accused-of-using-phone-to-look-at-10-year-old-girl-in-sheetz-restroom/.

23. Larry Flowers, "Man Accused of Filming Women in Smyrna Park's Bathroom," WKRN-TV Nashville, April 7, 2016, http://wkrn.com/2016/04/07/man-charged-after-allegedly-filming-in-smyrna-womens-restrooms/.

24. Brooke Magnanti, "Why Are Most Peeping Toms Men? Aren't We All Spies Now?," *Telegraph*, November 14, 2013, http://www.telegraph.co.uk/women/sex/10450005/Sex-spying-Why-are-most-peeping-Toms-men-Arent-we-all-spies-now.html.

25. Steve Helling, "Chicago Man Choked 8-Year-Old Girl in Restaurant Bathroom, Police Say," *People*, May 13, 2016,

http://www.people.com/article/chicago-man-allegedly-chokes-girl-jasons-deli-bathroom.

26. Chris Isidore, "Target's $20 Million Answer to Transgender Bathroom Boycott," CNN Money, August 17, 2016, http://money.cnn.com/2016/08/17/news/companies/target-bathroom-transgender/.

27. Peter Hasson, "Security Guard Arrested for Removing Man from Women's Bathroom," Daily Caller, May 19, 2016, http://dailycaller.com/2016/05/19/security-guard-arrested-for-removing-man-from-womens-bathroom/.

28. "Man Dressed as Woman Arrested for Spying into Mall Bathroom Stall, Police Say," NBC Washington, November 17, 2015, http://www.nbcwashington.com/news/local/Man-Dressed-as-Woman-Arrested-for-Spying-Into-Mall-Bathroom-Stall-Police-Say-351232041.html.

29. Ramisha Farooq, "University of Toronto Alters Bathroom Policy after Two Reports of Voyeurs," Star, October 2, 2015, https://www.thestar.com/news/crime/2015/10/05/university-of-toronto-alters-bathroom-policy-after-two-reports-of-voyeurism.html.

30. Wudan Yan, "Seattle's Absurd, Discriminatory Trans Bathroom Panic," Daily Beast, February 5, 2016, http://www.thedailybeast.com/articles/2016/02/05/seattle-s-absurd-discriminatory-trans-bathroom-panic.html.

31. Alison Morrow, "Seattle Man Tests Gender Rule by Undressing in Women's Locker Room," *USA Today*, February 17, 2016, tp://www.usatoday.com/story/news/nation-now/2016/02/17/transgender-rule-washington-state-man-undresses-locker-room/80501904/.

32. "Dear Colleague Letter on Transgender Students," U.S. Department of Justice and U.S. Department of Education, May 13, 2016, http://www2.ed.gov/about/offices/list/ocr/letters/colleague-201605-title-ix-transgender.pdf.

33. Bill McGurn, "Obama's Transgender 'Guidance': The White House Starts Another Culture War to Drive Liberal Turnout,"

Wall Street Journal, May 17, 2016, http://www.wsj.com/articles/obamas-transgender-guidance-1463438713.

34. Yezmin Villarreal, "ACLU Director Quits, Says Trans Rights Threaten Women's Safety," *Advocate*, June 2, 2016, http://www.advocate.com/transgender/2016/6/02/aclu-director-quits-says-trans-rights-threaten-womens-safety-video.

35. Zack Ford, "An ACLU Attorney's Ugly Transformation into an Anti-Transgender Pundit," ThinkProgress, June 6, 2016, https://thinkprogress.org/an-aclu-attorneys-ugly-transformation-into-an-anti-transgender-pundit-b41bce02edaf#.g399o34fq.

36. Noah Michelson, "What to Do If Your Kid Is 'Frightened' by a Trans Person in the Bathroom," Huffington Post, June 3, 2016, http://www.huffingtonpost.com/entry/maya-dillard-smith-transgender_us_575179a7e4b0eb20fa0d9475.

37. "Maya Dillar Explains Why She Left the ACLU over HB2 Law," ABC News, http://abcnews.go.com/Entertainment/video/maya-dillard-smith-explains-left-aclu-hb2-law-40223461.

38. "The Gender Identity Movement Erases Women," Delaware Online, June 22, 2016, http://www.delawareonline.com/story/opinion/contributors/2016/06/22/gender-identity-movement-erases-women/86252424/.

39. Meghan Murphy, "Rape Relief v. Nixon, Transphobia, and the Value of Women-Only Space: An Interview with Lee Lakeman," Feminist Current, May 14, 2012, http://www.feministcurrent.com/2012/05/14/rape-relief-v-nixon-transphobia-and-the-value-of-women-only-space-an-interview-with-lee-lakeman/.

40. Interview of Kathleen Sloan by the author on July 29, 2016.

41. Melissa Hogenboom, "A Tipping Point in the Fight against Slavery?," BBC News, October 19, 2012, http://www.bbc.com/news/magazine-19831913.

42. Amanda Walker-Rodriguez and Rodney Hill, "Human Sex Trafficking," Federal Bureau of Investigation, March 2011, https://leb.fbi.gov/2011/march/human-sex-trafficking.

43. "UNDOC Report on Human Trafficking Exposes Modern
     Form of Slavery," United Nations Office on Drugs and Crime,
     2016, http://www.unodc.org/unodc/en/human-trafficking/
     global-report-on-trafficking-in-persons.html.
44. Malika Saada Saar, "Girls, Human Trafficking, and Modern
     Slavery in America," ThinkProgress, October 6, 2012, http://
     thinkprogress.org/health/2012/10/06/971401/girls-human-
     trafficking-and-modern-slavery-in-america/.
45. "Decision on State Obligations to Respect, Protect, and Fulfill
     the Human Rights of Sex Workers," Amnesty International,
     https://www.amnesty.org/en/policy-on-state-obligations-to-
     respect-protect-and-fulfil-the-human-rights-of-sex-workers/.
46. "Q&A: Policy to Protect the Rights of Sex Workers,"
     Amnesty International, https://www.amnesty.org/en/
     qa-policy-to-protect-the-human-rights-of-sex-workers/.
47. "Note on Sex Work, Sexual Exploitation, and Trafficking,"
     UN Women, October 9, 2013, http://www.nswp.org/sites/
     nswp.org/files/UN%20Women's%20note%20on%20sex%20
     work%20sexual%20exploitation%20and%20trafficking.pdf.
48. "Sex Workers," UNAIDS, October 16, 2014, http://www.
     unaids.org/en/resources/documents/2014/Sexworkers.
49. Emily Bazelon, "The Everyday Faces of Sex Workers, *New
     York Times*, May 7, 2016, http://www.nytimes.
     com/2016/05/07/insider/the-everyday-faces-of-sex-workers.
     html.
50. Emily Bazelon, "Should Prostitution Be a Crime?," *New York
     Times*, May 8, 2016, http://www.nytimes.com/2016/05/08/
     magazine/should-prostitution-be-a-crime.html.
51. Mac McClelland, "Is Prostitution Just Another Job?," *New
     York* magazine, March 21, 2016, http://nymag.com/
     thecut/2016/03/sex-workers-legalization-c-v-r.html.
52. July 22, 2015, public letter to Amnesty International, http://
     catwinternational.org/Content/Images/Article/617/attachment.
     pdf.
53. Emma Brockes, "Gloria Steinem: 'If Men Could Get
     Pregnant, Abortion Would Be a Sacrament,'" *Guardian*,

October 17, 2015, https://www.theguardian.com/books/2015/oct/17/gloria-steinem-activist-interview-memoir-my-life-on-the-road.

54. Bazelon, "Should Prostitution Be a Crime?"

55. Naomi Schaefer Riley, "Making Prostitution Legal Doesn't 'Empower' Women—It Turns Them into Commodities," *New York Post*, May 15, 2016, http://nypost.com/2016/05/15/making-prostitution-legal-doesnt-empower-women-it-turns-them-into-commodities/.

56. Brockes, "Gloria Steinem."

57. Anonymous, "I Was a Real-Life 'Sugar Baby' for Wealthy Men," *Marie Claire*, May 9, 2016, http://www.marieclaire.com/sex-love/features/a20381/i-lived-the-girlfriend-experience/.

58. Gabriela Andrea Bien Lagunzad, "Candace Kashani: Law Student Gets Sugar Daddies to Pay for Law School?," Morning Ledger, May 31, 2016, http://www.morningledger.com/candice-kashani-student-gets-sugar-daddies-to-pay-for-law-school/1375969/.

59. "More Students Opting for Sugar Daddies to Ease College Costs," WMAL, June 1, 2016, http://www.wmal.com/2016/06/01/more-students-opting-for-sugar-daddies-to-ease-college-costs/.

60. Cass Mudde, "The Paternalistic Fallacy of the 'Nordic Model' of Prostitution," Huffington Post, April 8, 2016, http://www.huffingtonpost.com/cas-mudde/the-paternalistic-fallacy_b_9644972.html.

61. Roland Martin, "Obama's Big Transgender Restroom Diversion," *Wall Street Journal*, May 20, 2016, http://www.wsj.com/articles/obamas-big-transgender-restroom-diversion-1463769156.

62. Eugene Volokh, "Prominent Feminist: Bans on Sex Discrimination 'Emphatically' Do Not 'Require Unisex Restrooms,'" *Washington Post*, May 9, 2016, https://www.washingtonpost.com/news/volokh-conspiracy/wp/2016/05/09/

prominent-feminist-bans-on-sex-discrimination-emphatically-
do-not-require-unisex-restrooms/.

CHAPTER 10: GENDER REVEAL

1. Michael Blackmon, "This Couple Had an Insanely Unique Baby
    Gender Reveal: Prepare for a Cuteness Overload," Buzzfeed,
    May 7, 2016, https://www.buzzfeed.com/michaelblackmon/
    baby-gender-reveal?utm_term=.qn5bWy90BQ#.xadxQ6d0g5.
2. Miranda Bryant, "Target Practice! Special Forces Member
    and His Fiancée Discover the Sex of Their Unborn Baby in
    Dramatic Gender Reveal by Shooting a Box with a RIFLE to
    Expose Blue Powder," *Daily Mail*, May 10, 2016, http://www.
    dailymail.co.uk/femail/article-3582920/Target-practice-
    Special-Forces-member-fianc-e-discover-sex-unborn-baby-
    dramatic-gender-reveal-shooting-box-RIFLE-expose-blue-
    powder.html.
3. Alex Williams and Kate Murphy, "A Boy or Girl? Cut the
    Cake," *New York Times*, April 7, 2012, http://www.nytimes.
    com/2012/04/08/fashion/at-parties-revealing-a-babys-gender.
    html?_r=0.
4. "Explore Baby Bertrum, Tay Baby, and More," Pinterest,
    https://www.pinterest.com/pin/68257750580543909/.
5. Jasmeet Sighu, "How to Buy a Daughter," *Slate*, September
    17, 2012, http://www.slate.com/articles/health_and_science/
    medical_examiner/2012/09/sex_selection_in_babies_
    through_pgd_americans_are_paying_to_have_daughters_
    rather_than_sons_.html.
6. Jane Ridley, "We Spent $100K to Guarantee a Baby Girl,"
    New York Post, July 6, 2015, http://nypost.com/2015/07/06/
    we-spent-100000-to-guarantee-a-baby-girl/.
7. See chapter two. Christin Scarlett Milloy, "Don't Let the
    Doctor Do This to Your Newborn," *Slate*, June 26, 2014,
    http://www.slate.com/blogs/outward/2014/06/26/infant_
    gender_assignment_unnecessary_and_potentially_harmful.
    html.

8. Georgia Graham, "MPs Vote to Make Sex Selection Abortion Illegal," *Telegraph*, November 4, 2014, http://www.telegraph.co.uk/news/health/news/11208011/MPs-vote-to-make-sex-selection-abortion-illegal.html.

9. Ed O'Keefe, "Bill Banning 'Sex-Selection Abortions' Fails in the House, *Washington Post*, May 31, 2012, https://www.washingtonpost.com/politics/bill-banning-sex-selection-abortions-fails-in-the-house/2012/05/31/gJQAaWFd5U_story.html.

10. Motoko Rich, "Old Tactic Gets New Use: Public Schools Separate Girls and Boys," *New York Times*, November 30, 2014, http://www.nytimes.com/2014/12/01/education/single-sex-education-public-schools-separate-boys-and-girls.html?_r=2.

11. Melinda D. Anderson, "The Resurgence of Single-Sex Education," *Atlantic*, December 22, 2015, http://www.theatlantic.com/education/archive/2015/12/the-resurgence-of-single-sex-education/421560/.

12. Amy Novotney, "Coed ver[s]us Single-Sex Ed," American Psychological Association *Monitor on Psychology* 42:2 (February 2011): 58, http://www.apa.org/monitor/2011/02/coed.aspx.

13. "The National Association for Choice in Education," National Association for Choice in Education, http://www.4schoolchoice.org.

14. David Holthouse, "Gender Segregation: Separate but Effective?," *Teaching Tolerance* 37 (spring 2010), http://www.tolerance.org/magazine/number-37-spring-2010/feature/gender-segregation-separate-effective.

15. Susan Kovalik, "Why Gender Matters: Education vs. the Wiring of Boys and Girls," Federal Way Mirror, October 14, 2008, http://www.federalwaymirror.com/life/why-gender-matters-education-vs-the-wiring-of-boys-and-girls/.

16. Leonard Sax, "Sex Differences in Hearing: Implications for Best Practice in the Classroom," *Advances in Gender and Education* 2 (2010): 13–21, http://www.leonardsax.com/wordpress/wp-content/uploads/2015/01/2010-Sax-hearing.pdf.

17. Novotney, "Coed."
18. Cindy Hirschfeld, "Six Women-Only Ski Clinics Go Way beyond the Snow Plow," *New York Times*, December 9, 2011, http://www.nytimes.com/2011/12/11/travel/womens-ski-clinics-around-the-united-states.html?_r=0.
19. Sally Newall, "Hit the Slopes on a Women-Only Ski Break in Chamonix," *Independent*, February 22, 2016, http://www.independent.co.uk/travel/skiing/a-women-s-only-ski-break-in-chamonix-amazon-creek-rachel-kerr-a6884656.html.
20. "How Curves Fitness Centers Became One of the Fastest Growing Franchises Ever, Franchise Help, February 2, 2011, https://www.franchisehelp.com/blog/how-curves-fitness-centers-became-one-of-the-fastest-growing-franchises-ever/.
21. Curtis Mock, "Are Women-Only Gyms Guilty of Discrimination?," Fitness Marketing, http://fitnessmarketing.com/2011/04/are-women-only-gyms-guilty-of-discrimination/#sthash.ppOJD17H.dpuf.
22. Kafi Drexel, "Women-Only Crossfit Classes Are Popping Up All over the Country," *Self*, April 8, 2014, http://www.self.com/flash/fitness-blog/2014/04/fitness-women-only-crossfit-classes/.
23. Laura Bates, "Women-Only Gyms Are a World Away from Boys' Clubs Such as Muirfield," *Guardian*, May 23, 2016, https://www.theguardian.com/commentisfree/2016/may/23/women-only-gyms-muirfield-men-male-privilege.
24. Kristin Dizon, "So Far, Women-Only Gyms Are Allowed by the Courts," *Seattle Post-Intelligencer*, January 1, 2004, http://www.seattlepi.com/lifestyle/article/So-far-women-only-gyms-are-allowed-by-the-courts-1133532.php.
25. Carey Goldberg, "Lawsuit Challenges Women-Only Gyms," *New York Times*, January 26, 1998, http://www.nytimes.com/1998/01/26/us/lawyer-s-suit-challenges-women-only-gyms.html.
26. "Gain New Skills and Go Further with Lean In Circles," Lean In Circles, http://leanincircles.org/.

27. Lisa Bonos, "A Year after 'Lean In,' These Are Sheryl Sandberg's Truest Believers," *Washington Post*, March 7, 2014, https://www.washingtonpost.com/opinions/a-year-after-lean-in-these-are-sheryl-sandbergs-truest-believers/2014/03/07/407b0e8e-9dac-11e3-a050-dc3322a94fa7_story.html.

28. Katherine Goldstein, "My Year of Leaning In: It Made Me a Better Professional and a Better Boss," *Slate*, May 6, 2014, http://www.slate.com/blogs/xx_factor/2014/05/06/lean_in_circle_a_year_later_what_i_got_out_of_participating_in_one_of_sheryl.html.

29. Jessica Bennett, "I Leaned In: Why Sheryl Sandberg's 'Circles' Actually Help," *The Cut*, March 7, 2013, http://nymag.com/thecut/2013/03/what-i-learned-at-the-lean-in-sandbergs-right.html.

30. Mackenzie Dawson, "Female Entrepreneurs Are Flocking to This Women-Only Work Space," *New York Post*, September 5, 2016, http://nypost.com/2016/09/05/female-entrepreneurs-are-flocking-to-this-women-only-work-space/.

31. Jared Shelly, "New Co-Working Space for Women Now Open," *Philadelphia Magazine*, February 1, 2016, http://www.phillymag.com/business/2016/02/01/co-working-space-women-bizzy-mamas/.

32. http://herahub.com.

33. Marcus Noland et al., "Is Gender Diversity Profitable? Evidence from a Global Survey," Peterson Institute for International Economics, February 2016, https://piie.com/publications/wp/wp16-3.pdf.

34. "Companies with More Women Board Directors Experience Higher Financial Performance, According to Latest Catalyst Bottom Line Report," Catalyst, http://www.catalyst.org/media/companies-more-women-board-directors-experience-higher-financial-performance-according-latest.

35. Jena McGregor, "More Women at the Top, Higher Returns," *Washington Post*, September 24, 2014, https://www.washingtonpost.com/news/on-leadership/wp/2014/09/24/more-women-at-the-top-higher-returns/.

36. Dorothee Enskog, "Women's Positive Impact on Corporate Performance," Credit Suisse, September 23, 2014, https://www.credit-suisse.com/us/en/articles/articles/news-and-expertise/2014/09/en/womens-impact-on-corporate-performance-letting-the-data-speak.html.

37. Samantha Olson, "Gender Differences in the Workplace: Women Prefer Collaboration, While Men Distrust Their Coworkers and Desire to Work Alone," Medical Daily, August 22, 2013, http://www.medicaldaily.com/gender-differences-workplace-women-prefer-collaboration-while-men-distrust-their-coworkers-and.

38. Kelly Wallace, "What Changes with Women in the Boardroom?," CNN, October 23, 2013, http://www.cnn.com/2013/10/23/living/identity-women-management/.

39. Jon Birger, "The Woman Who Called Wall Street's Meltdown," *Fortune*, August 6, 2008, http://archive.fortune.com/2008/08/04/magazines/fortune/whitney_feature.fortune/index.htm.

40. Drew Gannon, "How Men and Women Differ in the Workplace," Fiscal Times, May 25, 2012, http://www.thefiscaltimes.com/Articles/2012/05/25/How-Men-and-Women-Differ-in-the-Workplace.

41. Ed O'Keefe, "Gillibrand Works to Elect More Women," *Washington Post*, August 1, 2012, https://www.washingtonpost.com/politics/gillibrand-works-to-elect-more-women/2012/08/01/gJQAsftTQX_story.html.

42. Therese Huston, "Are Women Better Decision Makers?," *New York Times*, October 17, 2014, http://www.nytimes.com/2014/10/19/opinion/sunday/are-women-better-decision-makers.html?_r=0.

43. Pamela Wilcox Rountree and Barbara D. Warner, "Social Ties and Crime: Is the Relationship Gendered?," *Criminology* 37:4 (November 2009): 789–814, http://onlinelibrary.wiley.com/doi/10.1111/j.1745-9125.1999.tb00505.x/abstract.

44. "Who Are Family Caregivers?," American Psychological Association, http://www.apa.org/pi/about/publications/caregivers/faq/statistics.aspx.
45. "Daughters Provide as Much Elderly Care as They Can, Sons Do as Little as Possible," American Sociological Association, August 19, 2014, http://www.asanet.org/press-center/press-releases/daughters-provide-much-elderly-parent-care-they-can-sons-do-little-possible.
46. "Senior Care Cost Index," Caring.com, September 2014, https://www.caring.com/research/senior-care-cost-index-2014.
47. Ross Doutht, "The Daughter Theory," *New York Times*, December 15, 2012, http://www.nytimes.com/2013/12/15/opinion/sunday/douthat-the-daughter-theory.html.
48. Rich Morin, "Study: Having Daughters Makes Parents More Likely to Be Republican," Pew Research Center, November 25, 2013, http://www.pewresearch.org/fact-tank/2013/11/25/study-having-daughters-makes-parents-more-likely-to-be-republican/.
49. Douthat, "The Daughter Theory."
50. Shafer and Malhotra, "The Effect of a Child's Sex on Support for Traditional Gender Roles," *Social Forces*, September 2011, quoted in Sarah Yager, "How Women Change Men: as Daughters, Sisters, Wives, and Coworkers," *Atlantic*, December 2013, http://www.theatlantic.com/magazine/archive/2013/12/how-women-change-men/354682/.
51. Adam Grant, "Why Men Need Women," *New York Times*, July 2, 2013, http://www.nytimes.com/2013/07/21/opinion/sunday/why-men-need-women.html?module=ArrowsNav&contentCollection=Opinion&action=keypress&region=FixedLeft&pgtype=article.
52. James Andreoni and Lise Vesterlund, "Which Is the Fair Sex? Gender Differences in Altruism," *Quarterly Journal of Economics* 116:1 (2001): 293–312, http://qje.oxfordjournals.org/content/116/1/293.short.
53. Grant, "Why Men Need Women."

54. Michael S. Dahl et al., "Fatherhood and Managerial Style: How a Male CEO's Children Affect the Wages of His Employees," *Administrative Science Quarterly*, October 31, 2012, http://asq.sagepub.com/content/57/4/669.abstract.
55. Grant, "Why Men Need Women."
56. http://www.iza.org/en/webcontent/publications/papers/viewAbstract?dp_id=9904.
57. Justin Wolfers, "A Family-Friendly Policy That's Friendliest to Male Professors," *New York Times*, June 24, 2016, http://www.nytimes.com/2016/06/26/business/tenure-extension-policies-that-put-women-at-a-disadvantage.html.

EPILOGUE

1. Jackie Kucinich and Martha T. Moore, "Hilary Rosen Says Ann Romney Never Worked 'Day in Her Life,'" *USA Today*, April 12, 2012, http://usatoday30.usatoday.com/news/politics/story/2012-04-12/ann-romney-hilary-rosen-work/54235706/1.
2. Inés San Martín, "Pope Calls Gender Theory a 'Global War' against the Family," Crux, October 1, 2016, https://cruxnow.com/global-church/2016/10/01/pope-calls-gender-theory-global-war-family/.
3. Catherine Rampell, "U.S. Women on the Rise As Family Breadwinner," *New York Times*, May 29, 2013, http://www.nytimes.com/2013/05/30/business/economy/women-as-family-breadwinner-on-the-rise-study-says.html.

INDEX